TERMAN'S KIDS

By Joel N. Shurkin

Helix (with Desmond Ryan)
The Invisible Fire
Engines of the Mind
Intensive Care
Terman's Kids

TERMAN'S
KIDS

THE GROUNDBREAKING STUDY
OF HOW THE GIFTED GROW UP

JOEL N. SHURKIN

Little, Brown and Company

BOSTON TORONTO LONDON

First Edition

Library of Congress Cataloging-in-Publication Data

Shurkin, Joel N., 1938–
    Terman's kids : the groundbreaking study of how the gifted grow
up / Joel N. Shurkin. — 1st ed.
    p.   cm.
    ISBN 0-316-78890-2
    1. Gifted children — United States — Longitudinal studies.
2. Gifted — United States — Longitudinal studies.   3. Terman, Lewis
Madison, 1877–1956.   I. Title.
BF723.G5S48   1992
155.45′5′0973 — dc20   91-37572

10 9 8 7 6 5 4 3 2 1

RRD VA
*Published simultaneously in Canada
by Little, Brown & Company (Canada) Limited*

Printed in the United States of America

To my beautiful — and gifted — sisters,
Susan Sicola and Mimi Heyman

CONTENTS

ACKNOWLEDGMENTS

The idea of doing a book on Lewis Terman's study of the gifted originated with Irv Goodman, my editor at Little, Brown. I broached the idea to Al Hastorf, the keeper of Terman's flame at Stanford, with considerable trepidation. No journalist has ever been allowed into Terman's files; indeed, not that many researchers have. Even the subjects of the study can't see the files, not even their own. Yet a book about the study that did not probe deeply into the lives of the subjects wouldn't work. The subjects, the "Termites," weren't just numbers or files to Terman, and they can't be that to us if we are to understand what he found and how. The story couldn't come alive if we did not learn about their lives.

Hastorf and I discussed the problem of confidentiality, and then, happily, he agreed to let me do the research. The rules were that I would name *or contact* only those subjects whose participation in the study is already public knowledge, unless I found them through outside sources and they agreed to help. I could not use the files to track down other Termites. The restrictions were to apply to the subjects' families as well. I accepted the conditions. The next week Hastorf's assistant, Eleanor Walker, handed me the list of subjects and the keys to the office and told me to have fun.

The book could not have been done without that cooperation, and I shall always be indebted to Hastorf and Leonard Horowitz, the two principal investigators, and to Ms. Walker.

I was aimed in the right direction initially by Karen Klinger, former science writer at the *San Jose Mercury-News*, who had done one of the most extensive newspaper reports on the Terman study. She shipped me her files. I stumbled on the family of another subject while researching another project—pushing the small world concept to the limits.

Consequently, before I began the research, I already knew the identity of several subjects whose participation was not public. They or their families proved to be of great help. They know who they are and know my debt to them. In a few cases they were asked to recall unhappy times and did so willingly. Some of the subjects or their families asked for anonymity, and I have abided by their wishes.

Shelley Smith Mydans and Ancel Keys, of those I can mention, gave me hours of their time on the telephone and then went through my drafts to correct mistakes. The family of Jess Oppenheimer, particularly his son Gregg, was wonderfully kind, letting me read and quote from Oppenheimer's unpublished, and regrettably unfinished, memoirs. The family also checked the manuscript for factual errors. Joel Greenberg of the *Los Angeles Times* provided useful background material on Oppenheimer as well. I'm also grateful to Rodney Beard for his insights.

Kristin de Voe, a Stanford undergraduate and friend, acted as my assistant with the Terman files, saving me hours of time and aggravation. Being a freshman adviser at Stanford has the great joy of introducing me to students like Kristin. Thanks are also due to Stanford for granting me a leave of absence to work on this project.

Two biographies of Lewis Terman were invaluable. The more extensive is *Lewis M. Terman: Pioneer in Psychological Testing* by Henry L. Minton. A more personal view is *Terman and the Gifted* by May V. Seagoe.

I am indebted to Dr. Bob Howard of Bass Lake, Wisconsin, for a number of reasons, not the least of which is putting me in touch with Dr. Keys, a most remarkable man.

And finally, my profound thanks to Carol Howard. Without her love, support, wisdom, and recklessness, this book would have been impossible. When her turn comes, I hope to be as wonderful.

Joel Shurkin
Ben Lomond, California
September 1991

TERMAN'S KIDS

INTRODUCTION

The future welfare of the country hinges in no small degree upon the right education of . . . superior children. Whether civilization moves on and up depends on the advances made by creative thinkers and leaders in science, politics, art, morality, and religion. Moderate ability can follow, or imitate, but genius must show the way.

Lewis M. Terman, 1919

IN 1922 a round-shouldered, bespectacled, red-haired, forty-four-year-old professor of psychology at Stanford University began a study of genius. Lewis M. Terman, who practically invented psychological testing and who developed the Stanford-Binet intelligence test, had a serious agenda. He firmly believed that the future of the United States lay with discovering and nurturing its brightest children. He believed that intelligence was inherited, that parents passed genius on to their children, and that not enough of the very bright children were being produced. He felt that many common ideas about those children were wrong. He believed that they did not suffer from "early ripe, early rot," that is, they did not peak early and then descend into insanity, frustration, and melancholy. They were not physically weak and socially maladjusted.

To prove his ideas, Terman began the granddaddy of all longitudinal psychological studies, the first scientific study that attempted to divine the origin and outcome of genius. Terman's goal was nothing less than to identify as many child geniuses as he could and follow them *the rest of their lives.* He wanted to see how these children turned out, if they succeeded, and if they failed, why they did so. His files have become one of the great icons of social science. They constitute one of the largest assemblages of information ever collected about a group of individuals. Now seventy years old, they are still being used by sociologists and psychologists because of their scope and Terman's nearly pathological attention to detail.

The study is still going on. Hundreds of "Terman's kids" are still alive, in their seventies and eighties. They call themselves "Termites." You know some of their names and some of the things they accomplished. They altered what you eat, what you read, what you watch on television, what you know of the world. Some of them saved lives. And some of them failed, failed miserably.

Besides being part of a scientific study, many Termites found that they had become part of a huge extended family, one that sometimes meddled in their personal lives. Terman's meddling was, indeed, one of the defects of his study. Their participation sometimes yielded benefits that gave them an advantage in life others did not enjoy. But some of the subjects found the experience onerous, believing that having been singled out as geniuses (a word Terman eventually abandoned) was a burden. The inability to live up to self-imposed expectations may have contributed to more than one suicide.

The Terman study is flawed and controversial in many respects, but it precipitated further studies of "gifted" children (a term Terman found more comfortable) and attempts to determine the proper educational environment for very bright youngsters. It also triggered one of the most vociferous debates in all of science, about the definition of intelligence, the value of psychological testing, and the roles of heredity and the environment in determining intelligence. Much of the continuing nature versus nurture debate began with this study.

The author of this book was granted unprecedented access to Terman's confidential files. The readers will get to meet several of the Termites and to follow them through their lives. When Terman originally tested the children, he promised that their files would remain forever confidential and that no one except legitimate researchers would have access to them. He and his successors have kept that promise, even to the point of denying living subjects or the relatives of those who have died access to their own files. The condition upon which I was given permission to see the files was that I, too, would protect that privacy. Consequently, except where noted, I have adhered to standard journalistic practice in medical and social science reporting and have changed the names and some of the biographical details of the gifted people in the study to blur their identities. I have, however, made every effort to stay true to the subjects and to their lives. Everything in quotation marks is taken from the files or from interviews, with only names altered.

Chapter One

INTELLIGENCE TESTING

TESTING FOR INTELLIGENCE has a relatively short and somewhat disreputable history. It was frequently associated with racist pseudoscience, such as a mid-nineteenth-century theory known as polygeny. Polygeny holds that humans derived from more than one ancestor and that the races are separate species. The theory was used to bolster the tenet that some races were inherently superior or inferior and to justify slavery.

The belief that the races differed in intellectual capacity even gathered some "scientific" support. Louis Agassiz (1807–1873), the great Swiss-American naturalist, believed in this racial difference and developed a number of theories to support it. Samuel George Morton (1799–1851), a noted Philadelphia physician and naturalist, collected human skulls and measured the size of the brain to support the theory that brain size and intelligence are related. He concluded that blacks had smaller brains than whites and were therefore inferior intellectually. In fact, as Harvard biologist Stephen Jay Gould points out, Morton "cooked" the data; he altered the results.[1]

Charles Darwin's cousin, Francis Galton (1822–1911), who believed everything in life could be quantified, also measured skulls for brain size. He even set up a stand at the International Exposition of 1884 where for threepence visitors could have their heads measured and receive a scientific analysis of what the measurement showed. The French surgeon and anthropologist, Paul Broca (1824–1880), who became famous for identifying the site in the brain in which thought is translated into articulate speech, was also known for his theories relating brain weight and intelligence. In his studies of brain size and weight, he concluded that women are not as smart as men, hampered as women are by their smaller physical size.

Agassiz, Morton, Galton, and Broca were not racist cranks, but were famous, respected, even leading scientists of their day.*

Testing for intelligence, or what was perceived to be intelligence, was pioneered in Europe by Alfred Binet and his student Théodore Simon. Binet had begun studying Broca's work, but being a better scientist, he noticed two things: the data he gathered himself did not support the theory, and the more he tested the more he found an unintentional bias creeping into his work to make the facts fit that theory. He abandoned measuring bulk and turned to using psychological assessments to ascertain intelligence. Binet believed that intelligence, which he declined to define specifically, was a multifaceted phenomenon involving such things as memory, suggestibility, sensory perception, and imagination, all of which could be separated from the influence of education. He did not believe that intelligence was a singular entity to which anyone should put a number or that testing a group of people told anything about any person outside that group.

In 1904 Binet and Simon were asked by the French ministry of public instruction to measure children who were slow in school or were suffering from what is now called learning disabilities. The two designed a scale for more than thirty tests to be used on children three to eleven years of age.† The scale essentially determined which tests "normal" children passed at each age. Grades were fixed as "mental levels," the scores that 60 percent of normal children should achieve at each age. By applying the tests to the slow children, Binet could quantify the differences among them. Binet's latest revision was in 1908. German psychologist William Stern (1871–1938) adopted the notion of a mental quotient, and using a different mathematical procedure, he produced an index he called an "intelligence quotient," or IQ, similar to Binet's levels.

Binet never intended the test to be used as a mass screening device, nor did he feel comfortable with the idea that it should be used to

---

* Men like Broca went to great lengths to make the data fit the theory. He had great difficulty in explaining how Germans wound up with heavier brains than Frenchmen. He blamed the sample. After he died, Broca's brain was measured and it turned out to be only slightly heavier than average for a Frenchman.

† "One might almost say, 'It matters very little what the tests are so long as they are numerous,'" Binet once remarked.

categorize people. His test was designed for one purpose only, to measure children who were having problems in school so the schools could help them. He felt that categorizing people tended to limit expectations others had of them. He did not take sides in the heredity-environment debate and did not believe his tests would prove the issue either way; he had no illusions his test proved any theory or had any cosmic importance. He was only trying to measure the mental competence of a group of slow students. It was left up to American psychologists, including Lewis M. Terman, to distort the purpose of his test.[2]

Lewis Terman's life's work derived from his own childhood experiences. If his interests and sympathies lay with children of exceptional abilities, it was in part because he had been one himself and had felt the loneliness and sense of difference that can torment the exceptional.

Terman was the twelfth of fourteen children, the son of James William Terman and Martha Cutsinger, born on the family's Indiana farm on January 15, 1877.[3] That put him halfway between the presidency of John Adams and Dwight Eisenhower, he once remarked.

Terman was tended by his older siblings, the usual practice in large families. His brother John, fourteen years his senior, was surrogate father and later his teacher. The family was busy, close, and generally happy, except for the grief that came from a predisposition to tuberculosis. Mourning for the young was not unknown in his boyhood home. The death of a sister at the age of twenty-four deeply affected the three-year-old Lewis, who would always remember her convulsions and coughing. Well into his maturity, he would lie in bed at night in terror, fearful of the same fate.

Terman entered the one-room, bookless schoolhouse in Clark township at the age of five and a half. He completed the eighth grade by the time he was twelve. With no high school in the neighborhood and unable to afford to live away from home, Terman moved to another one-room school nearby, this one taught by his brother John, one of the few teachers in the area with any college training.

Besides attending school, Terman helped work the farm. His father kept to strict sexual stereotypes: the boys helped in the fields and the girls helped in the house. Terman appears to have accepted these stereotypes. Terman's attitudes toward sex would color both his science and his personal life, skewing his research in ways that weakened his credibility. His attitude toward women involved strange inconsistencies, on the one hand supportive and paternal, on the other exploitative and sexist.

Terman the scientist concluded that his intelligence was the lucky result of heredity, but to reach that conclusion he had to ignore the influence of his environment and chance events. Few farmhouses had libraries to match his father's; his brother John was a superb teacher with more education than most people in the neighborhood; his parents and siblings happily let him dwell in his own fantasy world and encouraged his drive for education. He claimed his interest in psychology began when a visitor to his house studied the bumps on his head to analyze his intelligence.

The only college his family could afford was a state "normal college," set up to train elementary school teachers. Terman went to Central Normal in Danville, west of Indianapolis. The teachers he found there were exceptional. Overworked, underpaid, and unappreciated, many of them had ambitions for advanced degrees at universities in the East. "They took raw country boys fresh from the grammar school and in a few ten-week terms made them into teachers," he remembered.[4] The curriculum was rigorous; Terman read Darwin, Huxley, William James, and the ancient Greeks. He had a wonderful time at Danville, he recalled, living in a boarding house with other students.

At the age of seventeen he was ready to begin teaching, and the state assigned him to a one-room school just like the ones he had attended. After his first year, he went back to Danville for forty-eight weeks to obtain the equivalent of a bachelor of science degree. He moved to another one-room school the next year and then spent three years teaching and serving as principal at a forty-student high school. One more trip to Danville got him a second degree, bachelor of pedagogy. In 1899, at the age of twenty-two, he received a bachelor of arts degree. That was as far as Danville could take him.

In September 1899 he married a fellow student at Central Normal, Anna Belle Minton, described by friends as the prettiest girl in class. Nine months later, she gave birth to their first child, Frederick Emmons Arthur Terman, named in honor of a friend. Terman continued his education through a state reading program called Teacher's Reading Circle and was especially intrigued with books on education and educational psychology.

Throughout this period a specter stalked him, the family predisposition to tuberculosis. He had two bad episodes, and one doctor recommended he move to a more salubrious climate. But with a family to support, Terman had to take jobs where he could get them. Instead of moving he designed his own health regimen. He arranged his schedule to allow for a brief walk in the woods before breakfast and another walk after school, weather permitting. He took his temperature every day and his pulse after exercise. He moved into his own bedroom with large windows kept open every night. For most of his life he camped out in open bedrooms no matter what the weather, sometimes waking to find snowdrifts halfway across the room. He called it "outdoor" sleeping inside.

In 1901 Terman entered Indiana University as an undergraduate junior. He borrowed money from his family and he and Anna took in boarders to pay for school. Again, great teachers impelled him. One, Ernest H. Lindley, would prove crucial, instilling in Terman a love for psychology. To do an independent paper required in Lindley's seminar, Terman studied the psychology of mental deficiency, criminality, and genius and ran into the work of Alfred Binet, with whom Terman's name would be forever linked. He decided to study leadership for his master's thesis using a test for suggestibility designed by Binet. Terman took a group of one hundred white children and sixteen "colored" children in the Bloomington, Indiana, school system and split them into groups of four. He defined leadership as the ability to rise to a position of influence in a group, and then broke it down into several indexes such as the number of times a child answered test questions first, originality of the child's answers, the number of times others in the group imitated a child's answer, and how easy it was to catch a child with trick questions. He found that the children he identified as leaders were also independently identified as such by their teachers. Terman, following in the venerable tradition of social science, had learned to demonstrate the obvious. He followed up on his experiment with a questionnaire sent to teachers around the eastern United States to determine what they thought made a child a leader. The four hundred who responded seemed to feel that boys were more dominant and gregarious than girls and that leadership emerged early in life and reflected a feeling of superiority, skill, and high social position. His follow-up was completely unscientific and he later agreed his thesis was junk science,* but the study did point him toward his eventual field of research.

Three of his favorite psychology professors at the university had received their doctorates from Clark University, a small idiosyncratic school in Worcester, Massachusetts, and all had studied under G. Stanley Hall, the guru of American child psychology and president of Clark. Hall was the first person to receive a doctorate in psychology in the United States, and the American Psychological Association was founded in his house. Clark had fifty full-time students, thirty of whom were in psychology, education, or philosophy and almost all of whom were at the graduate level. To register for classes students simply gave their name to the president's secretary. No one had a major; no one took attendance; there were no grades. After finishing the required classes, students took a four-hour examination. If they passed, they were given a Ph.D.

Hall had studied under William James at Harvard and had taught at Johns Hopkins before becoming Clark's first president in 1888. He was, significantly, a firm believer that intelligence and most behavior were the products of heredity, a concept called "evolutionary." Children were as they came, and schools had to adjust to that. He believed in individualized instruction and special programs for the gifted from early adolescence on.

Terman's teachers recommended that he go to Clark to study under Hall. But how could he get there? In 1903, his last year at Indiana, his second child, Helen, was born. Terman believed that with a young family and the debt he owed his family for his education, he needed a serious job. Again, his father and brother came through with another $1,200 loan.

Hall had a profound influence on Terman. Hall designed a schedule for himself to maximize his time that Terman would imitate later in life. A prodigious worker, Hall served his administrative functions as president of Clark from eight to nine in the morning, he prepared for class from nine to eleven, and he lectured at eleven. He went home

* It was, however, his first published paper, being reprinted in the *Pedagogical Seminary* in 1904.

to work for the rest of the day and returned to work again after supper. The highlight of his teaching — and the aspect Terman loved the most and would later employ in his own teaching — was Hall's home seminars. Beginning at 7:15 on most Monday evenings, thirty interested and invited students (more than half the student body) would assemble at Hall's home to listen to and discuss reports on independent studies by two students.

The longer or more important report was read first. "It might be a review of the literature in some field or an account of the student's own investigation," Terman wrote. Hall would make a few "deceivingly generous comments about the importance" of the presentation, casting just a touch of doubt about the conclusions. Then, one by one, the students would join him in questioning and commenting, and the result would be a feeding frenzy, tearing the work apart. Hall would finally end the discussion by summing it up, and all would file into the dining room for refreshments. "I always went home dazed and intoxicated, took a hot bath to quiet my nerves, then lay awake for hours rehearsing the drama and formulating the clever things I should have said and did not," Terman remembered. "No educational experience I ever had was comparable to his seminar." Not everyone enjoyed it as much as Terman; at least one student had a nervous breakdown after having his research demolished. Terman wrote:

> I think the Clark situation . . . was of almost crucial importance in my development. I have never worked well under the restraint of rules and regulations, and it is hard to imagine a regime that would have been better adapted to my temperament than the one I found at Clark, if regime indeed it could be called. Because I was placed absolutely on my own responsibility, I was able to give my best with unalloyed enthusiasm.[5]

For all his respect, Terman soon grew skeptical of Hall's research methodology, particularly his emphasis on questionnaires. Terman was sure his own study of leadership in Bloomington was flawed for that reason. A follow-up study on leadership he did at Clark at Hall's urging, also using questionnaires, disturbed him even more. He felt there had to be a better way to test these things. However, whatever his doubts about Hall's methodology, he sank comfortably into Hall's evolutionary philosophy: mental abilities clearly are carried in the genes.

Terman launched into a project on precocity, which he addressed in terms of "prematuration," encouraging or forcing maturity on the very young. Largely, he was against it. He believed, drawing from Hall, that intellect best matures at its own pace and anything that artificially speeds up the process is harmful. Schools shouldn't push children to advance faster than they were meant to lest they be harmed by the stress. He was not thinking of gifted students; he excluded them from his research at this stage. He was decrying forced progression, not natural growth.

Almost a year into his schoolwork at Clark, he suffered another tubercular attack, provoked apparently by a game of tennis.

> When I informed the doctor of my desperate situation — a wife and two children, debts of more than $1,500, and the necessity of getting my degree the following year — I fully expected to be told to forget my plans and spend a year regaining my health. Instead, he suggested that I go to bed for two or three weeks to see how things developed. If there were no further symptoms, he thought it might then be safe to work a few hours daily provided I rested in bed the remainder of the day. I have always believed that if I had been sentenced to a year in a sanatorium I should probably have died of worry about the future of my family and my career. As it turned out, I was feeling so well within a month or two that I was working six or seven hours a day.
>
> Although no symptoms reappeared during the following school year, I developed something like an anxiety neurosis which remained fairly quiescent during the day but often woke me in the middle of the night and left me sleepless for hours worrying about my health, my debts, and my chances of getting the degree.[6]

By now, he was getting a clear idea of what he wanted to study for his dissertation, children who were either gifted or defective. He knew he would not use Hall's questionnaire technique, but would administer objective tests directly to the subjects. Hall disapproved, and Terman had to ask another professor, E. C. Sanford, to act as his adviser.

The idea of giving subjects psychological tests that withstood rigorous scientific standards was almost virgin territory. Most earlier attempts had failed. Terman wanted to study intelligence, both in children who were unusually bright and in children who were the opposite. In those days words like "dull-witted," "feebleminded," and "stupid" were considered scientific terms and were freely used by psychologists and teachers in referring to children. Terman wanted to see how the bright differed from the stupid.

Out of about five hundred children at three Worcester schools, principals chose twenty-four boys, ten to thirteen years of age, who represented the extremes of the intelligence scale measured by totally subjective criteria. It is not clear why only boys were chosen; perhaps Terman was trying to eliminate any gender differences. Twelve were called bright and twelve stupid. Out of each cohort of twelve, the parents of seven agreed to let their sons participate, and Terman besieged the boys with hours of tests. He came up with eight categories: inventiveness and problem solving, logic, mathematical ability, mastery of language, insight (determined by analyzing fables), ease of acquisition (determined by learning chess), memory, and motor ability. Some were off-the-shelf psychological tests; some he devised or revised himself — impressive stuff for a graduate student.

The bright boys won every comparison except for motor skills, and the results were unambiguous in every case, which shouldn't have surprised anyone considering the two cohorts represented the extreme ends of the curve. Terman was nevertheless intrigued by the consistency of the results among the bright boys. "While offering little positive data on the subject, the study has strengthened my impression of the relatively greater importance of *endowment* over *training* as a determinant of an individual's intellectual rank among his fellows," he wrote.[7]

Terman passed his orals and was handed his Ph.D. diploma by President Theodore Roosevelt at the Clark graduation ceremony in 1905. Terman was now a psychologist. He knew what he wanted to study, but he did not know where. His health would determine his fate.

Terman moved to California, taking a job in San Bernardino as a high school principal. He didn't particularly want to be a high school principal and missed the frenetic intellectual activity at Clark. Another bout of tuberculosis added to his unhappiness, but he was rescued by an offer from the Los Angeles Normal School (now the University of California at Los Angeles), which needed a professor of child study and pedagogy. It was his first chance to teach at a college level.

Terman's teaching load was light, and he had time to write articles on education in popular magazines, generally espousing the Hallian philosophy of letting children develop without stress. He stayed in Los Angeles for four years. He went back to Indiana University in 1909 to teach and see his family.

In 1909 Terman was healthy and reasonably happy, but felt intellectually stifled. He wanted to move on to a permanent university position. He was recruited by Ellwood P. Cubberley, chairman of Stanford University's Department of Education. Cubberley had met Terman the year before at an education meeting and had been impressed with what Terman had to say. Terman's appointment as assistant professor of education at Stanford meant a bit of a pay cut, but he was deliriously happy. The weather on the San Francisco peninsula, a cooler version of Southern California, was ideal for his health. Stanford was, he wrote, "the university that I would have chosen before any other in all the world."

Terman built himself a house on campus in what was known as the "faculty ghetto." In the ghetto, faculty members owned their own houses but leased the land from the university. He and Anna lived in that house the rest of their lives. It was a large, two-story, redwood shingled structure standing on over an acre of land. It had three bedrooms, a large study upstairs, and two sleeping porches. Terman's study was next to his bedroom, handy for working at home and popping off for an occasional nap. The ground floor was spacious, just right for Hallian student seminars, which Terman instituted almost immediately. He invited his brightest undergraduates to the graduate seminars (something almost unheard of at universities) and served alcoholic beverages.[8]

Terman was a man of medium height, five foot seven, although many who knew him thought him shorter because of his stooped posture. By the time he arrived at Stanford, he parted his red hair, just beginning to fleck with gray, in the middle and had taken to wearing round, professorial glasses. "He had a bit of a sport in him," remembered Ernest Hilgard, a colleague. "He loved to play golf and tennis, and suddenly one afternoon, he decided to play every week. Most of us found daytime a little hard to manage so we had to play under the lights." He built a putting green on the lawn. He would walk around wearing golfing clothes; his son, who became dean of engineering, was rarely seen out of a blue suit, dress shirt, and tie.[9]

His family life seemed to be conventional, but was in reality just a little odd. Terman could not get away from sexual stereotypes. Fred was clearly the favored child. Terman and Anna didn't send him off to school until he was ready for fourth grade. True to the philosophy of childhood development without stress, Terman did nothing to pressure Fred when he didn't seem interested in learning to read at what would have been considered a normal age in school. Neither parent forced the issue until he was eight, when Anna decided it was time and taught him herself. Fred clearly was bright and his lackadaisical approach to education didn't seem to bother his parents at all. He eventually justified their confidence, graduating Stanford Phi Beta Kappa with a passion for engineering. He would become as famous as his father. "Fred was a very strange man," said Olga McNemar, one of Terman's assistants. "Very brilliant but very strange."[10] Those who knew him remarked he had exactly two topics of conversation: engineering and football. His father lamented Fred was unlikely to marry, and according to family legend, Fred also feared his personality was not likely to attract a woman, so he asked his parents to fix him up. They introduced him to one of Terman's graduate students, Sibyl Walcutt, and to everyone's surprise, the two decided to marry. Sibyl turned out to be just as awkward socially as her husband. She learned to resent Anna's constant meddling in her family's affairs. The two women never became close.*

Bringing up Fred was Lewis's responsibility. Helen was a different story; Helen was a girl. Anna was in charge of her.† She started school at the normal time. Lewis would write his friends long letters extolling the intelligence and virtues of his son and referring to Helen as "happy," "average," and "attending more to the frivolities of adolescence than to academic learning." When she graduated Stanford "with distinction," her father seemed almost surprised. By the time

---

* According to McNemar, Sibyl tutored her children almost from the day they were born, in part to make sure they scored well on their grandfather's tests.
† When Terman produced the Stanford-Binet IQ test, he tested Fred, who measured in the genius category. Terman's biographers claim Anna did not want Terman to test Helen, but he did, and she also made the genius category. She was not part of the subsequent gifted study; her file consists mostly of material on her two daughters.

she left Stanford, all she wanted was to get married and have children, which seemed to be all her parents wanted her to do. She got a job teaching for one year in San Luis Obispo and then married a lawyer in Los Angeles. Terman was pleased with the marriage; her husband was partly Jewish and therefore, Terman assumed, intellectually gifted. Helen produced Terman's first grandchild. After Helen's divorce, she returned to Stanford and worked as a secretary at the university. "She was very quiet and retiring," said McNemar. "She was uninteresting to look at or talk to, but she was nice."

Terman's light teaching load allowed him to pursue his research. He concentrated at first on the problems of school hygiene. His interest grew in part from his concern about his own health and in part from his belief that good physical health was a prerequisite for intellectual and educational achievement. Sick children were wasting their time. Terman lamented the sorry physical state of many schools, particularly the poor lighting and ventilation systems. The result of Terman's interest was twenty articles on school hygiene published in his first four years at Stanford. In 1913 he wrote his first book, *The Teacher's Health*, in which he concluded (on little actual data) that the rate of disease, particularly tuberculosis, was unusually high among teachers and endangered the children. Somewhat more startling, although not out of character, Terman feared that certain undesirable traits, including "effeminacy, extreme docility, obsequiousness and lack of manly force" might be passed on by male teachers to their charges. He suggested that female teachers tended to be dogmatic and meddlesome.

In 1914 he wrote a textbook, *The Hygiene of the School Child*, for young people entering the normal schools, for teachers' reading groups such as the one he enjoyed in Indiana, and for parents. He combined Hall's attitude toward the relationship between health and education with Cubberley's insistence that schools serve a higher social purpose, in this case promoting good health. Later that year he coauthored a second book, *Health Work in the Schools,* with a Minnesota public health worker, dealing with teaching hygiene. The books sold well, and Terman began to feel the first signs of economic health.

In 1914 he changed direction and began to wonder about the possibility of testing for intelligence. That led him back to Alfred Binet.

Several other psychologists had tried to adapt and improve Binet's tests to study normal children, including a team from Clark University. In 1910 Terman began work on his own version. He first set about revising the mental levels based on data he thought more accurate and more appropriate to children in the United States. He added some tests of his own and borrowed others. He calibrated the tests in local public schools, revised the mental levels, and fine-tuned the components until he was satisfied that they were useful and accurate. When he was done, he and his graduate students had sampled 2,300 people, including 1,700 "normal" children, 200 children on both extremes of the intelligence curve (retarded and extremely bright), and more than 400 adults.

In 1912, with the help of graduate student H. G. Childs, he published his revision of Binet's test.* Because of the team effort involved (a legion of graduate students had spent hundreds of hours developing the revision), he called it the Stanford-Binet test instead of the Terman-Binet test. The complete Stanford-Binet consisted of ninety tests, at least six for each age group. Statistically, his tests produced what he felt was a normal curve, with the average score 100 and measuring both extremes, the gifted and the retarded. The test purported to do exactly what Binet had hoped testing would not do, categorize people.

The Stanford-Binet became the standard test of intelligence in the United States for more than fifty years, in part because Terman's colleagues were impressed by the amount of pretesting done, in part because Terman and his students modified the test almost every decade to keep it contemporary and to respond to criticisms.

Terman published the first results from the Stanford-Binet tests on a sample of 1,000 children in his monograph *The Measurement of Intelligence.* Terman thought he saw in his data confirmation of his assertion that intelligence was genetic. And, for the first time, he associated intelligence with class. He found that high school students from the upper classes scored on the average seven points above normal, while children from the lower classes scored seven points below normal. The difference, he claimed, was "probably due for the

---

* There is no evidence that Terman and Binet ever corresponded or met. Binet died in 1911, and Terman dedicated the first edition of the Stanford-Binet test to his memory. He earnestly felt Binet would have approved.

most part, to a superiority in original endowment." The quality of their schools or their home life had no part in his analysis.

Then Terman turned salesman. Mental testing for children was a tool of extraordinary value, he asserted in the monograph. Unlike Binet, Terman believed that he was measuring an innate quality and that the Stanford-Binet could be used to predict how well a student would do in school. He went even further in stating that, since he felt that mental development generally ended by the time a child reached sixteen, the tests could give a quantitative picture of how bright and successful the child would be when he or she grew up. A child scoring 100 would be an average student and lead an average life. A child scoring 130 or higher would excel in school and in life.

Terman could think of dozens of uses for his IQ tests. He could, for instance, foresee a time when people could take a test and be given the kind of jobs they were best qualified for, a quiet form of social engineering. And, by testing students, schools could individualize their instruction to be more effective. Not only was such testing good social policy, but, although he probably was not motivated this way, massive testing could prove to be good business. His tests could have particular utility in designing instruction for the retarded, there now being a way of quantifying the degree of retardation. Those who were only mildly retarded ("high grade defectives") would have much to gain from the tests, and so would society. Terman wrote,

> It is safe to predict that in the near future intelligence tests will bring tens of thousands of these high-grade defectives under the surveillance and protection of society. This will ultimately result in curtailing the reproduction of feeblemindedness and in the elimination of an enormous amount of crime, pauperism, and industrial inefficiency. It is hardly necessary to emphasize that the high-grade cases, of the type now most frequently overlooked, are precisely the ones whose guardianship it is most important for the state to assume.[11]

Terman's comments, which now seem astonishing, should be taken in historical perspective. Psychologists in the nineteenth and early twentieth centuries felt there were three gradations of retardation. The scientific term for the most retarded group was "idiot." Idiots were defined as those who could not learn to speak well and generally had IQ levels of infants. The term "imbecile" was applied to those who could not learn to read and write and who had the mental age of three to seven. The term applied to the third group created some taxonomic confusion. The "feebleminded" were those who could be trained to operate in society, but the term was also used more generally to describe all the retarded. Terman meant the third group when he spoke of high-grade defectives. To get around the taxonomic problem, psychologist Henry Goddard coined another term, "morons," from the Greek word for foolish.

Retardation (a term not used until the 1890s) was seen as a social illness, was generally assigned to the lower classes, and was considered responsible for everything from unemployment to crime and degeneracy. That perfectly normal people occasionally had a retarded child seemed to be an unexplainable anomaly that did not deter the theorists. The idea of eugenics, that the less intelligent lower classes were reproducing much faster than the brighter upper classes to the detriment of society, was hardly new. Galton, whose work Terman knew well, promoted selective breeding and coined the word eugenics in 1883.

But Terman's advocacy of mass testing raised other issues that would turn out to be subjects of excruciating public and scientific debate (although he could not have believed that at the time). For one thing, he thought intelligence testing, such as his IQ tests, provided the perfect tool for finding out if intellectual ability was mainly the product of heredity or environment. He asked whether the "so-called lower classes" suffered from that unfortunate position because nature had cheated them or because a poor home environment and bad schools kept them there. His data hinted it was the former, and even without statistical evidence, he firmly believed that that was true.

He also felt that intelligence testing could determine if there is a relationship between intelligence and race. "Are the inferior races really inferior, or are they merely unfortunate in their lack of opportunity to learn?" he asked. Using two Portuguese boys who scored poorly on the Stanford-Binet test as a data point, he suggested that their low IQs were "very, very common" among Spanish-Indian and Mexican families in the Southwest and among African-Americans. "Their dullness seems to be racial, or at the least inherent in the family stocks from which they came. The fact that one meets this type with such extraordinary frequency among Indians, Mexicans, and Negroes suggests quite forcibly that the whole question of racial differences in mental traits will have to be taken up anew and by experimental methods."[12] He predicted that further research would show "enormously significant racial differences in general intelligence."

That he used a universe of two to make general statements went far beyond what statisticians call an "environmental fallacy." It was inexcusably bad science. However, he had no context in 1916 by which to anticipate how future scientists would respond to such a thought and how those people he so disdainfully dismissed would feel about the idea of their genetic inferiority. He could not begin to understand scientists who would fiercely object to even having the question raised or who would challenge anyone's right to do such research. Terman was reflecting the attitudes of his time.

The Stanford-Binet test was a howling success. Even Terman was surprised, especially that his colleagues were so uncritical. He knew it was imperfect; in fact he began almost immediately to think about revisions.* Stanford was impressed and eager to retain him. He had been promoted to full professor and the Board of Trustees added a large raise to $5,000 a year "to retain Prof. Terman at the University." When trustee Herbert Hoover heard Terman was being courted by the University of Iowa, he pushed for another raise.

Terman's scientific interests had now coalesced and he applied for his first outside grant, to the Rockefeller Foundation's General Election Board (GEB). It was an excellent choice; the GEB was run by a soul mate, Abraham Flexner, who had completely reformed American medical education and was pushing the educational efforts of the board in ways that were criticized for being elitist. Flexner believed that society was served best when it best served the brightest of its citizens, especially among the young. He believed that it was the most intellectually gifted who had to lead civilization, who would solve society's problems. He believed all citizens had a right to go as far as their abilities could take them, but saw nothing undemocratic in paying special attention to the gifted. He was, in short, the ideal ally.†️ Unfortunately, the grant was held up by outside forces. In April 1917 the United States entered World War I.

---

* Most of the revision was done with Maud Merrill James, who came to Stanford as a graduate student in 1919 and later became a member of the faculty in psychology. She did the next two revisions under Terman's supervision.

† Flexner went on to found the Institute for Advanced Study in Princeton.

Like most other American scientists and intellectuals, psychologists gathered to consider ways in which they could use their skills for the war effort. Harvard psychologist Robert Yerkes, then president of the American Psychological Association, called a meeting in Philadelphia on April 21. Yerkes, a close colleague and friendly competitor to Terman, had already been at work trying to get the military to adopt some of the modern tools of psychological testing. The leading lights of psychology formed a committee to develop tests that could be used by the army to evaluate recruits and draftees, to put them to the best use, and to weed out ones likely to cause problems.

The committee got space and funds from the Philadelphia-based Committee on Provision for the Feebleminded at Goddard's school for the retarded in Vineland, New Jersey, and met for two weeks to work out plans. They decided it was in the army's best interests to test everyone entering the service. Using group tests based on those developed by one of Terman's graduate students, Arthur S. Otis, the committee created the Army Alpha and Beta tests. Terman, Anna, and Helen moved to Washington to work full-time for Yerkes's group. Fred, then a Stanford undergraduate, remained behind.

Each army recruit took either the Alpha or Beta test. Those deemed illiterate by interviewing officers and those who failed the Alpha were given the Beta, which was less verbal and required fewer writing skills. Those who failed the Beta were given further tests, including the Stanford-Binet. The psychologists divided the recruits into six groups running from the brightest, called A, to the least bright, called E. The E group was dismissed from service; the A group went to officer training school. Assignments for the rest were determined by their ranking from B to D. By the end of the war 1,750,000 men had been tested, an unprecedented achievement. Almost 9,000 men were dismissed from the army and another 10,000 found themselves in a labor battalion because of the tests.

The Army Alpha test is the ancestor of all written mental tests. Although Yerkes declared the experiment a complete success, the procedure was full of holes. The most devastating critique of the tests has since been written by Stephen Jay Gould, who produced a long list of fatal flaws.[13] The tests were given in rooms with bad acoustics. Many of the recruits did not understand the directions.

Officers found that many of those with the lowest scores were immigrants or illiterates who did very well if someone took the time to help them with the language problem. Worse, the content of the tests was marred by systematic discrimination and cultural biases toward the upper and middle classes. And most fatally, many of the officers in the field thought the testing unnecessary and did their best to be uncooperative. Gould writes that the army made almost no use of the results except as an adjunct to selecting officer candidates.

The results of the test were shocking. The average intellectual age of those tested was thirteen years old, which meant that by the definition of contemporary psychologists most American males were slightly smarter than morons, but not by much. Terman's tests had set the average age at sixteen. Naturally, with the biases built into the test and the testing, African-Americans scored much lower than whites. Immigrants were classified by the nation of origin, with the smartest ones coming from northern Europe, the dumbest from southern Europe. The lighter the skin, the brighter the recruit. Frenchmen scored higher than Poles. The results were used by opponents of open immigration to limit the number of non-Anglo-Saxon immigrants to the United States. They succeeded with the immigration law of 1924, restricting people from eastern and central Europe, the inferior Europeans. Those barred included Jews trying to flee Hitler in the 1930s.

The psychologists declared a new day had dawned; one described what had been accomplished as "mental engineering." They thought of innumerable ways in which group tests could be adapted to civilian life. Yerkes, for one, felt that if students could be tested, they could be classified by mental ability and given customized teaching. Terman had hinted at similar uses when he published the Stanford-Binet. Implicit in Terman's enthusiasm was the belief that on the basis of test scores people could be categorized (crammed in niches, although he certainly didn't think of it in those terms). Society could finally get itself organized! The possible undesirable consequences of such organization seem to have escaped many of the psychologists. Oddly, it was one of Terman's former doctoral students, Kimball Young, who sounded the first warning a few years later. Young denounced the trend toward this kind of testing as "part and parcel of the general trend toward mechanization and standardization of life." Terman ignored him.

The one sense in which the tests were an unmitigated success was that they proved a large number of people could be given complex psychological tests and classified accordingly. The era of psychological testing had arrived. Terman believed he now had the tools he needed to study the complexities of human intelligence.

Terman and Yerkes went back to Flexner for funding for more tests to be used in schools. Flexner agreed to $25,000 and teamed them with the National Research Council. Terman immediately began adapting what he learned from the Army Alpha tests to a series of tests for high school students, the Terman Group Test of Mental Ability, published in 1920, and the Stanford Achievement Test in 1923. The Stanford Achievement Test was pretested on 345,735 children in 363 schools in 38 states. The test became the most widely used in the United States.

Terman also began to publish books advocating the use of mass testing in schools and to lobby for their use in California schools. He pushed for the testing to be part of the college admission procedure, pointing to a student with the IQ of a twelve-year-old who had been admitted to Stanford and then flunked out, the implication being he would not have been admitted in the first place if the admissions committee had had test results.

The smell of racism in Terman's results could not be escaped. As a doctoral student, Kimball Young did the testing in San Jose, California, a city with a majority of Latins and immigrants from southern Europe. Young's task was to compare the "American" students with the "Latins." He found "extensive retardation of the Latins as compared to the Americans." The Hispanic children received the Army Beta and still scored below the white students. He surmised, therefore, that these students were inherently dumber than the "Americans," the same conclusion reached by the army testers with a similar population and for exactly the same reasons. Cultural differences that may have skewed the reaction of the Hispanic children simply were ignored.

Terman's influence extended to the National Education Association, a teachers' group. As chairman of a NEA subcommittee, he advocated customized curricula for students depending on their intelligence as determined by testing. In 1922 he published *Intelligence*

Tests and School Reorganization in which he advocated tracking students by assigning them to gifted, bright, average, slow, and "special" groups at least through the eighth grade. The next year in a speech to the NEA, he predicted those tracks would be standard in American schools. Within a few years Terman's prediction came true.*

* The author of this book was put in a moderately "bright" track in a junior high school in South Orange, New Jersey, in the early 1950s.

Chapter Two

THE STUDY

LEWIS TERMAN'S INTEREST in gifted children went back to his student days at Clark and Indiana, but his calling probably was piqued by a twelve-year-old prodigy he met named Henry Cowell.* Cowell was a musical genius and neighborhood pet around Stanford.

Cowell had been taken out of school at the age of seven and had been educated at home by his mother, a free-lance writer. His father was a writer who spent most of his time in San Francisco with Jack London and London's radical circle. The father left home permanently when Henry was quite young. Henry had been given violin lessons early in life, but after his father left, his mother could no longer afford the lessons; she sent Henry off to work, and he became her principal means of support, working as a janitor at a nearby school. It was at that school that he was noticed by J. Harold Williams, Terman's first graduate assistant. Williams observed that Cowell spent most of the time playing the piano, when he should have been sweeping and cleaning, and playing unusually well. The school kept him on as a janitor even though he didn't do much work because no one had the heart to fire him. Henry soon became known to members of the small Stanford community. Some families allowed him to visit their homes to use their pianos. On his own he taught himself botany. He couldn't make up his mind whether to be a composer or a scientist.

Economist Thorstein Veblen's wife arranged for him to have full-time access to a piano, and members of the Stanford faculty made financial contributions to get him out of the janitor business before he was fired. They arranged for music lessons in San Francisco and

* Cowell's real name is used here because Terman used it.

subsidized a year of formal training at the University of California at Berkeley. Henry was not a lad who took formal training — or formal procedures of any kind — well and soon dropped out of Berkeley. He conspired to get the time he needed on other people's pianos.

Even his piano playing was eccentric. He specialized in rhythms and tone, spending little energy on melodies. He got the tones and rhythms he wanted, not only by playing on the keys, but sometimes by climbing inside the piano and plucking or massaging the strings or banging them with his elbows or fists.

Cowell found himself informally adopted by Paul Farnsworth in Stanford's psychology department. Farnsworth collected piano rolls and recordings of modern music for him, and an engineer put together an electronic device that Henry could use to produce his weird rhythms. He eventually played this instrument, called a "rhythmicon," with the Paris Symphony Orchestra.

Williams told Terman about the boy. Terman knew nothing about music, but believed that no one could have this kind of talent without intelligence. Cowell's score of above 140 on the Stanford-Binet seemed to be a piece of evidence to support that belief. The score was all the more remarkable because of Cowell's unconventional childhood. The fact that he had not learned the things most children had learned before they took the test seemed to reflect well on the test. Terman found Cowell's mind among the most original he ever studied.*

Terman had been collecting data informally on child geniuses since 1911. By 1915 he could issue a report on thirty-one gifted children, all of whom had been identified by the Stanford-Binet test. Several were remarkable. One girl knew the alphabet at nineteen months, could recognize sentences at twenty months, and was reading primers at two years. Another girl was reading Dickens and Shakespeare by the time she was four years old and had written a hundred poems and seventy-five short stories by the time she was eight.[1]

More important — and this both pleased and intrigued Terman —

---

* Cowell became well known among avant-garde musicians for his experimentation. His work was too extreme to achieve any widespread notice outside the music community. His music was full of brilliant bursts of sound but minimal or no melodies at all. His compositions were known for their unusual titles, such as the opera *O'Higgins of Chile* and the ballet *The Building of Banba*. He eventually married a wealthy woman, which permitted him to compose without financial worries. He taught at various conservatories, particularly at the Peabody in Baltimore, and wrote several books, including a biography of Charles Ives. He died in 1965. His influence in modern classical music is still strong.

these amazingly bright kids were not the sickly, eccentric children conventional wisdom would have predicted. Terman's tests and the observations of their teachers indicated that these gifted youngsters were physically healthy and emotionally normal. In 1916, with the help of Margaret Hopwood Hubbard, he studied another fifty-nine kids with IQs above 140, going into greater depth in his interviews with parents and teachers. Again, the results flew in the face of conventional wisdom. The only thing that marked these children as special was their intelligence, or at least their ability to score high marks on the Stanford-Binet test.

Four years later, in 1920, Stanford established a fellowship for Terman for a ten-year program to study gifted children. The funding, $1,000 a year, consisted of $250 of Terman's own money (royalties from the Stanford-Binet and his books), $250 from Cubberley, and a matching contribution from the university. By the spring of 1921 Terman had gathered data on 121 children with IQs of 140 or higher. In addition to tests and parent and teacher interviews, he used an "interest blank," a form in which the children described the things that interested them in life. He had fewer data on another thirty children. The results supported the previous studies: there was nothing aberrant about any of the children. The results became the basis for his grant proposal for a major gifted children's study he was about to commence and, in some ways, anticipated the results of that future study. Terman found:

- There is probably a somewhat higher incidence of intellectual superiority among boys than among girls.
- In physical growth and general health gifted children as a group excel unselected children of the same age.
- Gifted children who attend school are on the average accelerated about a year and a half compared with unselected children, but on an average they are about two grades below that which corresponds to their mental development.
- Only a very small minority of intellectually gifted children have been subjected to forced culture or otherwise "pushed" in their development.
- Heredity is superior. Fifty percent of the fathers belong to the professional groups; not one to the unskilled group.

- There is an apparent excess of Jewish cases and a deficiency of cases from the Italian, Portuguese, and Mexican groups living in the vicinity of Stanford University.
- Trait ratings and social data give no evidence that gifted children tend more often than others to be lacking in social adaptability or leadership. However, they are probably less superior in social, emotional, and psychological traits than in intellectual and volitional traits.[2]

He was wise enough not to draw profound conclusions from the study, but he clearly stored away the results in his mind.

Because of Terman's interest in highly intelligent children, members of the Stanford community regularly introduced him to children who impressed them (that is how he had met Henry Cowell). Among other children who captured Terman's imagination was a boy who did a whole quarter's work in physics in one day and went on to be a famous scientist and university president.

Additionally, enough time had elapsed to watch the children in the 1911 study grow up to fulfill their potential. One had already attained a doctorate and was teaching at a "great" university, and at least two others were following the same path. One young man was thrown out of the Stanford Law School for alleged cheating. He explained to Terman that he had quoted long judicial opinions in an exam, but said he couldn't help it — that's how he always thought. Terman found he had extraordinary visual memory and interceded with the law school, which reinstated the youth.[3]

Terman decided to formalize and expand his work on the gifted.

In 1921 he received a grant of $20,300 from the Commonwealth Fund with an additional $14,000 for the next year matched by $8,000 from Stanford to test 1,000 subjects for a longitudinal study, the first of its kind anywhere. Calling on his experience with gifted children in the last decade, he designed a program in which each child was to get two intelligence tests, the Stanford-Binet and the National—Form B; the Stanford Achievement Test; a fifty-minute test of general knowledge; a fifty-minute test of games; and several personal questionnaires. The parents and teachers (Terman called them "lay experimenters") were to be questioned extensively about the subjects. The subjects themselves had to keep a two-month log in little yellow notebooks of what they were reading. The subjects' homes were to be evaluated by a test called the Whittier Scale. The second Commonwealth grant was used to pay for medical or "anthropometric" studies of the children. Although Terman began calling his prospective subjects "geniuses" (and retained that word in the title of the published report *Genetic Studies of Genius*), he soon adopted the term "gifted" to describe who he was studying.

Terman spent three months setting up his study. Truman Kelley was named his assistant director. Four women were hired to do the crucial fieldwork: Florence Fuller, who came from a smaller project at the University of Minnesota; Florence Goodenough, who was working toward her doctorate at Columbia University in New York; Helen Marshall, recruited from Ohio State University; and Dorothy Yates, who had studied a small group of gifted children at Berkeley. Yates had a doctoral degree, and the other three had master's degrees. All had experience with intelligence tests; all had taught school. The office assistant was Giles Ruch, one of Terman's doctoral candidates.[4]

The team began special training. Every morning at nine, Jessie Chase Fenton, a Stanford professor, presented case studies done earlier on gifted children. At ten, L. L. Burlingame, another Stanford professor, lectured on heredity, and J. Harold Williams of the state Bureau of Juvenile Research taught a class on methods for collecting data in the field. Maud Merrill, from the Stanford psychology department, lectured on the Stanford-Binet. The team then spent hours poring over the forms they were to use, honing them until they were satisfied the answers would produce the information needed. At the end of the training period, Terman marched them off to the Stanford bookstore for supplies, fountain pens, and cameras.[5]

Terman decided to set the bottom limit for subjects at an IQ of 140, which meant he would be studying the top 1 percent of the population. Because money was limited, the cutoff was lowered to 135 in some cases to make finding subjects easier. Subjects were drawn mainly from the larger population centers of the state because such areas were easier and cheaper to sample than more sparsely populated rural and suburban areas. Terman knew he couldn't test every child in California either; there were 500,000 children between grades one and eight spread over 158,000 square miles. Merely paying for the questionnaires for that many children would have wiped out his grant. He limited the study to the big cities; rural and many suburban schools simply were not queried. Volunteer assistants spread out to some of the areas the four field-workers could not reach, but while they were energetic and competent, their sampling was not as good as that of the four professionals.

Fieldwork began September 1921. Goodenough and Fuller went to Los Angeles, Marshall to San Francisco, and Yates to Oakland, the bay island of Alameda, and Berkeley. The volunteers and local assistants hit Santa Barbara, Fresno, San Jose, Santa Ana, Pasadena, Redlands, Santa Rosa, Palo Alto, Burlingame, Kelseyville, Irwin, Sebastopol, Burbank, San Mateo, San Bernardino, a few other cities, and rural schools in San Bernardino county, the only rural area canvassed.

Terman's plan for locating his gifted students was complex and ingenious. He knew he needed to get as broad a representation as possible if his data were to have any validity. Previous literature, he insisted, was flawed by general statements based on anecdotal evidence. He knew some of the weaknesses the limitation on his sample entailed.

> Such limitation has undoubtedly affected the findings in various important ways, especially with respect to racial and social origin of the subjects, their scores on the various achievement tests, their grade achievement, their interests, their reading, and their recreational habits.
>
> The next problem was to secure a group of subjects who would be as representative as possible of all gifted children in the territory covered. A satisfactory solution of this problem would have required the application of a perfect measure of intelligence to all the children. A perfect measure was not available, and even if it had been, the cost of its application would have been too great. It was necessary, however, to find some kind of criterion for the selection of an experimental group.[6]

In the larger cities Terman's army went to the local high schools, ninety-five in all, mostly in Los Angeles, Oakland, and San Francisco.

The procedure for the elementary schools was to give each teacher a questionnaire asking him or her to name the brightest child in class, the second brightest, the third brightest, the youngest, and the brightest child in the class the previous year. All the children so nominated were given the National—Form B test. Terman reported that in grades three through eight, 6 to 8 percent of the children were tested, "but the proportion varied from school to school. In a few of the best schools as high as 20 percent of the pupils enrolled were tested; in the poorest schools, as low as 2 percent." He did not state why he was getting this discrepancy, but he felt that the wealth of the neighborhood and the quality of the school were somehow linked.

Then the winnowing process began. Terman's researchers had statistics on how each child should do on the National by age group, culled by Terman himself from an earlier study in Vallejo, California. They sorted out test results for the top 5 percent of the nominated students, but that produced too few. They then sorted out the top 10 percent (the ninetieth percentile). A few exceptions were made for those who came close but did not quite meet that criterion, although Terman later lamented that perhaps he still lost some subjects by not bending the rules enough. There were, it turned out, some children who did not do quite as well on the National as they did on the Stanford-Binet.

Those who made it that far were given an abbreviated version of the Stanford-Binet, and those scoring 130 or higher were given the full battery of the Stanford-Binet tests.* Terman seemed sensitive to the problem of foreign-born children who might have problems with the language-intensive aspects of the Stanford-Binet, but thought the nomination process more than compensated for that; teachers were likely to see beyond the language problem when they made the nominations. Additionally, the abbreviated version of the test was less dependent on language. He also used that part of the National that was least language-dependent.

Terman feared he would be missing some children, so he had his field researchers also test the siblings of children who passed the tests, which added several children to the main study group, including most of those below school age. Casual, anecdotal information provided a few others. Someone would hear of an unusually bright child in the neighborhood and Terman researchers would track down that child for testing. An accident provided one subject; a teacher incorrectly

---

* Terman knew the Stanford-Binet did not always give reliable results with older students, so children over the age of fourteen were given his group test, which he felt was more accurate for that age group. Children in grades one and two skipped the National test, which was too advanced for them.

reported the name of a child on the list adjacent to the youngest. That child was the only one in the school who scored higher than 140.[7]

Experiences at the schools varied, sometimes depending on how cooperative or bright the principals were. Marshall's first school, with 600 students, was so well organized she was done in a week. She found two gifted children. In her next school a series of bureaucratic snafus, including the insistence that no child could be tested without permission from the parents, and her own inexperience greatly delayed testing. In her third school, with 1,800 children, she found not a single child who qualified as gifted. In the next she found several. She reported to Terman that the socioeconomic class of the school had a great effect: schools in poorer neighborhoods produced few gifted; schools in wealthier areas did much better. She did not say why she thought this was so. She worked in San Francisco for nine months and found 350 gifted children for the study.[8]

Goodenough seemed somewhat daunted by her assignment in Los Angeles. She asked Terman if she really needed to search the fourteen schools for juvenile delinquents, and he responded that she should use her own judgment. She seemed to feel that these children would not be as bright as children who had not gotten into legal trouble, a dubious assumption but one Terman was hardly likely to contradict. She also assumed — and again he was not likely to disagree — that since delinquents tended to come from the lower classes, the pickings would be lean. Terman's bias became a self-fulfilling prophecy.

To evaluate his sampling process, Terman selected seven schools in Santa Barbara and tested every student with the Stanford-Binet to see how many gifted children he was missing. He found he was getting about 75 percent of the gifted children in each school. "The field assistants estimate, however, that the efficiency was nearer 90 percent," he wrote, but he didn't say why there was disagreement. As an additional check, he retested one school in Los Angeles with 350 children and one in San Francisco with 800 pupils, both schools among the most productive in the initial screening. In the Los Angeles school the first run-through produced twelve subjects (one for every twenty-five students), and the San Francisco school produced twenty-eight (one for every twenty-eight enrolled). In both cases teachers at the schools protested that the researchers had missed too many very bright children, so Terman asked them to nominate the brightest and second brightest from among those not nominated before. These were then tested. The Los Angeles retest failed to produce any new subjects, but the San Francisco school came up with ten. Terman reported that meant that of the total of fifty subjects "thus located in these schools, 20 percent would have been missed but for the second survey." That might have given him cause to worry, but Terman did not suffer from self-doubt. "It is entirely improbable," he reported, "that the general loss was anything like as great, for the chances of loss would be lower in schools attended by average or inferior populations." These, of course, meant those of the lower socioeconomic class. He therefore adjusted his methodology.

> After a little experience the field assistants adapted the method of search somewhat according to the type of school in which they were working, and as a result were both able to save time and to make the search more effective. In the best schools more pupils were tested than the scheme called for, while in the poorest schools it was not necessary to test so many. In the good schools much testing was done in grades one and two, but if a large school had netted no cases in grades three to eight, it was deemed safe to omit grades one and two.[9]

In other words, in schools where he felt it unlikely to find many gifted children (that is, poorer schools), he dropped testing in two grades, thus ensuring a serious bias in the study. His only acknowledged loss was that he did not study private schools, especially in Los Angeles, where they tended to be "numerous and patronized by the superior social classes," but somewhat less so in San Francisco, where most of the private schools were parochial.

The survey turned up 643 cases out of a school population of 168,000.* This group constituted what Terman called the main experimental group. Terman believed if the worst case were true, that he was missing 20 percent of the gifted children in California, the group used for the study should be about 812 children, about 0.5 percent of the children in the state.

The nomination blanks contributed almost 70 percent of the chil-

---

* Terman's figures are used here. Terman also lists these 643 cases by city, and the figures are a bit odd. He finds the ratio of gifted within the student body to be 1 in 235 in San Francisco, 1 in 330 in Los Angeles, but 1 in 100 in Alameda, which is inexplicable. Alameda was and is a working-class city adjacent to a navy base.

dren; the rest were siblings of the nominated pupils or were found by accident or retesting. Teachers' estimation of the smartest kid in class produced 15.7 percent of the total. Among the categories recommended by teachers, oddly, the most productive was the youngest in the class, yielding almost 20 percent. That category contributed more to the study than did the teachers' nominations for the brightest. It is not clear why; certainly Terman never considered the possibility the youngest in the class were also the most challenged, which contradicted the educational philosophy of Hall, his mentor. But he admitted puzzlement about the finding. "If one would identify the brightest child in a class of thirty to fifty pupils, it is better to consult the birth records in the class register than to ask the teacher's opinion."[10]

Sometimes the testing simply missed extremely bright children. Two youngsters who were tested but failed to make the cut grew up to become Nobel Prize winners: William Shockley, who coinvented the transistor, and physicist Luis Alvarez. Terman didn't live long enough to know that. None of those who made the study became Nobel laureates.[11]

Sometimes the parents created problems. Six refused to allow their children to participate in the study. Many thought mental testing somehow implied their children were not "normal," and some fought the notion that some children were intellectually superior or inferior to others. Terman did his best to proselytize parents when he could. He did not want the study to get too much publicity, fearing, correctly, that parents whose children were not tested would volunteer their kids en masse. More than two hundred did, and Terman had to turn them down. Children found in the smaller towns far from the metropolitan areas, such as Sebastopol, well north of San Francisco, had to travel considerable distances to complete the testing program, and parents were sometimes reluctant to make the trip.[12]

In addition to the main experimental group, Terman formed three smaller groups. The second group consisted of 128 cases from his previous study, whom he called the "Outside Binets," and another 228 located between 1921 and 1922 by volunteer assistants from outside the search area, including some from outside California. Data for this group were incomplete and Terman did not count them in his first report. A third group came from a cooperative study carried on with help of California high school and junior high school principals based on group intelligence tests. This group included 444 cases. A fourth group, called "special ability cases," consisting of children who had special talent in art, music, manual training, "domestic science," and agriculture. Terman was disappointed to note that few of these prodigies, just three boys, had intelligence that measured high enough to be included in his study. Henry Cowell had been an exception. The average score of the special ability cases on the Stanford-Binet was only 114. Of a total of fifty exceptional art students in Los Angeles, only fifteen were deemed worth testing, but Terman found that they ranged from an IQ of 79 to 133, with an average of 109. Terman concluded that musical prodigies tended to be brighter than artistic prodigies.[13] Only one became relatively famous, the actor Dennis O'Keefe.

The total study group consisted of 1,444 children, with 831 boys and 613 girls. The main experimental group (643 cases) included 14 children between the ages of two and four. Two girls in this age group had an IQ of better than 190. Most of the subjects ranged in age between eight and twelve. A nine-year-old girl recorded a 185.

The second group, those from previous studies, included a five-year-old boy and a seven-year-old boy who both scored 190 and several other children who reached 185. Two children, both girls, scored 192.

Terman's first report on his gifted study showed even he was struck by the differences between the sexes: his cohorts were far too unbalanced toward boys to go without some kind of explanation. The difference in the ratio of boys to girls in the three groups is shown in the table below.

Terman went to considerable effort to find out just how skewed his

GENDER DIFFERENCES IN GIFTED CHILDREN GROUPS

Groups	Boys (Number)	Girls (Number)	Total	Boys (Percent)	Girls (Percent)	B-G Ratio
Main group	363	313	676	53.6	46.3	116-100
Second group	197	159	356	55.3	44.7	123.9-100
Junior and senior high school	257	121	378	68.0	32.0	212.3-100

data were and why. Using 1907 figures compiled by J. B. Nichols, he reported that the ratio of males to females in living births of whites in the United States was 105.9. The excess in males in stillbirths was even greater. He added that this was so for other mammals as well, not just white American humans. Terman, however, decided to be conservative and use the ratio of boys to girls in the pre–high school population of the cities he surveyed: 104.5 boys to every 100 girls, far smaller than the boy-girl ratio in his sample. "Our problem is," he admitted, "to explain the difference between this ratio and those found for the gifted groups." He proposed four explanations: (1) biased sample, (2) more boys in families with gifted children, (3) differential death rate of embryos, (4) differences in variability between boys and girls.

As to the first explanation, Terman doubted that the nominating process produced the skewed sample; after all, almost all the teachers making the recommendations, particularly for the main group, were women. So, too, he might have noted, were almost all his research assistants. Only one of his female assistants, Leta Hollingworth, suggested bias in the sample.[14] He seems to have ignored her remarks. Going back to the original nominating forms to look at names would not solve the problem, he admitted, as it was sometimes difficult to tell the gender of a nominated student by a name; but even with that caution, he went back to the forms and found that the apparent ratio of boys to girls nominated by teachers (not including those brought into the survey in other ways) was 109.7-100. That's slightly above what it should be, but nowhere near the kind of distortion in the gifted groups. Additionally, the ratio of those selected from the nominated group, those who passed the test, was 135.3 boys to 100 girls. The teachers, he concluded, were not the problem. That left the tricky question of whether the Stanford-Binet test itself was biased. He did not think that was the case, citing "the numerous investigations that have been reported on this point in the literature of mental tests. . . . The results have shown fairly consistently that, age for age and grade for grade, girls do fully as well on this test as boys." Since he did not adequately survey private schools, he floated the idea that if he had, it might have tilted the ratio back toward females — perhaps private schools enroll more gifted girls than boys. But he conceded that that was not likely to make a difference.

The second possible explanation for the difference in ratios was that families with gifted children have more boys. At the time Terman began analyzing his data, he had the family profiles of 502 families, which had produced 317 gifted boys and 274 gifted girls, a ratio of 115.7 boys to 100 girls. The ratio for all the children in those families was slightly higher, 119.5-100, still unusual. But the gifted boys tended to have more brothers than the gifted girls. "It has been suggested that superior vigor or vitality of parents favors maleness of offspring, and that this factor might at the same time exert a favorable influence upon the nervous structure and mental development of the offspring," he wrote.[15] He said there was some evidence for this, including one study of pigeons. Female pigeons determine sex, unlike in mammals where the males have that responsibility.

> If the female is stimulated by removal of eggs from the nest to keep on laying, the eggs later produced result in an excess of female offspring. By analogy, one might infer that in the case of human beings, superior vigor of fathers would result in an excess of male births. It need hardly be said that analogical reasoning in the biological field has no value except in so far as it suggests investigation. It is true, however, that the medical and anthropological data which we have secured indicate that gifted children come from families of more than average vigor.[16]

He added that since his data indicated that gifted children were healthier than the norm, infant mortality was likely to be very low. The children also had grandfathers whose longevity was higher than normal. The answer then might be that vigorous families were more likely to produce gifted boys. But the data didn't support that conclusion, he lamented. The longevity records of the families involved showed no statistical difference from the records of other families. Going back to a biographical reference book, Terman found 478 of the men in the book produced 716 sons and 668 daughters, a ratio that almost exactly matched the general population. It had to be something else.

If the figures for stillbirths were factored in, would that explain the preponderance of boys to girls? This question implies that his data are real, that there are more gifted boys than gifted girls and that Terman was merely explaining that fact. Unfortunately, data were lacking, but Terman noted that there were far more boys in families reporting no miscarriages than there were girls and suggested that might be significant. "If mothers of the gifted group on the whole have excelled mothers of the generality [the normal population] in the ratio of live births to conceptions, the excess of gifted boys would readily be accounted for."

Terman wrote that a gender skew could have been caused by greater variability among males than females, but that the data showed boys were slightly less variable in their IQ scores than the girls, and the statistical difference was negligible. That explanation didn't work. Terman had only one conclusion left: "exceptionally superior intelligence occurs with greater frequency among boys than among girls."

> The true cause of the sex ratio found can not be determined from our data. It may be either variability or the differential death rate of embryos. Both of these factors may be involved and possibly others. Biased selection due to the method of nomination and testing is probably not responsible.[17]

The demographics of the sample were interesting for other reasons as well. Here again, even Terman was troubled by the skew in the sample, but he used that to bolster his theory of the inheritability of intelligence rather than worry about other possibilities.

He broke down the sample by "racial origin," which in this case meant finding the national origin of the children's grandparents for whites and the race of the grandparents for African-Americans and Hispanics. The data came from questionnaires filled in by the parents. All those from the British Isles together accounted for about 67 percent of his sample. Almost 31 percent of the grandparents were of English origin, the largest single national group. Jews accounted for 10.5 percent of the sample, while African-Americans, "Mexicans," Syrians, and Icelanders were 0.1 percent each. The rest were generally of European stock. He did not have census data on the cities covered in his survey (although it's not clear why), but he suspected the general population was considerably different from his children.* The overrepresentation of Jews in the sample troubled him, and he thought their number was even larger than it appeared: "There is reason to believe that the presence of Jewish blood has in some cases been concealed," he wrote. The best estimates he could get from Jewish

---

* California did not have the extensive minority populations in 1922 that it has now, so the difference is somewhat less than it would appear in some cases.

social workers was that the Jewish population of Los Angeles, San Francisco, and Oakland was about 5 percent, so his sample contained at least twice the number of Jewish children it should have.

African-Americans, on the other hand, were underrepresented in light of their number in the general population. The population of the three cities plus Alameda and Berkeley was 2 percent black, yet Terman's researchers found only two African-American kids and these children were "part white."

There were no Chinese children in the sample because the Chinese typically went to their own schools and Terman's researchers did not sample there. Japanese children accounted for 0.6 percent of the sample, also below what it should have been, but quoting another researcher, Terman reported that Japanese children were not believed to be inferior to California white children.

The lack of "Latins" in the sample shouted for attention, and Terman could not help but notice. By "Latins" he meant not only Hispanics (almost always Mexican in California in the 1920s), but, reflecting his time, Italian and Portuguese as well. Terman wrote that IQ testing of those groups has shown "consistently low scores" in the past, with a median of between 75 and 85—80 being "a liberal estimate." He wrote, "How much of this inferiority is due to the language handicap and to other environmental factors it is impossible to say, but the relatively good showing made by certain other immigrant groups similarly handicapped would suggest that the true causes lie deeper than environment."[18]

Terman investigated the social class of his children by looking at information supplied by the parents on a Home Information Blank. Here he slid into the morass of social science's penchant for quantifying what should be left unquantified. First, he listed the occupations of the fathers along the same lines as the U.S. Census. He did not consider the occupations of the mothers. He found that the fathers of his gifted children came largely from the professional and commercial occupations. The children of executives and managers predominated. More than 29 percent of the fathers were professionals, 46.2 percent came from the general commercial classification, 20.2 percent came from the industrial group (tailors, carpenters, mechanics, florists, and so forth), and only 4.5 percent came from the public service group (postmen, firemen, mayors, military personnel, and so forth). Terman then looked at how those occupational groups matched the general population, using 1910 census data for Los Angeles and San Francisco. He was not surprised by what he found (see table below).

OCCUPATION OF GIFTED CHILDREN'S PARENTS

Occupation Group	Proportion of Fathers of Gifted	Proportion of Men in General Population	Percent
Professional	29.1	2.9	1,003
Public service	4.5	3.3	137
Commercial	46.2	36.1	128
Industrial	20.2	57.7	35

Only one father in the gifted group gave his profession as laborer, although 15 percent of the male population in California were laborers. Terman then went through biographies of American men of science and men of letters and found they matched his statistics fairly closely.* And from that, Terman could reach a conclusion:

> It has often been argued that this superiority in achievement should be credited for the most part to the larger opportunity for achievement enjoyed by members of the favored classes. *Our data show that individuals of the various social classes present these same differences in early childhood, a fact which strongly suggests that the causal factor lies in original endowment rather than in environmental influences.* [italics in original].[19]

The effect, in other words, proves the cause.

His conclusion was bolstered by checking other factors. Using a scale created by another social scientist, Terman's lieutenants rated the neighborhoods in which his children lived on a scale of 1 to 5, with 1 being "very superior." The average rating was 2.25, slightly below "superior." He explored home environment. Terman found his sample had fewer divorces than the California average. Teachers were asked to fill out forms describing any "significant facts" they knew about the children's home lives. The questionnaires asked about the children's friends, whether they received any instruction at home, if

---

* A study by Havelock Ellis on British men and women of genius did not.

they traveled much, if they were spoiled or loosely controlled. He found that 85.1 percent of his children lived under "probably favorable circumstances." He checked the size of the home library (the average home had 328 books), the education of parents and grandparents, and their genealogy* and found what he expected to find: *"the data . . . offer considerable indirect evidence that the heredity of our gifted subjects is much superior to the average individual* [italics in original]."[20]

He collected everything he could find about the families of his gifted, even down to the number of miscarriages recorded and the causes of death of parents (most fathers died of accidental death; the mothers died from a variety of causes). He listed chronic illnesses of the parents (the largest number of mothers were listed as suffering from "nervous troubles"). Not surprisingly for Terman, he went into considerable depth on the history of tuberculosis in his children's families (31.5 percent of the families had it somewhere in recent generations).

Terman put together an altogether amazing amount of data about the physical attributes of his subjects. Bird Baldwin, a graduate assistant, handled this part of the report. Three centers were set up, in Los Angeles, in San Francisco, and at Stanford. The parents brought their children to the centers for examination. Almost every physical aspect that could be measured was, in examinations that took about twenty minutes. In a few cases, the parents had kept growth charts of their children, and Terman could use those for comparison as well. For many of the children, it was the earliest memory of being one of Terman's kids.[21] Appointments were set up; the children were excused from school on the days of the examinations. Six hundred twenty-three children, mostly from the main experimental group, were measured. Of those, the data on 594 were tabulated. (Some were left out because they were in other groups, including the specially talented who did not have IQs of 130.) Terman wrote:

---

* The children in the main study group included descendants, direct or otherwise, of John and John Quincy Adams, Benjamin Franklin, Samuel Clemens, Andrew Jackson, Henry Longfellow, Ulysses S. Grant, Harriet Beecher Stowe, Rube Goldberg, Hiram Johnson, Albert Michelson, John Alden, Ethan Allen, P. T. Barnum, James Buchanan, Ezra Cornell, Elbridge Gerry, Benjamin West, and George Washington. Twelve of those in the main experimental group had parents or grandparents in *Who's Who,* well above the statistical norm. Terman traced one family back through ten generations to someone who immigrated to the colonies in 1630; that family contained thirty-four people of fame and distinction.

The attitude and the cooperation of the parents and children were exceptionally good throughout the study. In general, the children appeared to be physically well developed and normal. Mentally they were alert and quick to respond. Socially they were well mannered and showed good spirit. The parents of the mentally superior children, as a rule, showed a great interest in the welfare and training of their children.[22]

Terman collected all the data he could find on the measurements, especially height and weight, of children the same age as his subjects, including national figures based on a sample of 124,000 and a control group in Oak Park, Illinois. His published report contained several pull-out charts with the data in minute type, all gathered, analyzed, and correlated thirty years before the invention of the electronic computer, an impressive feat.

He found to his undoubted pleasure that his sample of the brightest of California's children were somewhat physically superior in terms of growth and size to the average American child. The boys "surpass the girls in the averages of all traits" until they are twelve; then the girls pass the boys. The girls are more physically variable than are the boys.

So much for the notion that very bright children are smaller and weaker. Terman then attacked another crucial question: were gifted children more sickly, frailer, less robust than average children? To his glee, he found out the answer was no.

Terman compiled data from questionnaires filled out by school personnel, parents, and the physicians who examined the children. The forms left nothing unasked, down to whether the children sleep with a bedroom window open. The researchers compared the subjects to a control group of children from the same schools, usually from the same class. The teachers also were encouraged to try to match each control kid with a gifted kid of nearly the same age.

Terman even collected data on the length of pregnancy of his children's mothers (94 percent went full term) and the mothers' health during the pregnancy. He checked how many of the births were normal, involved induced labor, were breech presentations, and required cesarean section. Why he thought any of that was pertinent is not clear in his report, but Terman was, if nothing else, thorough once he got going. He asked whether the children were breast feeding (only

8.2 percent of the gifted were bottle-fed, much lower than the national average), and asked how long breast feeding went on. Every disease was tracked, again with a special emphasis on tuberculosis. He listed injuries, surgical procedures (tonsillectomies, circumcisions, etc.), frequency of headaches, urinary problems, eating habits, and even frequency of mouth breathing instead of nose breathing. Hearing and vision were checked. The children were examined for pubic hairs, one doctor concluding that if the pubic hair appeared kinky or twisted on boys, the boys had reached puberty. Menstruation of the girl subjects was tallied.

Of particular interest to Terman was the general category he called "nervous disturbances." They ranged from nail biting through restlessness, excitability, teeth grinding, restless sleep, sensitiveness, and stuttering. Both the home and school questionnaires asked: "Is the child especially nervous?" Again, Terman was investigating, and hoping to disprove, the commonly held belief that very bright children tended to be more sensitive and nervous than other youngsters. He found that the boys in the gifted sample seemed to be slightly more nervous than boys in the control group; the girls less so.

"IS THE CHILD ESPECIALLY NERVOUS?"

	GIFTED			CONTROLS		
	Boys	Girls	Total	Boys	Girls	Total
School report	16.3	9.6	13.3	15.9	16.4	16.1
Home report	24.7	15.0	20.4	—*	—*	—*

* Parents of control children did not fill out this questionnaire.

His conclusions put a major dent in the stereotypes of "genius" children.

- The gifted walked on average one month earlier than the control children and talked three and a half months earlier. They also got their teeth a bit earlier.
- The gifted suffered no more or less from contagious diseases than did the less gifted.
- The gifted had slightly more surgical operations than did the controls, mostly adenoids and tonsillectomies.
- Half as many gifted had headaches.
- The gifted had better nutrition.

- The gifted had the same number of colds and had fewer hearing problems.
- Indications of "nervousness" and stuttering were reported less frequently for the gifted than for the control group. "Excessive timidity" and "tendency to worry" were reported with about equal frequency for the gifted and control groups.
- Pubescence seemed to arrive a little earlier for gifted boys, although Terman admitted the small number of cases made this idea "tentative."
- A greater percentage of girls in the gifted group than of girls in the control group menstruated (48) before the age of thirteen.

Terman found that the children in his sample seemed to be slightly larger, healthier, and better adjusted than the children in his control group. He did not attempt to explain why.

Terman, however, didn't leave it at that. Some 780 children from various of his groups underwent intensive physical examinations. These included 87 percent of the 578 families in the main experimental group.* Everything was probed and studied. The results were the same: Terman's gifted children were healthier than average children. One physician called the examinations

the most satisfactory of any series of examinations I have conducted. The quickness of these children in comprehending what was desired of them in the various tests was a delight. As a whole, there was unusual ability to concentrate attention, and self consciousness was less noticeable than in the average child. The home care, cleanliness and health habits, such as diet, hours of sleep, etc., indicated superior intelligence on the part of the parents.[23]

Terman seems to have found something in his sample that rises above the obvious biases. That his children had "superior" genes is debatable; that they lived in a superior environment compared to that of other children was not. The controls came from the same schools, even the same classrooms, apparently selected at random. Terman was not comparing his children to children of different social classes and radically different environments; they were more or less children

---

* He lost some of his children because their parents were Christian Scientists and refused to let the doctors near their children.

drawn from the same socioeconomic class. Separating out heredity from environment now becomes more difficult.

It is easy to dismiss aspects of Terman's study because of the manifest flaws in his sampling technique, even if the flaws more or less reflected the state of social science in the 1920s. But whatever he was measuring intellectually seemed to be repeated in his physical data. Although the physical differences between his kids and the controls were not great, they did exist; they were statistically significant and meticulously documented.

Once Terman felt he had dismissed the folklore about the physical characteristics of the gifted, at least for childhood, he finally turned to their intellectual — or at least academic — accomplishments.

Not surprisingly, he found none that could be called "retarded" by the normal definition of the word to mean a much lower grade level than would be expected at a given age. Although it's not clear why he felt it necessary, he went to great lengths to prove that a genuinely retarded child could not score 130 on the Stanford-Binet.

Terman found that 85 percent of his kids were accelerated in class, on average 14 percent ahead of their ages. They generally skipped a full grade. He found 4 percent, however, who had been held back. They did best in classes of intellectual substance, according to their teachers, while they shone less brightly in such courses as penmanship, sewing, manual training, and physical education. About half excelled in math. Generally, they wracked up impressive scores on the Stanford Achievement Test and other similar tests, but their intelligence level was higher than the level of their achievement scores. Oddly, Terman's gifted seemed to be underachievers.

Nearly 50 percent could read before they entered school, at least 20 percent could read before the age of five, and 6 percent could read before the age of four. Interestingly to Terman, who passionately believed children should not be pressured, 70 percent of the parents said they let their children proceed at their own pace, 20 percent said they pushed, and 10 percent actually tried to hold their children back.

The children tended to read much more than other children; 90 percent read more than the average, and the average gifted child at age seven read more books during the two months in which the group kept logs than any of the control group up to age fifteen. More striking to Terman was what they read. Few children in the main experimental group or in the control group cared much about reading fairy tales. The gifted tended toward science, history, biography, travel, nature and animal stories, "informational fiction," and the classics. Their reading was more catholic than the controls.* Of the twenty most liked books, the gifted boys and girls agreed on five: *Ivanhoe, Treasure Island, Call of the Wild, Three Musketeers,* and *Tale of Two Cities. Treasure Island* topped the boys' list, *Little Women* the girls'.†

When the gifted child played he or she was more apt than the ordinary child to pick games with some mental challenge. Terman concluded that gifted boys tended to be somewhat more "masculine" in their approach to play than boys in control groups, but his girls showed no difference from control group girls.

And what kind of kids were they? Terman and his associates gave each one a battery of character and personality tests, a relatively new field of psychology at the time. One test, to see if the children overstated their achievements, presented a list of book titles and asked the child which ones he or she had read. The list contained a number of ringers, such as *Scouting in Strange Lands.* Another test asked about the kind of friends the child would most like to have. Another test attempted to measure trustworthiness.

In almost every category the boys in the study (both gifted and control) did better than the girls. But the gifted showed a "significant superiority" over the controls in every category.‡

The gifted child of nine years has reached a level of character development corresponding roughly to that of unselected children of fourteen years. . . . Although these tests do not make possible a very reliable comparison of individual children, they warrant the conclusion that in the traits which they measure, the gifted group is decisively superior to the control group, and that this superiority is greater for girls than for boys.[24]

* The boys' tastes in both groups tended to be broader than the girls'. By the age of nine or ten the boys tended to change to more realistic or serious books, while the girls did not, probably more a reflection of sexual roles than anything biological.

† The Oz books were not counted because they were a series, not a single book, but they were immensely popular.

‡ He also reported a similar study of his high school group, which tended to show similar findings.

He reported happily that although he admitted the children had superior home lives, he found nothing in this aspect of the study that showed any impression made by superior environment. Again, their superior development had to be in their genes.

He went back to the same group two years later and found nothing dramatic had changed in their lives. "Prediction as to the probable future of these children," he wrote finally, "would be profitless. We can only wait and watch."

CHILDHOOD

Beatrice

FROM THE DAY SHE WAS BORN, it was obvious that Beatrice Carter was going to be a most unusual child. Her mother certainly thought so. Gladys Carter began keeping a precise, detailed, hand-written journal of Beatrice's life before she was a year old. She noted that Beatrice was large; at birth on January 20, 1912, she weighed eleven pounds twelve ounces; at six months she weighed nineteen pounds and was twenty-seven and a half inches long.

"Always had a strong back," Gladys wrote. "Turned in bed when two days old to the nurses' great excitement. Tried to stand at two months. When three months old, her father said, 'Do not let her stand. She is too young.' When she was given to him, I was delighted to hear him say, 'Bend, Beatrice, bend,' for she had braced herself against him and was standing upright. At six months, danced while her mother held her."

By seven months Beatrice was trying to walk and could say "papa." She refused a high chair after eleven months and spent most of her time looking at scrapbooks her parents made for her containing copies of the art of the masters and bird pictures. She was lulled to sleep at night with English, French, and German folktales.

Beatrice's father, Henry, was a prominent lawyer in Belmont, California, a wealthy suburb south of San Francisco. He did appellate work for the Southern Pacific Railroad. While his wealth did not match that of some of his neighbors, the Carters were comfortable. Henry was fifty-four years old when Beatrice was born. Gladys was thirty-nine.

If Beatrice was physically advanced, it was apparent that her mind was also remarkable. By nineteen months she spoke clearly and knew the entire alphabet. By twenty-two months she could recite Mother Goose and gave every sign of having total recall. At two years she started reading. "In fact, each new stride she made was a complete surprise to us for we thought she was too young to do anything definite," Gladys wrote in her journal. "When not playing there was an incessant 'read to me' and 'all over again' with patient grandmother willing to yield." A few months later, Beatrice began making up her own stories, simple little tales of rabbits, frogs, fish, and squirrels. She began pecking out tunes on the piano.

Beatrice became the light of Gladys's life. She saved all of Beatrice's works, not only out of doting pride, but also because she thought Beatrice would be famous. Her pride was hardly misplaced. By the age of seven Beatrice had read over seven hundred books, in most cases more than once. "They include," her mother wrote, "all the great works of fiction that I know of, most of the great poets (she has loved Burns since she was four), though she has read only parts of Shakespeare so far, science, art and history. I am grateful that she loves all kinds of literature for that makes her education so broad." She was cited in Ripley's *Believe It or Not* for having read fourteen hundred books by the age of ten. Beatrice was writing her own works as well, usually poetry. At age seven she wrote:

A PRAYER

O Master of Fire, O Lord of Air,
O God of Waters, hear my prayer.
O Lord of ground and of stirring trees,
O God of man and of pleasant breeze,
Dear Father, let me happy be,
As happy as a growing tree.

The Carters felt Beatrice was better off not to be in school, where she might be held back, so they began her education at home, an education centered on the mountain of books Beatrice was collecting and reading. But worried that their daughter had little or no contact with other children — not that she had anything in common with children her age — her parents somewhat reluctantly sent her off to a private girls' school in Palo Alto at the age of ten. There Lewis Terman's researchers found her. She was tested on August 2, 1922.

Terman could not have done better than Beatrice Carter, who scored 192 on the Stanford-Binet test. She had one of the four highest IQs recorded by Terman in his study.

The researchers also gave Beatrice Terman's test of masculinity-femininity factors, which was designed to measure a subject's interests against those of the general population (see page 79). Beatrice was found to be "noticeably masculine." Field-workers who visited the Carter home wrote that her play interests "resemble those of [a] much older child."

By this time Beatrice's fame had grown, and the fact that she was accepted for Terman's study of the gifted quickly became common knowledge. Terman was sure he knew the source of the information. A San Francisco newspaper did a feature story on Belmont's "wonder child," describing how "the writing of poems comes as naturally as the play instincts. . . . The study recently made by Prof. Lewis Terman . . . of this phenomenal child, who has read 1,400 books and written hundreds of verses and stories, showed that her inspirations come from incidents in her 'play life.'. . . 'The majority of Beatrice's poems have been written in less than ten minutes,' says Prof. Terman in his report on Beatrice. . . . "Several of Beatrice's poems completely fooled an English class at Stanford where they were presented anonymously with some of the little known work of Tennyson, Longfellow and other masters."

The Carters gave the newspaper the results of Terman's studies. Terman was probably livid. But in Beatrice, Terman got more than he bargained for. He got Gladys as well.

Jess

PREDICTING the achievers and nonachievers in Terman's study of the gifted was a risky proposition. Children do not necessarily become merely older versions of themselves when they become adults. People change as they grow. Luck is a factor. And the adults who do the predicting can miss or misjudge a child's traits and abilities. All of the above was true of Jessurun Oppenheimer, better known as Jess.*

"A conceited, egocentric boy," one of Terman's field-workers sniffed after an interview with the teenaged Jess in San Francisco. "Ruined by mother. Has her attitude of fault-finding in others, looking for someone else to blame."

"Too playful, too socially inclined in school," wrote one of his teachers. "Doesn't study at home. Does poorly in arithmetic. Very careless."

"Gave the impression of being very pushy and forward although he did not show these characteristics during the interview," wrote Melita Oden, one of Terman's assistants. And, in what would prove to be the single funniest line in all of the Terman files, she added, "I could detect no signs of a sense of humor."

"I had a rotten childhood," he remembered later. "And I deserved it. I was a self-centered, sarcastic, un-sharing little brat. I was also bright. I delighted in telling others they were wrong, and then proving it. Knowing from past history that I would need ammunition for future fights and arguments, I carefully inventoried all the weak points of everyone I knew, and worked them into carefully worded

* His real name is used with permission.

phrases calculated to inflict the most pain. I was ostracized by my playmates, beaten up frequently, and constantly humiliated."

Jess was the son of a young German-Jewish immigrant who got into the luggage trade after the 1906 San Francisco earthquake. Told to evacuate his apartment, James Oppenheimer went to a luggage store to buy a suitcase. The proprietor was so terrified by the quake that he decided to flee the city. He turned over the store and the inventory to Oppenheimer at ten cents on the dollar. Jess's father eventually had the largest luggage store in San Francisco and was known as "Oppenheimer the Trunk Man."

Jess was tested by Terman's assistants at the age of eight with an IQ of 141, just high enough to make the study. That he did even that well on the tests is amazing because Jess had a first-class handicap, what would now be called a learning disability. The handicap was one of the reasons he was so unhappy as a child and had so much difficulty coping with other people.

"I had very little communication with other people. I didn't seem to know how to act with them. It later turned out — not until I was in the service in 1942 did I discover it — that my eyes had always looked in two different places, and not constantly, so I just assumed since I'd always seen this way that this was normal, that everybody had two heads. When I played baseball I'd see two balls coming toward me, but since I had four hands and two gloves it wasn't too difficult to catch both of them. I can joke now, but it was very sad. I had never seen a third dimension; I couldn't study because every time my eyes jumped to read, the page would go apart and come together again, but I didn't know it. . . .

"I had no stereopsis. I couldn't locate sounds in space. I couldn't hear music. I couldn't hear two tones together to form a third tone, a harmonic."

His brain insisted on reading the impulses from both eyes and both ears, but was incapable of putting the impulses together. He drove very carefully because if a truck was approaching, he saw two trucks. The world was constantly in motion. When his eyes moved in one direction, the world moved in the other. He suffered from vertigo.

Jess was average size, the field-workers reported, with very heavy dark black eyelashes, very dark complexion, brown eyes, and brown hair.

His ambitions during childhood were unclear. At one time he listed law and advertising. If he had any talent it was as a tinkerer, and for a while he seemed interested in becoming an engineer, particularly an aeronautical engineer. His favorite subject was Latin, and his parents thought he should be a Latin teacher. When he took Terman's aptitude tests, nothing stood out. "This is directly in line with the difficulty you have been experiencing in coming to any decision regarding your life work," Terman wrote him. The vocations listed in the results seemed "awfully trivial to me," Jess replied. "Hasn't any responsibilities," a field-worker wrote when Jess was in high school. "Anxious to get a job now to earn money for a cut-down Ford."

He did have one other interest: radio. He bought his first radio with the winnings he earned as the "house" in a crap game he ran on the grounds of the Presidio, the army post near the Golden Gate. He was fascinated by the idea of radio, the notion that politicians could talk directly to the public instead of through newspaper reports, that an entertainer could reach a million people at one time. He became a "go-for" at a San Francisco radio station and even tried his hand at writing a sketch or two.

The family survived the depression because the day before the market collapsed, James Oppenheimer, thinking the financial markets had gone stark raving mad, sold all his stock — over the loud objections of Jess's mother.

James Oppenheimer died in 1931 when Jess was seventeen. That left Jess and his sister (who also made the Terman study) with their mother, Stella.

"I don't remember much about my father," he said. "I do remember that he loved to laugh, and I remember wrestling with him, especially when I was able to pin him for the first time. He was a very easy-going man. I recall an argument he and my mother once had about an employee of his, the store manager, who was, if not stealing, indulging in some very questionable accounting practices. My mother insisted — and she had an insist that would fell an ox — that he be fired. But my father, who almost always gave in to her, said, 'Look, he runs the store better than I can. I make more with him pocketing the money than I would if I fired him and ran it myself.' "

Jess's mother never flinched from dominating her children. "In the beginning," Jess once joked, "there was mother." Stella thought life was a battle, she against the world. One evening the grown Jess and his wife took his mother to a restaurant. The entrée had just been served when Jess noticed his mother looking around.

"What do you want, Ma?"

"Nothing. Do you see the waitress?"

"What's wrong?"

"It's nothing. These string beans are cold, that's all."

"Okay, let me handle it."

"Why do you always do that? Don't you think I know how to be tactful? The beans are cold. I want to ask her to bring me some warm ones. Does that take the secretary of state to handle?"

"No, it's just that—"

"Well, I'll take care of it, thank you. Oh, there she is. Miss."

The waitress came to the table. "Yes, ma'am?"

Jess's mother held out the dish of beans. "I wouldn't serve these to a dog!"

Jess was accepted by the University of San Francisco, but because he then thought he wanted to get into aeronautics, he asked Terman to help him transfer to Stanford. Terman wrote to the admissions committee saying that Jess was in his gifted group and that Jess's academic work so far was "only fairly good, but this does not represent his grade-getting abilities. I think he will make a creditable record if he is admitted to Stanford University."

As usual, the letter worked, but Jess left Stanford after three years, apparently by invitation. (He was not the only Terman kid to leave Stanford under such circumstances, and not the only one to discover that this was not necessarily one of life's great tragedies.)

He tried his hand at several jobs, including being a fur salesman, until in 1936 he decided to leave San Francisco to find his fortune in Hollywood. A friend, Ralph Freud, who produced plays at the San Francisco Jewish Community Center, helped him overcome the objections of his family by working out a deal: Jess would go to Hollywood and if he did not earn a minimum of $500 in six months, he would come home. He left for Los Angeles in a ten-year-old yellow Packard convertible, leaking oil all the way.

Jess remarked several times that he had incredible luck. It took him exactly one day to find a job and an apartment. No sooner had he arrived when by chance he ran into an old friend who told him that the Young & Rubicam advertising agency was looking for writers. Young & Rubicam, like all major advertising agencies of the day, controlled the content of radio programs. While he was waiting in the reception room at the agency for an appointment, he heard two writers talking about scripts they had written that had been rejected. By the time the conversation was over, Jess had learned exactly why the scripts had been rejected and what the agency was looking for. He dashed from the office, found and rented an apartment, set up his typewriter, and returned to the office by six that same day with a completed script. He was hired at $125 a week to work on the Fred Astaire radio program. On his first day in Hollywood he knew he would not have to return home to his family.

Ira

IN 1912 psychologist Henry Goddard reported on a New Jersey family, the progeny of a Revolutionary soldier, whose retarded mistress seemed to carry the genes for criminality and insanity. While some members of the family appeared normal and bright, generation after generation produced people who were criminals, people who were seriously insane, and some who were criminally insane (known to their neighbors as "Horrors"). Most of the "Horrors" were retarded. Goddard called the family the "Kallikaks," a fictitious name. Ignoring any possibility environment was at least partially to blame, Goddard surmised that they carried demon genes.

Ira Seaburg seemed to carry such a burden. Ira came from a long line of people who were genuinely crazy. One aunt was institutionalized for "epileptic furors" which turned her into a homicidal maniac. Other aunts, uncles, and cousins were almost as mad, many of them institutionalized. Indeed, four collateral branches of Ira's family were in asylums. Social workers said they suffered from insanity and criminality, and as if they were being punished for sins in a prior life, some bore the ghastliness of elephantiasis. Ira's mother was in and out of state institutions. One social worker called her "insane" and a psychiatrist described her as suffering from "constitutional inferiority but no psychosis," but whatever the diagnosis, she was incapable of surviving by herself in the real world or caring for her children.

Nothing is recorded about Ira's father. He had abandoned his wife and two children perhaps to escape the lunacy in his wife's family. Ira and his sister Molly became wards of the juvenile court and lived in the Pacific Hebrew Orphanage in San Francisco. They spent their nights and weekends at the orphanage, their days at public school in the city. It was at school that Terman's researchers found Ira. He was eleven years ten months old when his teacher listed Ira's name as the youngest child in her class. When the Stanford-Binet tests were completed, it was found that Ira had an IQ of 143. Since a general characteristic of the "bad Kallikaks" was retardation, the people running the orphanage had hopes he would escape his bad seed.

A picture of Ira, taken about the time of his test, shows a serious, dark-haired boy with an oval face and troubled brown eyes. He wears a jacket and tie, his shirt collar open. Ira bit his nails. He spoke too much and too quickly and showed a tendency for braggadocio. His teeth were yellow and old-looking, and he was described as "an *institutional* child." He was in poor physical condition, suffering from psoriasis patches on his arms, legs, and chest.

When he was admitted to the gifted study, a doctor reported to Terman that at the age of thirteen years four months Ira was 57.6 inches tall and weighed 79.1 pounds, slightly underweight.

The orphanage was not something out of Dickens; the Jewish community in the Bay Area provided sufficient funds to keep several dozen children living comfortably, at least physically. The director, Dr. John Lang, was described by a Terman field-worker as "cold-blooded, regarding his charges more as guinea pigs than as humans. The physical environment of the institution is ideal, there is a great deal of money available for providing the needs of the children, but the atmosphere is a bit too rare and intellectual for comfort. I think he [Lang] was quite just to Ira at all times; I question whether he was ever kindly."

If Lewis Terman was going to research genius, he eventually had to confront the connubiality of genius and madness. He found it in Ira.

Ira did poorly at school, showing an occasional glimmer of the genius recorded in Terman's test, but beginning many things and finishing few. He would appear genuinely surprised when he found other students, obviously less bright than he, getting better grades, and he would apply himself vigorously for a few months showing what he could do, and then what he would not do. His interests, a teacher wrote, seemed mechanically oriented, and Ira announced he would be an electrical engineer. One of his high school teachers wrote,

"Fond of 'confidential' chats with a single person — boy or adult — but will not mix in games or company. Fond of attracting attention. Will not stick to assigned tasks in school or at home. Therefore has a poor to bad record in nearly all subjects. Has real musical ability, but won't practice and has had to give up music. Models in clay and draws well."

He went to the best high school in San Francisco, Lowell, where he seemed to have friends, enough so that he was elected class treasurer in his senior year. School administrators soon found he had "misappropriated" the class funds, and Lang, who was legally responsible for the boy, called the juvenile court. It was not the first time Lang worried about how closely Ira would follow his heritage: he was found to have made lewd advances to some of the younger girls in the orphanage and was thrown out.

Ira was too clever for the juvenile court. He fled to Los Angeles to avoid prosecution, and he got a job (perhaps with Lang's assistance) on a shipping line and went to sea for several months. Then he disappeared.

His sister Molly was still in the orphanage. She provided the only source of information for the authorities and the Terman office about her brother's whereabouts. He visited her occasionally, she reported, "looking filthy and smelling worse."

"One gets the impression," Terman's field-worker said, "that this may be a case of beginning dementia praecox," an old word for schizophrenia. The researcher felt that Ira's genetic trap was about to spring.

In May 1929, Ira fell in love with a girl in New York City. When she rejected him, he walked into a Greenwich Village bookstore and swallowed cyanide. He was eighteen at the time.

The Tadashi Family: Emily

EMILY RENEE TALBOT was the beautiful young daughter of an Episcopal bishop in San Francisco. She had brown hair hanging almost to her waist, deep green eyes under thick, dark brows, and a bent, whimsical smile. Her ancestry could be traced through most of American history and back to twelfth-century England. She could count as her relatives signers of the Declaration of Independence Charles Carroll and Elbridge Gerry, six colonial governors including John Winthrop and William Bradford of Massachusetts, and scores of writers and artists. The family had almost a half dozen ancestral estates all over the British Isles. Emily lived in a lovely house near Pacific Heights with her parents, a brother, and a sister, surrounded by love, culture, and the kind of liberal tradition nurtured by this most liberal of Episcopal bishoprics in this most liberal of American cities. Coddled, admired for her wit, beauty, and intelligence, she was unprepared when the love of her young life entered through the kitchen door.

Akio Tadashi had received little formal education in Japan, but had studied silk culture and lectured widely on silk. He was large for a Japanese man, about five foot four, an inch smaller than Emily, with a round face, wide dark eyes. In 1911, at the age of twenty-nine, he immigrated to California and scoured the streets of San Francisco looking for work. He found that there was little demand for his main area of expertise. He also fancied himself an expert on eastern philosophy and occasionally talked his way into giving a lecture on that subject. Akio found his income did not begin to cover his living costs, and he liked to gamble a bit at race tracks. He realized he would have to find a steady job, no matter how demeaning. He found one, in the kitchen of Bishop Talbot's San Francisco home.

No one knows how it happened, but one day Emily, then aged twenty-three, was seen kissing Akio at the Corte Madera depot. Emily was getting on the train back to the city. They had fallen in love, a difficult thing for them to do as Akio spoke little English and an inconvenient thing for them to do at a time when racial discrimination flourished. Her parents were distraught. They were not the kind of people to take extreme action; they did not order Akio out of their home or forbid their daughter to see him, but they made clear their displeasure.

When it became evident that the couple were serious, they tried to reason with Emily. They talked about the harsh reality of racism and prejudice, how difficult the two would find it. California forbade interracial marriages. No white woman had married a Japanese man in California or, to their knowledge, anywhere in America. Where would they live? Who would rent to them? And what about their children? Even if Emily and Akio thought they could cope with racism, they were dooming their children to a world they did not ask for and could not understand. Was that fair? Fairness, however, is not necessarily an impediment to love. All Emily could think of was Akio. Emily's parents had no idea what Akio was thinking, but they did know that the two were determined to get married.

The California laws on miscegenation were explicit: they could not marry in the state. On August 14, 1913, the two took a train to Portland, Oregon, where, they had been told, there were no laws forbidding their marriage. Not only could they find no one who would marry them, but they were warned by a justice of the peace that if they persisted, they would be run out of town. A week later they boarded another northbound train and got off in Seattle.

Seattle was still a small town, living off its glorious past as the great supplier for the Klondike. By and large Seattle didn't much care what people did with their personal lives as long as they were quiet about it and didn't overtly break any laws. There were no laws against miscegenation. Emily and Akio found a minister willing to perform the ceremony, and Emily became perhaps the first Caucasian woman to marry a Japanese man in the United States.

They took the train back to San Francisco in something resembling triumph. Emily was quickly pregnant. She produced five children in six and a half years. Although the law forbade interracial marriage, it said nothing about cohabitation. They were not violating the law by living together, but they certainly were violating the mores of the times. Newspapers wrote stories about the family.

"Thinking back," she wrote later, "we now feel glad that the publicity happened for this reason: Our marriage has always been a public affair. At the time it took place it was prophesied that the children of such a union would be monstrosities physically and sub-normal mentally. Perhaps it is just as well since that idea was given wide publicity that these articles should appear in confutation of that."

Ten years later visitors reported the Tadashis to be a large, boisterous, happy family. Akio was now working as a nurseryman and gardener. Emily's mother had moved in with them to help after the bishop died. "All adult members of the household have made it their aim to bring up the children in the best possible way. The father as well as the mother is much loved by the children."

The family loved camping, hiking, and studying nature. The children eagerly collected caterpillars and observed them as they went through their different stages to emerge as butterflies or moths. The children loved acting and dramatics, playing charades and producing playlets for the family.

For reasons unknown, the family moved to a chicken ranch near Placerville, in the foothills of the Sierra, in 1920. The ranch, which turned out to be a disastrous financial venture, was two miles from the nearest town and school. "Conditions are such," Terman reported after a field-worker visited the family, "as to make a natural social unit out of the family, and as there are enough members of it for evening games and amateur dramatics, they find great enjoyment in their own pursuits."

Soon after, Akio left home, unhappy and penniless. He could not support his family, and was too far from the nearest race track. He did not come to America to live on a chicken ranch. He went back to San Francisco and eked out a living as a "character reader" and insurance salesman. Character reading didn't pay, and he was a failure as a salesman because he simply didn't believe in insurance.

"He found it far more interesting to describe in an excited way the various deeds of valor he had performed on behalf of California

Japanese," Terman wrote after meeting Akio following the separation, "the lotteries that he had started in Japanese districts through impassioned newspaper appeals, the silk worms he nurtured in Japan, than to discuss the future of his children. He seems to have lost all interest in his family and remarked during our talk, apropos the separation: 'I don't worry about it, and neither do they.' "

He died of a heart attack in 1932 or 1933. No one knows for sure.

After Akio left home, the task of raising the five children fell to Emily. Emily had almost no money. She did not need much, she thought, just enough for food and clothing. Poverty, she said, was a state of mind, and she didn't happen to be that way. It required real inner strength, she said, to survive being poor, and she firmly believed she had it. Terman's field-workers were less philosophical, reporting back that the family was living in real poverty. The field-workers, however, reported that the family was still happy and "in full harmony" despite Akio's absence and the poverty. A visitor described the home as "extremely plain. The ceilings are peeling, wallpaper is fading to nothing, but the living room has a fireplace, the room is adorned with wild flowers and gives a cozy impression."

After Terman's assistant Barbara Ramsperger and her husband visited the Tadashis, she wrote back to Emily: "We both left with the feeling that we had made lasting friends in you and your mother and the children. Once in a long time one meets friends whose strength and poise and gaiety give something of permanent value to every one they touch, and meeting you has meant that to me."

When Ramsperger asked about the relationship between the children and their father and his race, Emily wrote back: "I really do not believe they were conscious of the racial element. Unfortunately, he was more and more a failure as a husband and father for reasons which I believe were quite personal and had nothing whatever to do with race. It was rather a pity that I did not choose more wisely, but any way, the children are delightful. So perhaps, the urge of the heart results just as well as the decisions of the head."

Emily had met some of her Japanese relatives, liked some, disliked others. There was even a young Japanese man she wouldn't mind as a son-in-law, although her daughters expressed no interest.

The children undoubtedly suffered because of the move from the city.

"In San Francisco," Emily wrote, "the children early formed a small, select circle of friends who advanced with them from grade to grade through grammar school and into high school. In a large community there was no occasion for them to be brought into contact with any who were violently antagonistic. In Placerville, the situation was different. New contacts had to be formed in a community sufficiently isolated to be extremely reserved in its attitude toward all newcomers. The children had reached an age when they had come to recognize the fact that prejudice might and probably did exist. Young children are usually happily ignorant of this. Their very recognition of this fact probably affected (quite involuntarily) their own attitude toward their new associates."

Her daughters told her they thought the prejudice was a test that separated the "sheep from the goats." They had no intention of having as a friend someone who could be that bigoted, they said. Their racial background would filter out such a person, leaving only people they could be close to.

Newspapers wrote about the children after one of the teachers in their school revealed to a reporter that they were in Terman's study of genius. A former United States senator, James T. Phelan, wrote to the president of Stanford ranting against the peddling of such nonsense as a study showing an extremely bright brood of children arising from a mongrel family. The senator quoted Herbert Spencer as saying that hybrids from race crossings were always inferior to either of the parent races. (The Terman office sent a strangely weaseled response to the senator. A letter apparently not from Terman — no signature appears on the carbon copy — assured the senator that the tests were not conclusive; that although the Tadashi children did well, "the test scores were by no means as high as many white children"; and that one can't make any conclusions about mixed marriages from the results.)

"I am reconciled to being an experiment and to the fact that any affair must always, to some extent, seem public property," Emily wrote.

The newspapers wrote kindly about the children, noting that "each morning they drink a glass of salt water and take a cold bath" and that this regimen constituted the only rule of the house. The children were well behaved even without discipline. No one was ever spanked or scolded. They were good children.

What they were not were "monstrosities." Physically, they seemed to range the spectrum. Ronald, the youngest son, looked classically Japanese; Sophie, the oldest, was an American beauty like her mother.

And they most certainly were not "sub-normal mentally." Teachers had recommended to Terman four of the five as the brightest in their classes. Delores, the youngest, was not yet in school. When the Tadashis were tested, they were substantially above the cutoff. When Delores was old enough to be tested, she too made the main experimental group. Their IQs ranged from 143 to 154, and when Terman got to test Emily, she was almost off the scale. Emily Talbot Tadashi was five for five, having produced the largest family of genius in the Terman study.

"One naturally awaits with eagerness and some anxiety the outcome of the struggle which these children must wage against the handicap of poverty and yet greater handicap of race prejudice," Terman wrote. "That such children should not have a fair chance in a country which boasts of its democracy is enough to bring a blush of shame to anyone who is not utterly lacking in fair-mindedness."

Chapter Three

GENIUSES OF THE PAST

WHILE TERMAN WAS SETTING UP his longitudinal study, one of his graduate students, Catharine Cox (later Catharine Cox Miles), was beginning a collateral study that must rank as one of the silliest experiments in the colorful history of social science. It earned her a Ph.D. from Stanford.

Cox and Terman were fascinated by the idea of going back through history and studying past geniuses with the hope of determining their IQs. One of Terman's predecessors provided the model. Francis Galton (see page 6) had done his own study of genius and was one of the first to conclude genius was hereditary.

Galton was himself an easy subject for such an enterprise. Galton's biographer, Karl Pearson, painted a picture of an astonishingly precocious child who could read at age two and a half and could write letters before he was four. By age five he could read almost any book written in English and a few in French, could add any sum, had mastered all the multiplication tables except for the nines and elevens, and could tell time. Pearson seemed only mildly impressed: "I do not think we can say more than that Francis Galton was a normal child with rather more than average ability." Terman was more impressed. Psychologists had measured other children who could perform such feats, and extrapolating backward, Terman concluded that Galton must have had an IQ of at least 200, a level reached by perhaps one child in fifty thousand. Could researchers measure other historical characters? Terman said he thought it would be valuable to understand the childhoods of certified geniuses of history, and that justified Cox's proposed dissertation topic. More important, it might be guessed, showing that these monuments of the past had had high IQs might be taken to substantiate Terman's claim that he was in fact measuring something discrete and quantifiable.

Cox had to find subjects for her dissertation and to decide how to do retroactive IQ testing. The difficulties were daunting. She chose inclusion in a biographical dictionary as a criterion for selecting possible subjects. Terman wrote:

> Although possessing the merit of objectivity, this criterion, admittedly, is far from ideal in that eminence is influenced by circumstances other than intellectual achievement. The population it affords is the result of innumerable selective factors which vary from age to age, and from culture to culture. The genius who survives as such has successfully run the gauntlet of premature death, the stupidities of formal education, the social and ethical pressures of his immediate environment, and the more general cultural influences that have given direction and content to the civilization in which he was born. Moreover, a man's eminence is not a static thing; it rises and falls with the value transformations that cultural changes inevitably bring. Genius in the sense of eminence is not a biological concept, though it does have biological prerequisites in ancestral genes, nutrition, and escape from mortal disease.[1]

Terman knew that studying geniuses we know of from the past tells us nothing about the geniuses we don't know about. But Cox pursued her project.

First, how to find these geniuses. James M. Cattell, one of Hall's students at Johns Hopkins, had compiled a list of the one thousand most important men of history according to the amount of space they received in bibliographical dictionaries. He literally took out a ruler and measured the length of the biographies; the longer the biography, the more important the person. From the five hundred with the longest biographies, Cox eliminated those born before 1450, those from hereditary nobility or royal families, and a few whose fame had nothing to do with mental prowess. That left her with 282 men. She then went about trying to discern the IQs of her sample, dividing them up into A1 IQ to measure birth to age seventeen and A2 to measure age seventeen to twenty.

Using the biographies and other sources, she looked for interests, education, school standing and progress, friends and associates, reading, and achievement. Most weight was given to documents such as dated letters, compositions, poems, mothers' diaries, and other evidence. She and her researchers accumulated 6,000 typed pages of data, a victory of volume over common sense. She then gave the data to three psychologists who knew about intellectual age and mental performance. Their role was to estimate the minimum IQ that would account for the subjects' childhood performances and to rate the credibility of the evidence on which that IQ estimate was made. The IQ was to be the lowest possible level considering the evidence. The average of the estimates was the primary data used for the study.

The average A1 IQ was around 135, the A2 almost 145.[2] For the entire group the estimated minimum IQ ranged from 100 to 200, with an average of 155. Terman reported to a scientific meeting:

> The latter figure is more than three standard deviations above the mean of the generality. . . . Low estimates in the range of 100 to 120 IQ occurred only when there was little biographical information about the early years. The mean was highest for philosophers (170), and next highest for poets, novelists, dramatists, and revolutionary statesmen. The lowest was for soldiers (125), the next lowest for artists (140), and musicians (145). The mean for scientists (155) was identical with that for the total group.[3]

He assured his audience that these figures represented estimates and were "not to be taken too literally." He admitted that in most cases biographical information was insufficient to do better. "Despite the inadequacies of her study, I believe that the author's main conclusion is warranted: namely that the genius who achieves highest eminence is one whom intelligence tests would have identified as gifted in childhood."

Not necessarily. Stephen Jay Gould points out that Terman fudged the data in his report. Cox actually took her results to *five* psychologists. Three of them agreed substantially in their estimates of the IQ; the other two disagreed considerably, one well above the score, one below. Cox simply discarded the two anomalous authorities.[4]

She, of course, was not measuring IQ; she was measuring the length of biographies in a book. Generally, the more the information, the higher the IQ. Subjects were dragged down if there was little information about their early lives. As Gould points out, the premise is that all the subjects had childhoods that were equally observed and noted or that if there was no information, it was because the child did nothing notable enough to attract anyone's attention. Also, if IQ is not supposed to change through time, why is the A1 score substantially lower than the A2? Why did Michael Faraday, the great English scientist, have an A1 of only 105, but an A2 of 150? The reason, Gould believes, is that there was more information about him as a youth and young adult than as a child. Cervantes and Copernicus came out with average scores, 105, because little or nothing was known about their childhoods.

Further, no consideration was given to external influences. If John Stuart Mill could learn Greek as a child, is it possible that others could have learned it too but simply never had the chance? Cox accepted Terman's tenet that intelligence was inherited and looked at the professions of her subjects' parents. If the father or mother was a professional, she added to the subject's score. Consequently, subjects from the poorer classes were handicapped in her study.

Cox's extrapolations were extraordinary. Napoleon's general André Masséna came in at the bottom of the class with a rating of 100, just an ordinary man. His problem was that all anyone knew of his childhood was that he served as a cabin boy on his uncle's ships. Cox remarked that "nephews of battleship commanders probably rate somewhat above 100 IQ; but cabin boys who remain cabin boys for two long voyages [as Masséna had], and of whom there is nothing more to report until the age of 17 than their service as cabin boys, may average below 100 IQ."[5] She did not say how she knew that. Masséna was lucky; Cox massaged the data for several subjects, including him, to get them over the 100 IQ mark.

Some were penalized for being rambunctious children (Jonathan Swift, to name one). She seemed prejudiced against performing artists such as musicians, throwing off Mozart as "above the average level of his social group."

Terman crowed:

We are justified in believing that geniuses, so called, are not only characterized in childhood by a superior IQ, but also by traits of interest, energy, will, and character that preshadow later performance.

The ancient saying that "the child is father to the man" probably expresses a truth far more profound than anyone has hitherto suspected.[6]

Cox got her Ph.D. and Terman used her study to bolster his beliefs for years. Terman told a scientific meeting that Cox "has made a substantial contribution to our knowledge of the early mental traits that underlie prodigious achievement in adult life." She, of course, did no such thing.

Chapter Four

THE BATTLE OVER TESTING

IT DID NOT TAKE LONG for intelligence testing to attract dissenters; a number of critics came forward after the war, some of whom were upset by the elitism and racism that showed in the results of the army testing and the possibility that the results would be misused. The expanded use of the Stanford-Binet also kicked up controversy. The study of the gifted was not in itself considered dangerous, but the credibility of the testing that served as the scientific underpinning of the study was the target of criticism. What was Terman measuring? How were these children different from other children of the same age? Were they the beneficiaries of a genetic gift or an advantaged life? Or both? If the tests used to select these kids were invalid, who and what was Terman watching? In other words, how much attention should be paid to Terman's study of the gifted?

What bothered the critics primarily were the implications of mass intelligence testing and the dangers inherent in the use of the results. And what results! Was it really true that 47.3 percent of white male Americans were borderline morons? What are the ramifications in a democracy if a fair portion of the potential electorate is not very bright? Do you restrict the franchise to those who can understand the issues and candidates or do you let just anyone vote? One writer in the *Atlantic Monthly* suggested that "we may have to admit that the lower grade man is material unusable in a democracy, and to eliminate him from the electorate." The data that caused the rumpus were drawn from Yerkes's report, and no one involved in the army testing, including Yerkes and Terman, was willing to contradict publicly either the data or the conclusions drawn from the data.

For a while Terman stayed somewhat removed from the fray. The severest critic of this "scientific" categorizing of humans was the young Walter Lippmann, who would later become the dean of liberal American columnists. Lippmann took after Terman specifically, pointing out the discrepancy between the average intelligence level established by Terman's Stanford-Binet and the much lower level demonstrated in the Army Alpha test. Lippmann, writing in the *New Republic* and *Century Magazine*, concluded that the discrepancy destroyed the credibility of the Stanford-Binet. More important, he challenged the notion that Terman was measuring any innate ability that could be called intelligence, a position not dissimilar to one Binet himself took. Lippmann wrote: "Without offering any data on all that occurs between conception and the age of kindergarten, they [the researchers] announce on the basis of what they have got out of a few thousand questionnaires that they are measuring the hereditary mental endowment of human beings."

He assaulted the statistics in the Stanford-Binet work and spoke out heatedly about the dangers of categorization.

> The danger of the intelligence tests is that in a wholesale system of education, the less sophisticated or the more prejudiced will stop when they have classified and forget that their duty is to educate. They will grade the retarded child instead of fighting the causes of his backwardness, for the whole drift of the propaganda based on intelligence testing is to treat people with low intelligence quotients as congenitally and hopelessly inferior.
>
> If it were true, the emotional and worldly satisfactions in store for the intelligence tester would be very great. If he were really measuring intelligence, and if intelligence were a fixed hereditary quantity, it would be for him to say not only where to place each child in school, which to college, which into the professions, which into the manual trades and common labor. If the tester would make good his claim, he would soon occupy a position of power which no intellectual has held since the collapse of theocracy.[1]

Terman did not take this criticism lightly. Besides attacking Terman's livelihood, Lippmann was assailing the foundation of his science and his reputation. He immediately suggested that Lippmann, a journalist, not tell scientists how to do their work. In a classic *ad hominem* attack, he heaped scorn on the writer and then defended, but only in general terms, his science. He said the discrepancies between the tests could be attributable to the different amount of time allotted to the tests. He denied the tests indelibly marked children. He admitted the tests did not measure pure intelligence, but rather intellectual ability plus other factors.

His colleagues applauded his counterattack, which was published in the *New Republic*. Some of the praise was from psychologists circling the wagons in defense. Some of it was simply support from friends of Terman. Some of it was disreputable, such as that from the biologist E. G. Conklin, whose letter to Terman was openly anti-Semitic. No less a light than John Dewey pitched in to attack this quantifying of human worth. The idea of

> abstract, universal superiority and inferiority is an absurdity. Now we welcome a procedure which under the title of science sinks the individual in a numerical class; judges him with reference to capacity to fit into a limited number of vocations ranked according to present business standards; assigns him a predestined niche and thereby does whatever education can do to perpetuate the present order.[2]

Terman concluded that fighting about scientific matters in the popular press was a losing proposition; the average American could not comprehend the complexities of the issues. "I think that answers in the future will be confined to presentation of data in scientific periodicals," he said.

But scientific journals, even in his own field, gave him no peace either.

The most serious scientific debate was with George D. Stoddard of the University of Iowa's Child Welfare Research Station. The battleground for the opening rounds was a yearbook project of the National Society for the Study of Education (NSSE). In 1928 Terman chaired the yearbook committee and the topic that year was the nature versus nurture debate. Both sides felt they came out of it victorious, and as is usual in this kind of debate, no minds were changed. In 1940 Stoddard was chairman. He wanted to reopen the debate and invited Terman to serve as a committee member. The Iowa scientist had data that directly contradicted Terman and the hereditarians.

Bird T. Baldwin, Stoddard's predecessor at the station, had collected longitudinal data on IQ tests. After Baldwin's premature death, his work was carried on by Beth L. Wellman beginning in 1932. Wellman found that mental growth, at least as measured by IQ tests, increased as a result of education. In short, a child's IQ could be increased by the educational environment. In one case Wellman found a group of preschool children who increased their IQ by an average of about twenty-seven points. Moreover, a control group of children locked in an orphanage showed a decrease of 20 points. Terman would find the same thing years later, but didn't know it at the time.

Stoddard, as the station chief, acted as spokesman for his researchers. He felt that the only valid use for IQ tests was to measure change and that the tests should not be used as a mass screening process. Terman believed exactly the opposite, that IQs *don't* change to any large extent. How could they if they were measuring something that was largely genetic? Battling a lay columnist like Lippmann was one thing; here was a respected scientist doing work that could not be sloughed off. Terman appropriately took it as a direct threat to his career and reputation. He immediately launched his graduate students to scientific meetings to counter the Iowa scientists. Florence Goodenough went to meetings about the yearbook. A year later another Terman student, Quinn McNemar, was commissioned to find holes in the Iowa report. He succeeded in finding so many that Terman asked that his paper be independently published. Wellman was invited by the journal in which it was published, the *Psychological Bulletin*, to respond, which only raised the level of invective.

An open public meeting was held at Stanford in July 1939. Terman arranged it so he had a full hour to speak, Stoddard only ten minutes. Terman's speech was loaded with sarcasm and vindictiveness, to the extent, according to Stoddard, of making faces when he mentioned any of the Iowa psychologists. Even Terman's friends thought he behaved poorly. He then tried, and succeeded, in preventing Stoddard from enlisting federal officials in a plan backed by the Iowa group to make use of their findings in the nation's educational system. When he was invited to a meeting on the same subject later that year at Columbia University, he sent Goodenough with instructions not to "mince words . . . I think you know I was none too polite in my address here [at Stanford] in July." She reported to Terman that while she addressed the meeting, Stoddard was at the World's Fair talking to the "masses." Terman sent another student, Lowell Kelly, to the meeting of the American Association for the Advancement of Science, again to counter the Iowa speakers.[3]

The NSSE yearbook committee met first in St. Louis in February 1940. Terman reported he was astounded at the "propaganda" the Iowa researchers were promulgating. "They seem to think they have demonstrated that feeble minds can be brought up to average by their nursery school program and that the average can be made into the exceptionally brilliant. These preposterous contributions are not backed up by data at all convincing."[4] Actually, the Iowa researchers had not gone nearly that far in either their data or their conclusions.

Throughout the conflict Terman, in his virulence, greatly misrepresented the Iowa findings. Wellman never discounted a heredity component to intelligence, saying both genes *and* environment were factors. "In the life space of the child," Wellman wrote, "these two are never separated: he is a flexible, changeable, responding organism within wide limits set by heredity and other organic conditions, and within other wide limits set by environmental stimulations and opportunities."

Both sides discredited the other's research in the yearbook papers. Stoddard, somewhat stunned by the guerrilla warfare launched from Stanford, stuck to his conclusions, somewhat to the amazement of a number of observers. "I am inclined to agree," Terman wrote a supporter, "that Stoddard is a dangerous man." When Stoddard went before a convention of educators to recommend limitations on IQ testing, Terman wrote: "It seems to me as though he is willing to go any distance in the direction of distancing data to suit his needs."

"It wasn't stubbornness," Olga McNemar said, trying to explain the virulence of Terman's attack. "It was absolute confidence in his beliefs."

Fortunately for Terman, Stoddard's position failed to gain any popular support, either among educators — who seemed to like having complicated ideas simplified into numbers — or the general public. Stoddard finally left Iowa to become education commissioner of New York State. Terman told friends Stoddard had been forced out, but that is not true. Nonetheless, Terman, the hereditarians, and those committed (in some cases financially) to mass intelligence testing won the war.

In 1922 Stanford had moved its rising new star from the School of Education to the Department of Psychology. He replaced Frank Angell, an incompetent administrator but popular teacher, whose department had graduated exactly one Ph.D. student in the last thirty years. Terman had the resources he needed to rebuild the department. University founder Leland Stanford's younger brother, Thomas Welton Stanford, had left the university $500,000 which he wanted to be used for "psychical research." When he learned of the intended bequest before Stanford's death, David Starr Jordan, then Stanford's president, afraid that the money would be wasted, talked him into modifying his will to add the words "and psychological" after the word "psychical." That freed up some of the money. The first part of his bequest went to fund a fellowship in psychic research, which Terman gave to J. E. Coover,* a holdover from the Angell regime. Terman used the rest of the bequest to build one of the finest psychology departments in the United States.

"He was an ideal department head," Ernest Hilgard, one of his recruits, remembered. "He did just everything to help you get funded, and he didn't interfere with your work at all." Olga McNemar, who worked for him as an undergraduate and then came back as a researcher with a Ph.D. (she was the wife of his assistant Quinn McNemar), remembered him as "just about the nicest person that you could work for. He was kind, he was considerate." He was also a "disciplinarian" and he could be cruel if he was disappointed in a student's performance.

Terman had reached the apotheosis of his career, arguably the most influential psychologist in the country. They were happy days for him. He had the money and financial support to hire the faculty he wanted, some of them old friends, former students, students of friends. His personal life was generally calm and accommodating.

---

* Coover produced a respectable, scholarly book on ghosts, entirely skeptical of sightings and other reported phenomenon. He later branched out into extrasensory perception, also showing a high degree of skepticism.

Chapter Five

THE PROBLEM WITH SEX

SEX AND GENDER were the source of one of the great weaknesses in Terman's work, especially his study of the gifted. Considering the amount of research he did on sex and gender, the persistence and degree of the sex biases seem surprising. His initial sample was wildly skewed against girls, and his subsequent life studies emphasized the accomplishments of the men far more than those of the women. He seemed genuinely unable to measure the life satisfaction and successes of his female Termites; he didn't even know how to phrase the questions.

By 1925, perhaps bothered by the bias in his sample, he tried to find ways to quantify the differences between the sexes. Such quantification might help him to weight some of the results or perhaps even to modify the Stanford-Binet to counter the criticism that it is male-oriented. He hardly broke new ground here. Havelock Ellis pioneered sex studies in 1894, and hundreds of tests had been designed in the first decade of the century to measure sex differences, both physical and intellectual. Terman and Catharine Cox Miles (see page 68) decided to study differences in instinctual and emotional traits, the effect of age and maturation on masculinity and femininity, the effect on education of the fact that most teachers were women. Some of these tests were first adapted from his first study of the gifted. His only conclusions had been that women tended to be more subjective, men more objective.[1]

In order not to tip the purpose of the test to the subjects, Terman and Miles called it the Attitude-Interest Analysis Test, which could have meant anything. Terman believed that if subjects understood the nature of the test, they could deliberately bias the results. The test was designed so that "masculine" tendencies scored as a positive, "feminine" as negative, androgynous as zero. Terman and Miles were measuring personality; they made no claim they understood the causes of individual scores, although they thought the test could provide a tool for a study of that kind. They wanted an objective tool clinicians could use to measure how a person might deviate from the norm in matters of gender. Subjects had about 450 multiple-choice questions, divided into subsections such as word associations, questions about interests and emotional responses, and inkblots. For instance, in word association the subject had to select a word related to "jealousy." A choice of "lover" or "woman" was considered a masculine response; "angry" or "green" was considered a feminine answer. When the subject was asked to complete the sentence "Eggs are best for us when," the answer "fried" or "hard-boiled" was considered masculine, "deviled" or "soft-boiled" feminine.[2] Terman felt no discomfort with sexual stereotypes.

The results fit the cultural norms of the time. Better educated men scored as more feminine than men with less education; athletes of both sexes were more masculine than nonathletes. Engineers, lawyers, and salesmen tended to be more masculine than artists and clergymen (and presumably writers). Artists, in fact, just barely scored on the plus, or masculine, side. Among women, differences between housewives and those who worked (generally in traditionally feminine jobs) were not great. Teachers scored lower than housewives on the femininity scale.

To Terman's surprise, the study was widely criticized on the grounds that it was full of data without theory and that it simply reinforced cultural stereotypes. Terman countered that the study was necessary because teachers and psychologists often judged masculinity and femininity wrong when dealing with students or patients. The result was they did not fully understand the motivations behind what people did to compensate for confusion in sexual identity. Some children might be pressured into accepting what society deemed as the appropriate patterns of personality. "The less aggressively inclined males will be driven to absurd compensations to mask their femininity; the more aggressive and independent females will be at a disadvantage in the marriage market; competition between the sexes will be rife in industry, in politics, and in the home as it is today."[3]

In their various tests, Terman and Cox had found 134 male homosexuals. Studying homosexuals in the 1930s presented enormous problems, homosexuality being still hidden away. Terman brought in two of his assistants, Quinn McNemar and Lowell Kelly.* One of them was to go to San Francisco to do the fieldwork; the other was to stay at Stanford to handle the data. McNemar volunteered Kelly to do the fieldwork. Terman, who knew little about homosexual culture in San Francisco, which even then had a fairly large and relatively open population, suggested Kelly visit the jails and reform schools. Kelly located a prisoner who offered to locate other homosexuals, and Kelly produced a sample of eighty-eight, twenty-nine of whom were in jail.

Terman and Kelly wanted to find "passive" homosexuals rather than those they characterized as "active." By their definition the passive homosexuals played the female role during the sex act because they were somehow less ambiguous in their sexual orientation, Terman felt. He found seventy-seven in his sample, and the rest were ignored in the study. He found a group of "active" homosexuals through the army on Alcatraz to act as another sample. Terman and Kelly found that the passive homosexuals had by far the most feminine scores, exceeding women collegiate athletes. The men reported being interested in things the researchers described as feminine since childhood. "They are far lazier than any persons of similar age with whom we have come in contact, being inclined to shun any occupation which promises even a small amount of hard work," the two men concluded.[4] The men in the passive group loved to act like women, called themselves "the girls," and adopted a "queen" name. Terman and Kelly concluded that since the feminine traits in the men went back well into their childhood, the cause must be either biochemical or "psychological conditioning." With no obvious physical differences, they tended to support the latter explanation.

Because active homosexuals had masculine scores slightly higher than a random sample of soldiers and tended to like masculine activities as children, the researchers concluded that active behavior had a different cause from the cause of passive or "pansy-type" behavior. "In the making of active male homosexuals, it is probable that chance circumstances often play an important role . . . [as in] a willingness to experiment." Using psychological words first coined by Ellis, they

---

* Terman knew he was weak in the complexities of statistics. He hired Kelly because he was an excellent statistician.

described the passive homosexuals as inverts and the active ones as perverts. The inverts, the passive men, had inappropriate gender identification, probably the fault of parental influence. The perverts had approximately the proper identification but acted as homosexuals. Terman and Kelly concluded they were not really homosexual at all, but suffered from a gender role deviation.[5] The inverts suffered from a pathology but within their subculture were psychologically normal. Terman, certainly a creature of his times, could not accept that as normal behavior within the greater context of society.

Kelly instigated the next thrust, a study of sexuality and marital happiness. Kelly had proposed a longitudinal study of marital happiness as his dissertation, but Terman had convinced him it would take much too long. After Kelly got his degree, Terman found the funding for such a study. Kelly was impressed that all earlier studies linked marital happiness to sexual compatibility. He thought happiness went deeper than just sexual matters; he believed that psychological and temperamental differences provided the cause for marital unhappiness and these were manifest in sexual problems.

Terman and Kelly divided responsibilities. Terman at Stanford handled the short-term marital adjustment component; Kelly, then at the University of Connecticut, handled the longitudinal follow-up.

Terman studied 334 divorced couples over a three-year period for the preliminary study along with control married couples from the neighborhood. He measured the 100 happiest married couples with the 100 most unhappy ones from the divorced group. He followed this with a much larger study involving 792 married couples.[6] Again, Terman would get to prove the obvious.

The happiest married people had the happiest childhoods. They tended to be the most sensitive and accepting of their spouse's feelings. Happily married women were kind, did not take offense easily, and did not "object to subordinate roles." Unhappily married women were aggressive, ambitious, and not interested in traditional womanly pursuits such as volunteering in hospitals. Happily married men, however, had a more egalitarian view of women and were less domineering than those unhappily wed. Since Terman's data centered on individuals, not couples, it is impossible to draw conclusions about the relationships. Did unhappy, domineering husbands have rebellious wives?[7]

Where Terman did break new ground was in matters of sexuality. He found only two sex factors that related to marital happiness: how closely the sex drives of husband and wife matched and how often the woman had orgasms. For the 1930s this was strong stuff and controversial. He worked out a ratio of actual sex acts to the number of times each individual would have liked to have sex, along with a rating of each other's passion. This, however, he concluded to be less important than nonsexual factors in determining marital happiness.

What was more important was the female orgasm. The more the woman experienced orgasm, the happier the marriage. A third of the women in his study had no or very few orgasms (which matched other studies), and Terman concluded that the reasons were biological, possibly genetic, not psychological. Some women just didn't have the personality for frequent orgasms, he found. As evidence of that, he had guessed that as society became more liberal in the 1930s, the number of young wives happily riding frequent orgasms would rise, but his data showed no such thing. He, of course, totally ignored the fact that he was describing an act performed by two people, and in many bedrooms making love ended when the man was done.

Terman incorporated what he learned in his sexuality studies into his questionnaires to the gifted when they grew up. He used similar questions to ask about his kids' marital happiness and even managed to probe into their sex lives to see if they differed from everyone else in any way.[8]

His 1936 report on sexuality was widely acclaimed and stood as the most authoritative text on the subject until Alfred Kinsey published his report ten years later. Terman hated the Kinsey report.

Terman's biographer Henry Minton points out that his study of sexuality was replete with instances of data and conclusions skewed by Terman's own middle class, Midwestern biases. Terman felt he was being objective. He collected numbers; therefore he was a scientist. This blindness had certainly found its way into his study of the gifted.

What made this study interesting in relation to Terman's private life is that while he spent so much time investigating what made other people happy in marriage, his own was far from a model relationship. Terman was fond of bright, beautiful, young women, and many of his graduate students fit that description. Between 1925 and 1935 Terman indulged in that venerable tradition of the male-dominated world of academe: female graduate students. Terman had a house in the Carmel Valley, a cabin in the foothills behind the campus, and a "study" north of the campus.[9] And there were side entrances to his campus home. Rumors of his liaisons were common on the small, clannish campus, and Terman was often seen in restaurants with his young protégées.[10] One former student told Terman's daughter Helen that all Terman's female students were "in love with him."[11]

Anna apparently knew about the other women and told Helen, who in turn told her two daughters. Anna did not discuss it with their son, Fred; he learned of it only in May Seagoe's 1975 biography. Anna's diaries reported her depression when she first found out, once fleeing to the mountain cabin until things calmed down. Her diaries were later filled with sarcasm, once about the "fun" Terman was having working with one of his students at Carmel and another time about how cheered he was when a student dropped in when he was sick. Anna was bitter, feeling that she had sacrificed much to help her husband. She had given up teaching to raise his children. Helen was less than completely sympathetic with Anna, feeling that her domineering and meddlesome mother was getting what she deserved. Having somewhat more respect for her father than he had for her, she felt he was more the target than the chaser. He was fairly shy, but could be wonderfully charming. He seemed to restrict himself to women who were bright and interested in what interested him.

Terman's relations with his female students were complex. Men in that position — then and now — have enormous power over their students, and sexual relations between male professors and female students are so common at most campuses that some professors consider them fringe benefits. Unquestionably, these relationships can be, and frequently are, exploitative, particularly when graduate students are involved. But Terman also was intensely loyal to all his students, male and female, making great efforts to further their careers and provide counseling long after they left his classroom. He clearly relished their successes and his students returned his loyalty and help with uncommon loyalty and affection. In some regard, Terman and his women students seemed to be using each other, each for their own needs, apparently to their mutual satisfaction.

He could be hypocritical about infidelity with his students. Olga McNemar remembered one incident in which a graduate student was having an affair with a married woman. "He told [the student] that if he heard anything more about it 'You're out.' He just wouldn't stand for it."

Anna began traveling, leading a more independent life. She became more active in campus affairs, particularly among faculty wives (many of whom knew perfectly well what she was going through). She became extremely popular with his students and their spouses. She was pleasant, smiling, and supportive. She played her role well.[12] "Anna was a sweetie. Everybody loved her," McNemar said. "She ran [Lewis's] social life. She did everything that she should do, and he should have done, and she protected him as if he were a China doll. . . . She was very friendly with the graduate students." On Sunday mornings she and Lewis would drop by the homes of his students just to visit and chat. Eventually, as he got older, the affairs tapered off and he and Anna floated into a quiet, comfortable, and passionless relationship for the rest of their lives.

Yet Terman seemed peculiarly detached from that aspect of his life. Without a blink or a shudder of hypocrisy, he spent considerable time studying what made marriages happy (with no regard to the unhappiness of his own) and sex and sexuality (with no apparent introspection aimed at his own). In some ways, it was the single most insidious flaw in the Terman study of the gifted.

Chapter Six

THE PROMISE OF YOUTH

IN 1929, eight years after his first study began, Lewis Terman began his first follow-up. He knew that children change and that not even "the most extreme of hereditarians would accord only zero or negligible value" to all the environmental and "innumerable vicissitudes" of growing up. He felt that some attributes developed as children grew from childhood to adolescence, and he wanted to measure those changes as well. Not enough time had elapsed for Terman to measure any drastic changes in the lives of his kids, but he could measure how they were doing in school and see if the good things he predicted for them were coming true.

Terman had funding problems: the ideal longitudinal study would require more money than he could possibly raise. He would have loved to track down all the members of his main experimental group, give them a full battery of intelligence, psychology, and physical tests, and measure them with as much sedulity as he had the first time, but he lacked the resources. After his first volume was published, he could afford only a half-time secretary to keep track of as many of his kids as possible. He mailed out questionnaires in 1922, 1923, and 1924; 90 percent of the forms sent to parents were returned, but only 75 percent of the forms sent to schools came back. The data collected were useless, but at least Terman stayed in touch with his subjects.

In 1927 the Commonwealth Fund came through again, and so did the Thomas Welton Stanford Fund and a benefactor in San Francisco, Max Rosenberg. Terman launched his field-workers. The goal was to verify the results of his first study and to gain more data to add to the picture of gifted youth.

We do not yet know to what extent the superior achievement of relatives is indicative that the gifted subject comes of biologically superior stock. We do not know how much the IQ and school achievement fluctuate during the period of mental development. We do not know whether such unevenness of ability as is found tends to increase or decrease with age. We do not know whether age brings improvement or deterioration with respect to personality traits. We know all too little about the resemblances and differences between our gifted group and those individuals who in mature life achieve eminence of a degree that ranks them popularly in the class of geniuses. We know still less about the type of education that is best for gifted children.[1]

To retest his kids, Terman elected to give the Stanford-Binet to all those still below the ninth grade and, because the Stanford-Binet seemed less accurate for older children, to use the Terman Group Test of Mental Ability for the others. He could convert the numbers from the group test to IQ for the sake of comparison. He also could compare the results of another intelligence test administered to the forty-five gifted who had been admitted to Stanford. A whole array of other tests, depending on the age of the children, was to be given, including several designed to measure "nonintellectual traits" such as his masculinity-femininity test and a test of social attitudes. A batch of questionnaires, many similar to the ones originally employed, were aimed at the main experimental group.

Terman gathered a team together including Helen Marshall, who had assisted in the first study, and Melita Oden, a recent graduate student. Florence Goodenough could not get away from her post at the University of Minnesota, so she recommended one of her students, Alice Leahy, starting a second generation of Terman disciples. Dortha Williams Jensen, one of Terman's graduate students, pitched in with a dissertation comparing the literary output of the gifted with famous English and American literary lights at the same age. Her dissertation became an appendix to the study. She called her subject "literary juvenilia" (see page 101). Four field assistants were enlisted to do the actual survey.

One of the field-workers' tasks, Terman admitted, was simply to keep relations with the families as cordial as possible. He was dependent upon the families' cooperation, because, except for curiosity and pride, the parents and siblings of the gifted subjects got nothing for all the time they would be asked to spend and all the prying into their family life the study would require. Terman was hoping for a long-term, meaningful relationship with these families. He would succeed admirably. By the time the study was complete, he had exhaustive dossiers on almost four hundred children, and somewhat less data on most of the rest. In most cases the number of responses provided sufficient data points to draw acceptable conclusions. Many of the parents wrote long, sometimes quite personal letters to Terman, giving information and asking advice. His study gathered as much information about some of the parents as it did about the children. Sometimes even other relatives, who thought their children gifted, sought advice — and received it. Essentially, Terman created a large tribe, one that sometimes got so close and personal as to damage the validity of his research.

Terman's "universe," the number of children from which he drew his data, totaled 1,444, including 643 from the main experimental group (5 had died since the first study), 35 of their siblings, minus 6 children whose parents refused to cooperate and another 6 whose parents' cooperation Terman deemed insufficient or untrustworthy. The other groups, including the children with special talents, also were included in the universe. Most of the data in the original came from the main experimental group, and he limited his conclusions in his second study to those children. The others provided interesting case studies and anecdotal information. The field-workers visited every child who had originally been tested by the Stanford-Binet who lived in the San Francisco and Los Angeles metropolitan areas and the areas around Fresno and Palo Alto. Subjects living elsewhere in California and those who had left the state and the country were contacted by mail.

Terman's staff was able to track down 96.7 percent of the living regular subjects and obtained cooperation from the families of 91.7 percent of them, a total of 587 children. They called on 86.2 percent (552 children) and Terman received Home Information Blanks filled out for 78.6 percent (503 children). Their average age was nineteen.

First and most important, the children were given IQ tests, which Terman admitted was what most people cared about. "Do intellectually superior children become intellectually superior adults?" he

wanted to know. He also had three other more precise questions he
wanted to answer in this study:

- How well does the mental ability of these children hold up on
  average?
- How many of the children later show radical changes in intelligence rating, either positive or negative?
- How do the sexes differ from each other with respect to the two
  previous questions?

It seems quite evident that while any person with an IQ as high as 140
may have the sheer intelligence requisite for exceptional achievement,
only a very small proportion are likely to possess the total complex of
mental and personality traits that cause an individual to become eminent. If it were not that personality traits and other non-intellectual
aspects of endowment wield an enormous power to enhance or inhibit
the individual's use of his intelligence, we might expect in ten or fifteen
years, from our thousand California gifted children, such a corps of
geniuses as has never before graced the population of a single state.[2]

It's not clear whether what he discovered surprised him; some of it
certainly puzzled him. Terman found that the children tested with the
Stanford-Binet dropped an average of nine points in IQ. The drop for
girls was five times larger than the drop for boys, averaging thirteen
points. The trend was not restricted to those in the main experimental
group, but was evident across the groups. Age seemed to make no
difference, but sex did; the girls did much worse than the boys. Some
of the drops were precipitous, with more than two dozen children
falling as much as fifteen points and six cases (two boys and four girls)
dropping twenty-five points or more. Twelve even dropped below the
minimum for the Terman study, and one girl fell below 104, barely
above average for the general population. According to the hereditarian dogma to which Terman subscribed, that was not supposed to
happen.

Terman looked carefully at the children who showed a decrease
and could rarely find a reason. He reported several examples. One, a
girl he called "Bertha," scored 138 in her original test at the age of six,
two points below the putative boundary, but was included in the
study because her sister scored 141. Other tests by Goodenough

substantiated her inclusion. "A charming child, very chatty but not forward. Responds readily. Shows good knowledge of her own abilities and inabilities," Goodenough wrote at the time. But four years later, she had dropped to between 107 and 104, and one of the teachers asked a field-worker, "Why is Bertha included in the gifted children group?" Terman's crew studied everything they could about Bertha, including behavioral and health problems, but could find nothing to account for this decrease. She was sensitive and "tractable"; she fainted at the sight of blood, but was healthy; her family was stable and supportive. Terman had no explanation.

A boy called "Jerome," who was marginal in his first test but was included because of his musical talent, dropped thirty-three points. Jerome seemed to have a limited attention span when he was retested and had developed a personality that seemed to exclude intellectual pursuits. Perhaps Jerome's fall from grace was behavioral in nature?

Not all those who showed a decrease were marginal in the first study. "Clara" tested at 148 at age ten, but fell considerably by the time she reached sixteen.* A girl who was described as "beautiful, charming, intelligent, and studious" had become significantly less intelligent and less studious. Perhaps her home life had something to do with it, Terman hinted. The girl was the daughter of a psychic. She lived in a dingy home in a Los Angeles slum. Her parents were Italian in origin and had a somewhat chaotic marriage. "It seems reasonably clear that individual ambition among the three children of the family is not encouraged by their domineering, clairvoyant mother," Terman suggested. "On the other hand, several members of the gifted group have shown deterioration under extremely favorable environmental conditions."[3] He had no real clue as to what happened to these kids.

Interestingly, while his tests measured decreases in test scores, the parents of these children noted no changes at all. Of all the parents who filled out the home questionnaire, 45 percent perceived no change in their children; 54 percent thought their children were getting brighter, including the children whose scores actually dropped.

Terman remained confident in the validity of his tests. He developed them, after all, and felt that there was sufficient corroborative

---

* Clara was not given the Stanford-Binet at sixteen, so the drop was noted in her score on the group test. Terman could compare the two scores, but the numbers would be meaningless to the reader.

evidence to believe in what the tests were telling him. Nonetheless, the changes disturbed him profoundly, and he decided to go back to the Berthas and Jeromes of his universe to see if he could find out what happened. He retested the children, adding a test he had not used the first time around, the Herring-Binet test (a rival of the Stanford-Binet), and also more complex versions of his group test. The latter had an 80 percent correlation factor with the Stanford-Binet, close enough for his needs. Twenty-seven of the thirty-seven children were given the Herring-Binet. The results substantiated his findings. When Terman tested school achievement, he found the same thing: these children didn't seem as bright as they once were!

Why? Terman looked at several possibilities involving health, personality, race, environment, gender, and mental growth rate. He found no evidence that the children who suffered decreases in IQ had health problems. In fact, statistically, they seemed to be slightly healthier than the other children.

In exploring personality traits, Terman reported, "There is no clear evidence here for inferring that the children whose IQ's dropped have poor balance or undesirable personality traits as compared with the members of the entire gifted group."

Terman believed that some races and nationalities are "quick-maturing," by which he meant they tend to peak early. Children from these groups might do well early in their development, but wither quickly. He didn't say so, but he apparently meant minorities and Mediterranean types. He had a serious problem trying to prove this was so in his study because he had so few of these children in his sample. He looked at the kids whose IQs had decreased to see what races and nationalities they represented and came out empty-handed. Partly because the numbers were so small, he could find no statistically significant racial or national explanation for what he found.

In considering environmental factors that might affect test scores, Terman was on slippery ground. As a hereditarian, he could not accept that any major change in the children's IQs — up or down — resulted from environmental causes, but he admitted the thought did occur to him. Not to worry; using a battery of tests and home visits, he could find nothing in the home environment of his children to account for the decrease in test scores.

Terman was bothered by the fact that girls showed a greater

tendency to suffer a decrease in test scores. This came in the shadow of his unease about the gender imbalance in the original sample. He directly confronted the possibility of a sexual bias in the test. He was persuaded the test was not biased because the average IQ of girls not in the study was the same as the average IQ of boys not in the study. If it was gender, it had something to do with very bright girls, but he could not imagine what that could be. "It appears that boys not only are more likely than girls to have high IQ's, but are more likely than girls to retain the high IQ's which they have evidenced in their early school years," he concluded.[4] It did not occur to him that the girls had been socialized in such a way as to decrease their test scores or that the tests had a male bias to them.

Terman thought, but could not prove, that mental growth rate explained what he was seeing, that "fluctuations in IQ may be accounted for by changes in the rate of mental growth that are congenital or at least quite normal in character." He used the analogy of physical growth. A child who was quite small when young could suddenly spurt up to larger-than-normal size in his or her teens. Contrariwise, a relatively big baby could grow into a relatively small adult. Perhaps this happens with intelligence. "If no other theory can be made to account for the observed data, we feel that a normal-change-of-rate theory is reasonable and does no violence to established facts," he wrote.[5] Terman felt a bit better accepting this thesis because when he tested the siblings of those whose IQ fell, he found no similar decrease in their scores; indeed, they tended to rise, not fall. Hence, he doubted that what he observed was the result of "mysterious subterranean influences." His conclusion was that "gifted girls do not maintain their intellectual superiority in adolescence as well as boys do." Again, cultural conditioning did not enter his picture.

Despite the children who dropped in test scores, the children in Terman's study were still exceptional, at least by the standards he used to measure them. He found that 74 percent of the boys and 84 percent of the girls were accelerated in grade. The average Termite graduated from high school at sixteen and presumably entered college at about that age. Of the oldest group, most were either in college or planned on getting a college education (98 percent of the boys, 94 percent of the girls). Of those who were not considering college or who had dropped out, most gave lack of money as their reason. By the time Terman made his second study, sixty-eight boys and sixty-four girls were in college.

When studying the college students in his group, Terman got a lot of help. Besides being able to get the data he needed from Stanford, the University of California at Berkeley provided him with grades for all its students plus the transcripts of the large number of Terman's kids who went to Berkeley.

Generally, the gifted girls did better than the gifted boys, except in science courses. More important, his gifted students at Berkeley did better than the rest of the student body. Most of his kids were lower division (freshmen and sophomores), and they did better than most lower division students, many upper division students, and even some graduate students — and this at a relatively younger age.

At Stanford, even then a very selective college, the gifted freshmen boys did better than the average Stanford freshman, and the girls did better than their classmates who graduated high school as honors students. While that does not at first seem like a major accomplishment, Terman's kids were on the average two years younger than their classmates. And their classmates represented the cream of their high schools, the top 2 or 3 percent of the population. Terman added that he felt some of the instructors were underrating the achievements of students so young and that some of his gifted were trying not to appear too bright and were deliberately not working as hard as they might. Some of his students claimed they were being marked harder than their peers because their professors expected more of them.[6]

Terman could also account for fifty-four gifted youngsters from all his study groups who had already graduated from Stanford. About 33 percent had made Phi Beta Kappa, and 28 percent of his graduates from Berkeley also achieved that honor. Since only one student in ten at those schools made Phi Beta Kappa, Terman's kids were running three times better.

And what kind of students were his gifted children? Girls spent 7.6 hours a week reading, boys spent 7.2. Both boys and girls spent more time originally on outside reading than class-assigned books. The girls let their homework dominate at age thirteen, the boys at age fourteen. The gifted children generally preferred to read than to do anything else. If they had any failings as students, it was that they daydreamed too much and tended to have difficulties with structured programs.

Terman thought there was a lesson in that for educators when confronted with gifted students.[7] When they played games, they tended toward those that required great amounts of exercise. They were an ambitious lot; most had already decided on a profession. Terman did point out that they were no more ambitious than the average Stanford student, but the average Stanford student was very ambitious indeed.

Then there were personal attitudes. Terman gave his high school seniors and college freshmen the Watson Test of Fair-Mindedness, a test of prejudice. Like generations of social scientists who followed, Terman was capable of quantifying to the first decimal point human attitudes that would appear to the non–social scientist to be unquantifiable. Then he did statistical tests based on the numbers and drew conclusions. He found that his gifted boys and girls were somewhere in the middle of the road, certainly less prejudiced and more open-minded than a "men's Bible class in eastern city" and "Methodist ministers in middle western state" and even "newspapermen in large western cities" who had been given the same test, but more prejudiced and less open-minded than "faculty in journalism in a western university" and "students in an eastern theological seminary." As Terman pointed out, they were not remarkable in this regard.

He gave his masculinity-femininity test to his gifted again. Terman's psychology department had been refining this test since 1925 under a grant from the National Research Council. His conclusions supported an aphorism he quoted: "There are no women of genius; the women of genius are all men." He found that inverted tendencies, that is, tendencies of a person of one sex to have the desires and interests characteristic of the other, were not more common among his gifted boys than they were in the general population of boys; he didn't have an unusual number of "effeminate" boys. But the normal degree of inversion was not true of his girls; they tended far more to the masculine than the general population of girls. "Between men and women of genius," he reported, "sex differences in interests, attitudes, and thought trends are probably less extreme than they are for men and women of the generality, the *approchement* being due chiefly to the tendency of gifted women to vary from the norm toward masculinity."[8] It is not likely that a psychologist working now would make such a finding or at least announce it, but in the 1920s Terman's statement probably confirmed the common wisdom.

His report contained a number of examples of gifted subjects who had "inverted tendencies." "Renwick," a musician with an IQ of 150, was the most extreme example, clearly — although Terman did not say so — well on his way to becoming a transvestite. A child prodigy on the pipe organ, he had an "intense interest in playing 'dress up.' He inclined definitely toward the feminine in his interests. He composed playlets and operas, always casting himself for the leading feminine role. He played with dolls and amused himself by dyeing clothes and designing feminine garments." Renwick scored strongly toward the feminine the first time he was tested at the age of nine. By the time he was retested six years later, he scored in the zero percentile of boys and in the forty-eighth percentile of girls. Always fascinated by the "inverted," Terman, who felt this type of homosexuality was largely environmental, wrote:

> The etiology of his feminine tendencies is not clear. It may be significant that he has been closely associated with his mother and that the father was past middle age at the time of his birth. A medical examination given him at the age of ten years revealed an unusual distribution of fat and some enlargement of the thyroid gland. With the onset of puberty, however, a negative thyroid is reported.[9]

Terman had no idea what that meant and said so.

Terman sought data on what he called "social traits" in an attempt to see what kinds of teenagers his subjects were. Did other teenagers like them as well as they liked the nongifted? Yes, they seemed to. Were they teased more often than their peers? No, actually they were teased slightly less. Were they disciplinary problems? No, only 5 percent were listed by parents as being "headstrong." Were they considered by their peers to be "queer or different"? Not especially. He found that more girls were interested in boys than boys were interested in girls, but that was normal for the age he was testing. Only three of his group, two boys and a girl, showed any signs of abnormal sexual behavior, or what was abnormal behavior in 1927. The sexual behavior of one other kid was deemed questionable. When they were younger, the gifted seemed to gravitate toward children who were older than they, and Terman found this tendency increased as they grew older.

The children at the very top of his group, those with the highest

IQs, had the most difficult time adjusting socially. They also would have the most difficulty adjusting to life in general. What the most brilliant tended to become was what students today call "nerds." Take "David," who scored an 184 IQ at the age of seven years four months, before he had spent a day in school. He was educated at home until then. He went through junior high school in one year, entered high school at the age of ten, and graduated college, with honors, at sixteen. When tested for the second time, David was working on his Ph.D. David was described at the retest as a loner, rarely seeking companionship, frequently disappearing into a fantasy world or word games. He was well liked by those who knew him, but they were few in number. Slender, somewhat stoop-shouldered, and pale of complexion, David was almost the stereotypical intellectual. "Our records show that few of our gifted subjects have combined such intensity of mental life and such versatility of intellectual interests," Terman wrote. By Terman's standards, David came by his gifts honestly.

> D. is an only child. Conspicuous relatives beyond the first degree of kinship include a chief rabbi of Moscow, who was exiled for aiding the nihilists, a distinguished lawyer, a man who by his own efforts became a millionaire, a concert pianist, a composer and virtuoso, a writer, and a relative decorated for science in Poland. The maternal great-grandfather was a famous rabbi who compiled and published a Jewish calendar covering the period of 414 years. . . . This rabbi was also the great-grandfather of the four first cousins of D. whose intelligence quotients have been taken. These cousins yielded IQ's of 156, 150, 130, and 122, respectively. A second cousin in the maternal line yielded at the age of six years an IQ of 157.[10]

That's what Terman liked to see. The indications were, Terman wrote, that David would grow up to be a "man without eccentricity other than the retiring disposition that often characterizes scientists and scholars."

Most of Terman's kids were, socially at least, a lot more normal than David.

Terman's youths remained a healthy lot. Terman lacked the funds and resources to redo the extensive medical and physical testing of the original study. He believed that his first study had so demolished the notion that very bright children were sickly that he felt no need to pursue the subject further. Even without medical tests, he felt that the data from the questionnaires he sent to home and school confirmed the earlier results.

He found that very few members of his study had suffered serious illness other than the five who died.* He found that the teachers' comments on the children's health tended to be somewhat less sanguine than the parents', particularly for the girls, but Terman thought the teachers might have thought the girls were sick when their parents kept them home because of menstruation. The teachers reported that 77 percent of the girls had "good" health, while the parents reported that 90 percent did.

His subjects had no more frequent colds than they did as children, and they were still slightly healthier than his earlier control group. Terman was able to verify the truth of one cliché: gifted children were far more likely than nongifted to wear glasses. By the time they were teenagers or older, 25 percent of his boys were wearing glasses, compared to only 4 percent of the control group boys measured in the original study; for girls it was 20 percent of the gifted compared to 5 percent of the control group. He attributed his finding to two factors: advanced school work made it more likely children would have even minor sight weaknesses corrected and "superior parental intelligence and medical care of the gifted group." Only 2 percent of the boys and 1 percent of the girls were categorized as extremely myopic.

They were no more inclined to worry as youths than they were as children, he found. Two of his girls had married; none yet had children.

Terman also wanted to see if the socioeconomic status of his gifted children's families had changed. He admitted not enough time had elapsed since his first study to make any meaningful comparison, but he was curious. Using the same kind of test as in the first study, he found that the status of the fathers had increased slightly. He did not ask for the occupation of the mothers in the first study, but he did ask this time and found that one-fifth of the mothers were working. He did not compare that figure with the general population. Sixteen percent of the women were raising their children alone, because of

* One was a suicide. See the story of "Ira," pages 59–61.

widowhood, separation, or divorce. Some who had been widowed or divorced were remarried, but he had no figures. Sixty-one percent of the single mothers were working. Forty-three percent of the working mothers were professionals, by which Terman meant teachers, musicians, artists, or academics. One woman was a college president. None was a doctor or lawyer (it was, after all, 1927). Terman surmised that the mothers shared a tendency "to prefer homemaking to an outside career unless the outside career holds unusual inducements in the way of interest and compensation." He felt that was true because about 50 percent of the nonwidowed working mothers were professionals, while only 32 percent of the working widows were professionals. The latter, apparently, were working because they had to; the former because they wanted to. Proportionally, there were more professionals among the women in 1927 than among the men in 1922.

Terman was naturally curious about the brothers and sisters of his kids. If intelligence was hereditary, surely the siblings of the gifted would be likewise gifted, or at least on the high side. Also, if he could find enough siblings who did not make the cutoff, he had a handy control group. He could measure the lives of the two sets of children who had grown up in almost exactly the same environment to see if there was a difference. Terman gave the Stanford-Binet test to siblings under twelve and the group test to older siblings. When children were picked for the main experimental group in 1921, siblings old enough for testing sometimes were checked, and those who made the cutoff were added to the list. Terman did not retest any brothers or sisters who had been tested previously and had failed because that would bias the sample toward a lower number; Terman already knew they didn't make the minimum requirement. He found the mean IQ of these new children to be 123, considerably higher than the average, but below the level Terman dubbed gifted. He found the boys and girls tested about equally, but more boys were over the gifted mark than girls. Again, he had no explanation.

At the end of the second study Terman could conclude that:

• Gifted children come predominantly from family stocks of decidedly superior intellectual endowment and of slightly superior physical endowment.

- Children above 140 IQ are not as a group characterized by intellectual one-sidedness, emotional instability, lack of sociality or of social adaptability, or other types of maladjusted personality, and indeed may be socially superior.
- Boys maintain their intellectual superiority better than do girls.
- By the age of ten, the scores on achievement tests by the gifted bear no relationship to the actual grade in which the children study, and three-quarters of the total marks of gifted girls and one-half of the marks of gifted boys are A's.
- The most important single outcome of the follow-up investigation is the abundant and conclusive evidence that for the group as a whole, the picture did not greatly change in the period that elapsed between the studies.... With minor exceptions, what was true of these children in 1921–22 was true of them in 1927–28.[11]

Two things seemed to bother him. First, the families of the gifted were reproducing at a rate so low they were having trouble replacing themselves. Second, "data collected regarding the spouses of the gifted subjects who have married show that, notwithstanding a marked tendency toward marital selection in the usual direction, the spouses appear to be in a majority of cases less well endowed than the gifted subjects who have married them."

Terman ended his report on the second study with a reaffirmation of his belief in a meritocracy, in the need for superior minds to run the world.

That important scientific discoveries are sometimes made by fairly commonplace intellects may be freely admitted, also that this is probably more likely to occur today than in any previous time in the world's history. It does not follow from this that the role of genius has grown less important. . . . It is more reasonable to believe that the mounting quantity and growing complexity of knowledge call more insistently for the masterful genius today than ever before. . . . The air, the sea, and the bowels of the earth offer more powerful incentives to the engineer and the inventor than ever have been offered. Millions still languish and die of diseases which the brain of man now, for the first time, has some chance to conquer. . . . Lawmaking in most countries, and perhaps nowhere more than in the United States, is chiefly the product of fourth-rate minds. . . . The truth appears to be, not that superior ability is likely to go begging, but that it will become more and more at a premium.[12]

It was to Terman a question of eugenics, a problem that bothered him most of his professional life.

Chapter Seven

LITERARY JUVENILIA

TERMAN WAS FASCINATED by the relationship between talent and intelligence, but was disappointed when he found that his special group of children was not as bright as he had hoped. He wondered, therefore, if he could find special talents among his regular subjects, especially in the main experimental group for whom he had the most data. One of his graduate students, Dortha Williams Jensen, launched an experiment to compare the literary work of the best writers among Terman's gifted with the work of the best writers of the English language at the same age.

A number of the kids had been precocious writers. They — or more often their parents — mailed Terman copies of poems and stories, and he kept them in the files. Undoubtedly, many were quite good. "Beatrice" (see page 51) was very good indeed. She was so talented that Terman and Jessie Fenton did a study of her as writer for a paper in the *Journal of Applied Psychology*. Jensen wanted to determine just how good these most gifted of children were. How did these children compare in talent to children who later grew up to be lions of English literature?[1]

Jensen selected for study fourteen children from the main experimental group whose works she and her colleagues considered superior and twenty-eight prominent writers. Ten of the writers were in Cox's study of geniuses of the past (see Chapter Three). To make sure she was talking about geniuses across the board, she asked some of Cox's judges to estimate the IQs of the writers she selected in addition to those in Cox's study. She apparently felt that having the writers evaluated by the same judges would make her study more scientific.

That the whole approach Cox used was spurious didn't seem to bother her. The IQs of her Terman kids ranged from 141 up to 188. The estimated IQs of her famous writers ranged from Robert Burns's 140 to Samuel Taylor Coleridge's 180.*

All but three of her children were girls, but Jensen had no female writers in her list of the famous, not George Sand or even Emily Dickinson, who was by then recognized as one of America's greatest poets. Her famous poets included Robert Browning, but not his wife, Elizabeth Barrett. She listed Percy Shelley, but not his wife, Mary Wollstonecraft. She gave no explanation.

Jensen enlisted seven professors, mostly from the Department of English and the School of Education at Stanford, to serve as judges. She picked 151 poems, short stories, and essays, and retyped them without identifying the authors. Where the titles might be giveaways, they were omitted. She designed a mathematical formula to judge the poems and prose — an algorithm of literary quality — and gave her judges complicated forms to fill out.

Her dissertation was filled with formulas, charts, and tables, including tables with such titles as "Intercorrelations Corrected for Attenuation" and "Standard Deviations of the Judges' Ratings for Various Combinations of Judges." Jensen was sure of the efficacy of her methodology because her judges were experts in either literature or child development or both and when she measured the results from three of the judges against three of the others, she found they were statistically acceptable. Nothing to a social scientist is unquantifiable.

As absurd as the mathematical precision was in this study, the results were intriguing. In only twenty-five cases could the eminent judges spot the work of famous writers in the years before fame. An obscure poem written by Pope at the age of twelve was spotted by two of the judges. A poem called "To a Young Lady on Her Birthday," written by a sixteen-year-old Samuel Johnson, got three comments:

"I suspect it is Pope," said Judge C.

"Isn't it Pope?" asked Judge D.

"Samuel Johnson," sniffed Judge F.

The trick wasn't to see if the judges would mistake the work of

---

* Others were Poe, Keats, Browning, Shelley, and Pope, all at 165, and Thackeray at 145. Benjamin Franklin and Thomas Jefferson each had 160, according to Cox's research. Alexander Hamilton came in at 150.

Terman's kids for Shelley or Longfellow — and none did; Jensen wanted them to rate each work independently. She asked the judges to fit each work into a category such as "best work of the ten best authors in the English language," "average work of ten best authors," "average work in modern literary magazines," or "average work of children below school age" (none was placed in this category). When the results were tabulated, Terman's kids came up better writers in their early teens than the literary stars of the language. It was only after the age of sixteen that the famous overtook California's gifted. "Edith" had the highest score of all of Terman's kids, beating out selected works of Hawthorne, Wordsworth, Byron, and Franklin in the sixteen-year-old classification.

Edith was seventeen when Terman and Jensen did their study. She came from a long line of clergymen and engineers with no particular literary bent. Terman had measured her IQ at 148. By her sixth birthday she could read and had written her first poem. From the age of nine she spent two to ten hours a week writing everything from poems to stories to monologues. She had already been published in her college literary magazine although she was only a freshman when Jensen wrote her dissertation. She grew up to be a published poet and essayist.

Even for experts, spotting talent and being able to predict whether a person will grow up to be a famous writer are difficult. Just how difficult is demonstrated below. Here are five poems, two by famous poets and three by Terman's kids. The age of the author is given below the title. The authors are identified in the notes for this chapter at the end of the book.

NIGHT
(Author: Age Fifteen)

Miles o'er the emerald seas, and across the golden sand,
Beyond where the plumed palm trees give shade to a burning land,
Is a deep-mouthed, rocky cave, lost in the purple hills,
Still as a lonely grave, with a silence that awes and thrills,
In its depths, forlorn and weird, asleep on a massive throne,
Where a torch, as if it leered, makes a smoky, flickering zone
Of devil-dancing light upon the shadowy walls,
Sits the sable-winged Night, queen of those Stygian halls.

· · ·

Her skin is white as death, and her black cascade of hair,
Stirred by her gentle breath, gleams in the dull red glare.
Her arms are bound with chains which clank if she slightly stir,
For she, while Phoebus reigns, is the sun-god's prisoner.

The moon sleeps by her side, with her silver wings outspread,
White as a lace-clad bride, who lily-like, lies dead.

HOW WONDERFUL IS DEATH

(Author: Age Eighteen)

How wonderful is Death,
Death and his brother Sleep!
One, pale as yonder waning moon
With lips of lurid blue;
The other, rosy as the morn
When throned on ocean's wave
It blushes o'er the world:
Yet both so passing wonderful!

Hath then the gloomy power
Whose reign is in the tainted sepulchres
Seized on her sinless soul?
Must then that peerless form
Which love and admiration cannot view
Without a beating heart, those azure veins
Which steal like streams along a wave of snow,
That lovely outline, which is fair
As breathing marble, perish?

THE HAPPIEST DAY, THE HAPPIEST HOUR

(Author: Age Eighteen)

The happiest day, the happiest hour
My seared and blighted heart hath known,
The highest hope of pride and power,
I feel hath flown.

Of Power! said I? Yes! such I ween;
But they have vanished long, alas!

The visions of my youth have been —
But let them pass.

And pride, what have I now with thee?
Another brow may ev'n inherit
The venom thou has poured on me —
Be still, my spirit.

The happiest day, the happiest hour
Mine eyes shall see, have ever seen,
The brightest glance of pride and power,
I feel — have been!

DEATH
(Author: Age Sixteen)

And this is death? This carven marble face,
The effigy of one we loved so well,
Lies on its pillow, white as are the blooms
That early spring has heaped upon his bier.
His last sharp agony has wiped away
The furrows left by years of wearing pain,
And now he seems to sleep a dreamless sleep.

Joy is not there, nor woe, nor any look
Known to the world of which he was a part.
All mortal struggle he has left behind
Like broken shackles lying on the ground . . .

A GLOVE
(Author: Age Thirteen)

She left her glove, and cold and void it seemed
To fill the place where her warm hand had lain,
As empty as the heart of one who dreamed
And lost his dream, and found it not again.
The fingers, curved and grasping on the air
Made the same gesture that had bid farewell —
O poor illusion! There was nothing there!
Perhaps some vagrant breezes — who can tell?

.   .   .

This glove has compassed many times, I know
A dearer hand than many angels own:
I cannot kiss the kindly hand, and so
I kiss this quickly, now I am alone.
There! Lie there, little glove! But do not tell
Our secret to the one I love so well.

Jensen got her Ph.D. Terman was pleased enough to include her dissertation in his published volume on the follow-up study.[1]

YOUTH

Shelley

TERMAN did not have to look far to find Shelley Smith.* Shelley was the daughter of the head of Stanford's journalism department, the Smiths and the Termans were neighbors, and Shelley was enrolled in the campus elementary school when she was tested at the age of eight.

Terman was no doubt amused when her mother warned, "Ancestors on grandfather's side nearly all notorious for eccentricity, strong will, and quaint humor."

Shelley became the only known Termite to flunk the seventh grade.

"She seems to be a favorite," her mother added in the initial parents' report. "Usually is the one ordered about, though when alone she has plenty of initiative."

Shelley, her mother wrote, was not spoiled despite the relative comfort in which she lived. Her "brother, Sandy, is five years older than she, and her sister, Rosemary, is three years older. Consequentially, Shelley has been less carefully treated than they were, and her health from six months to now somewhat less good. At two-and-a-quarter, I deliberately sacrificed her nervous system to the educational advantage of Sandy because the chance came then for a year or two in the East, and I dragged her along and round on the sight-seeing trips. Also was obliged to feed her more carelessly than the others had been fed. It will be interesting to see if her after life shows effects from this."

She was a beauty. The physician doing the examination for the study wrote: "One of the most attractive of children. Artistic. Probably is going to be temperamental, but is not so yet. In good physical condition."

* Her real name is used with permission.

The Terman researcher who visited the Smith home in 1927 reported: "A winsome child, loved by everybody. . . . She also likes to play, climb trees, and be a tomboy." "A pretty child," wrote another, "cheeks pink through an outdoor tan, slim, rather graceful in her movements. Had been out playing just before I saw her. Face and eyes were glowing with suppressed fun."

"She definitely plans to be a poet," her mother wrote in 1922. Three years later Shelley said she wanted to be an archaeologist. Her independence (she played alone much of the time in games of her own invention) and her self-reliance were noted by the field-workers.

She had spirit too. When she had to leave the cozy campus elementary school, she found herself in a traditional, strict, rule-bound middle school. "The campus school was very small, four or five children per teacher, and it was sort of experimental. It was supposed to be for faculty children," she said. "It was a wonderful, wonderful, wonderful, wonderful school. In that school I got all A's . . . except in effort and deportment I got D's. Anyway, I did very well academically in the lower grades." Like a number of children who came from the campus school, Shelley did not like the atmosphere and approach of the public school. "These days we would call it rebellion, back then I just didn't like that school." She began the rebellion by "forgetting" to take her apron to cooking class, and it escalated from there until she failed seventh grade.

Her parents rescued her by sending her to Castilleja, a fine private girl's school in Palo Alto. She enrolled in the eighth grade, kissing the seventh off as a learning experience and was given a scholarship for four years of high school.

Shelley went to Stanford for three years. She didn't exactly flunk out; the depression was on and even well-endowed Stanford needed tuition money from students to keep it going. "My record was abysmal. I was really interested in the theater and that's what I did at Stanford and not much else." She dropped out when she was invited to join a theatrical stock company in San Francisco. After six months, when the company folded, she had no desire to return to school. She had decided to make a career on Broadway.

"Dreams of glory," she explained. "And in any case, I was not a serious student, and I have to tell you — I didn't do well in college. My father died very suddenly in the summer after my freshman year. I don't know if that had anything to do with my subsequent failures. He and I were close."

Shelley and three other women from California found an apartment on the top floor of a brick building on Morton Street in Greenwich Village and, in a life reminiscent of *My Sister Eileen* and *Wonderful Town*, tried to storm Broadway. She joined a dance company and spent a summer working as a dancer at Camp Unity, the International Ladies' Garment Workers' Union summer camp. "And so you can say I was a professional dancer. But being a professional dancer doesn't mean you can eat."

One of her father's former students got her a job at the *Literary Digest*, a distinguished news magazine, and she joined that publication in time to be an innocent victim of one of the most famous screw-ups in American journalism history. Making use of the newly developed techniques for public opinion polling, the *Literary Digest* confidently predicted that Alf Landon would win a landslide victory over Franklin D. Roosevelt in 1936. The result, besides setting back election polls for a generation, destroyed the reputation of the magazine. She left, returning to California to visit her mother and take her breath.

Shelley knew she had to return to New York, however, because she had a commitment to her roommates to help with the $55 a month rent. She had earned $18.50 a week at the *Digest*. "I was poor; but I was young. And it didn't matter if you are poor when you are young, especially in the Depression."

She was told that a new magazine had started up and was interviewing anyone with magazine experience. "A wonderful woman who hired me said, 'What do you know about photographs?' and I said, 'Nothing.' She said, 'Oh well, it doesn't matter.' So I was hired on *Life*."

She had a glorious time, working at *Life* during the day, dancing at night, still finding time to go to leftist political meetings and demonstrations, and "pretty well exhausting myself," she remembered.

Her job at *Life* was called "researcher." At *Time* and *Life* in those days men got to be "writers" and women stayed researchers. Today that job is called "reporter." "We did a lot of research out of books and interviews for background for the stories, and we also went out with the photographers. When they hired a man to be a researcher, he really didn't attend to detail — you had to be very detail-conscious. So when he didn't do it very well, they promoted him to writer. We resented that a lot, as a matter of fact."

The job had a number of benefits for her, however. She got in on the ground floor of a journalistic enterprise still unmatched in this country, the magazine that practically invented a whole new genre: photojournalism. Henry Luce, who founded the magazine, had hired many of the world's finest photographers, some of them refugees from Europe, and turned them loose on the world to take its picture. And so Shelley Smith of Palo Alto, California, got to meet the photographer Carl Mydans.

The researchers all worked together in a large bull pen, and Shelley's desk was near the desk of Margaret Bassett, who was in charge of national affairs. Bassett and Mydans had worked together on several projects. Chunky, good-looking Mydans was one of the few American-born photographers on the staff. A native of Boston, the son of an oboist, he had fallen in love with photography at Boston University. After working as a photographer for the Farm Security Administration, he joined *Life* when the magazine began and found himself with adventurous, sometimes dangerous assignments.

"He came in and sat down in [Margaret Bassett's] wastebasket which seemed to be comfortable," Shelley remembered. The first thing she noticed was his voice. "His voice is full of secrets. He speaks not too loud, not a whisper, it has a lot of vibrations, of energy inside it. It was mesmerizing to me, so I sat through lunch hour just listening to this voice.

"Then we met. And that was kind of nice. Six months later we got married." He was thirty-one, she was twenty-three.

Next year, when war broke out in Europe, they were sent as *Life*'s first photographer-reporter team to cover it. They had one brief detour when Carl was stricken with appendicitis and had to be taken off the Pan Am Clipper at Bermuda. Cars were barred from the island so he was carted off to the hospital in a surrey with a fringe on top.

After finally arriving in Lisbon, they traveled through fascist Spain and expectant France. This was the period of the "phony war" and not much was happening, so they continued to England where they both joined the Time-Life London bureau. "The office gave us each a gas mask, I guess from World War I. And money belts. We had lots of cash. When we got to London, everybody was carrying gas masks and putting up blackout curtains and sandbagging windows. They were digging trenches in the parks and blacking out all traffic lights at night."

Their first story in England was a *Life* essay on the Port of London, the lifeline of the Empire. Then Carl covered the Royal Air Force, while Shelley worked with another photographer on a story about mine sweepers. Then, together, they went to Stockholm for an essay on neutral Sweden. When the Russians invaded neighboring Finland, Carl was sent to cover the winter war there while Shelley, who was not allowed to go into a combat zone, remained in Sweden.

Carl photographed combat frequently after that, but Shelley said she did not worry much about him or about herself.

"I know that my mother never worried, and I got that from her. It's a very strange thing; I don't worry. I don't know why but I don't. Perhaps it's just a trust in God. It was very comfortable that my mother didn't worry because I could have put her through hell, I guess. . . .

"On rare occasions, I wrote a little piece with byline, but mostly my job was to find stories, get the background, and work with the photographer and write up the research and captions for the use of the editors in New York. Perhaps it was what you might call second-class citizen work. I won't say drudge work because it was very interesting to get the story and follow it through. But the primary role of a *Life* researcher in the field was to support the photographer."

"Carl has the whole show," she told Terman. She also said she thought that was the way marriage ought to be. She would change her mind later.

When they were still in Sweden, *Life* suddenly was given permission to photograph Mussolini's fascist state. Carl flew to the north of Italy and worked south while another photographer started at the toe of the boot and worked north. Meanwhile, Shelley was sent to Portugal to work with yet another photographer. When the Germans broke through the Maginot Line, Carl was rushed to France where he covered the fall of Paris and the French rout south. He and Shelley were reunited in Lisbon and flew home together in June 1940.

She was assigned to the Time-Life bureau in Washington; he was sent to photograph the naval base in Pearl Harbor.

Around Christmas of that year, Carl and Shelley were transferred to Asia. The Japanese were already at war with China, and while the

United States was not yet involved, U.S. interests certainly were affected. Their first assignment was China, where Chiang Kai-shek was holding out against the Japanese invasion. China was of particular interest to Luce and he wanted Chiang's efforts well documented. The Mydanses were assigned to Chungking (now Chongqing), the refugee capital of China. They went by ship to Hong Kong, and then by Chinese Nationalist Airlines over the Japanese lines to Chungking. The flight was crowded, but not with people. Because of an astonishing inflation rate, the Nationalist government was printing money in Hong Kong as fast as it could. It put the bills in sacks and sat the sacks in airline seats strapped down with the seat belts. The Mydanses found themselves the only human passengers; every other seat was occupied by sacks of money. The copilot had served as a model for a character in the cartoon "Terry and the Pirates," and Shelley, a comic page buff, was mightily impressed.

"We landed in a sandbar in the middle of the Yangtze," she recalled. "In Chungking, the Yangtze and the Jialing rivers come together and the city rises up like the bow of a ship, a rock. You go up I don't know how many steps, and the first time you do it, they put you in a sedan chair, though not so fancy, more like a pig being taken to market. Bamboo hammock kind of thing. And two men carry you up these steps. It's too horrible to believe; they've got callouses on their shoulders." The next time you try to walk, she said, but that is grueling.

They arrived in time for an air raid.

"They took us to the press hostel which had been bombed immeasurable times because they had the government's radio antenna there so it was a nice target. It was a group of re-built and re-built series of mud and wattle huts with straw roofs where the correspondents stayed.

"Carl couldn't sit still. He just went wild with his cameras, running through the streets. It was so full of exciting things. And I ran after him taking notes. Not only was Chungking oriental and different, but it was like going back in history 400 or more years. It was thrilling! It was so exciting!"

They were assigned to cover the front along the Yellow River. Luce wanted Mydans to photograph the Chinese army in action.

"First lap we got a car, which is unbelievable in Chungking — the government lent us a car — and everybody we knew, of course, jumped into the car to drive up to Chengtu [now Chengdu, in Sichuan or Szechwan Province]. From Chengtu, we got on a Chinese airline plane which was corrugated aluminum, like a flying bread box, and landed in Lanchow [Lanzhou], the terminus of the old silk route. Then we got on a bus made from a Russian truck body with a box built on top. Everybody, chickens and people and us, and inched our way up the mountains to Sian [Xi'an] — funniest trip I've ever taken." They got into little carts drawn by Mongolian ponies, then finally they went on ponyback to the front to see what was happening. They found only a desultory artillery shell lobbed from one side to the other. "The Chinese were not very eager to fight, to tell the truth," Shelley recalled. That probably was not exactly what Luce wanted to hear.

They returned to Chungking. The city was under constant air attack. They were not, Shelley recalled, large raids, at least not by the standards that would later be set in the war, but in those days waves of twenty-seven plane formations bombing a city without letup was a major attack, and Chungking suffered.

In the fall of 1941, after short trips out of China to cover the preparation for the defense of Malaya and Singapore, the Mydanses were told to rush to Manila, where General Douglas MacArthur had taken over the Philippine defenses. The Japanese were already in Indochina and were inching their way south.

"I don't know if the threat of an attack on the Philippines was foreseen very clearly," Shelley said. "The idea probably was that they would come down through Malaya and Singapore or into Burma and Thailand. Nevertheless, when MacArthur was named commander of the U.S. forces in the Pacific, he began to set up the defenses of the Philippines."

The Mydanses did a photo essay on these preparations and shipped it out on what was to be the last Pan Am Clipper to Honolulu. They were in Manila when the Japanese attacked Pearl Harbor, learning about it first when a Manila newspaper with the war headline was delivered to their hotel room. The Japanese bombed Clark Field in the Philippines and destroyed MacArthur's air force the same day, December 8, Asian time. The Mydanses went to work immediately covering the Philippine army and visiting Clark Field and the fortifications at Corregidor at the entrance to Manila Harbor. They had several chances to get out before Manila fell, but didn't take them.

"They had a chance to escape imprisonment by taking the last boat that left," Terman wrote for Shelley's file, "but felt that they shouldn't do so because it would deprive others of the opportunity. They also could have joined the army on Corregidor, but they refused that also because it would have meant taking food that should have gone to the army. Regarding the boat on which they could have escaped, they would have had to disguise themselves in Red Cross uniforms, which their consciences would not permit."

"That makes us sound so holy," Shelley protested. "I don't remember any of that." Nonetheless, they did choose to stay. Carl could have gone to Bataan with the Signal Corps and perhaps escape that way, but Shelley couldn't go along and he wouldn't go without her.

"Truth of the matter was, we just got trapped. And truth of the matter is, you don't know how much time you have. You still have a story to do," Shelley said, following a train of thought that has probably come to every journalist in harm's way, "and you don't actually visualize it until they surround the city, and then you're trapped. Then it was scary for a while. The city was burning from the constant air raids and the oil fires set by our retreating troops. I learned something. I was frightened. . . . I realize now that for a day and a half, when the Japanese were right outside the city on all sides, I couldn't stand up straight. I never had a back problem before, but now I went around stooped over. Isn't that interesting? It was a psychosomatic something. I must have been frightened. But fright is like pain; you don't remember pain and you don't remember fright. But I remember the symptoms. I was frightened. We knew how they had taken Nanking [Nanjing]. They had ringed that city and then they came in — the depths of brutality, thousands raped and murdered. When you visualize that and you're sitting around. . . ."

On Christmas Day, they cabled New York from Manila: "Christmas morning was very quiet. Three raids kept us close to our base. We opened our presents under a tiny tree in our room, while a Filipino serenader below sang 'God Bless America.' Manilans first choked on the words 'Merry Christmas,' but soon found the toast of the day: 'May this be the worst Christmas we ever spend.' Christmas night we can laugh because we are still free." Then the Japanese overran Manila and all contact with the Mydanses ended. *Life* expressed hope they were alive and prisoners of the Japanese.

Beatrice

BEATRICE CARTER spent three years at the private school her parents reluctantly sent her to and then applied to college. Her first choice was Stanford. She told Terman she had always dreamed of sitting in the student section during the "Big Game," the annual football game between Stanford and the University of California at Berkeley. Beatrice was only fourteen and would not be fifteen until the middle of her freshman year. Stanford was most reluctant to admit her because she was so young and because she had spent only three years in school. The university felt there could be serious social problems for a fourteen-year-old girl surrounded by girls two and three years older and vastly more sophisticated. But the admissions committee was confronted with the fact that she did unusually well in the admissions tests, better than almost any other applicant.

Offering to intervene on behalf of his kids to get them into college at a very early age was not unusual for Terman. One young boy, aged fifteen, rejected Terman's offer telling him he thought his going to college at his age was "silly." Terman intervened for Beatrice. First he wrote to the headmistress of the private school to ask what she thought. He mentioned Stanford's reluctance over Beatrice's age, but pointed out that there would be several freshmen girls who were sixteen and even a few who were fifteen. Her answer could not have pleased him, but it probably didn't surprise him.

"My fervent wish is that I had had her five years ago and had been able to offset some of the influence of her family," the headmistress wrote. "I realize that both Mr. and Mrs. Carter have been adoring of this child from the moment of her birth, and it would be strange if they did not feel Beatrice was a very unusual person." But Beatrice was an insufferable bore, having been too often told that she was a genius. The headmistress related several examples of life with Beatrice.

"A little incident that happened about two weeks after the beginning of the term will indicate Beatrice's feeling about herself. We had changed tables, and when Beatrice noticed an eighth grade girl at the same table with her, she said quite airily: 'Oh, we have a little girl at our table this month!' One of the older girls said immediately, 'Why, Beatrice, Janice is not very much younger than you are, is she?' And you can imagine the consternation of the others at the table when Beatrice quickly responded, 'No, but what an intellectual difference.' "

"Of course there is no doubt about Beatrice's being able to do this work in college next year," the headmistress wrote, "but personally, I hate to see her go into that larger group before she has gotten a little more social balance. Her father and mother in their love for her have omitted so much that would have been valuable to her that it is very hard now to give her all that she needs. She is less of an individualist than when she came to us but she is not socially mature enough to hold her own with girls of college age."

The headmistress wrote that her mother constantly intervened with Beatrice's teachers and that one teacher called Gladys the most obnoxious parent she had ever met.

Terman thanked her for the letter, admitting he was not surprised. His files had already grown full of long letters from Gladys describing each of Beatrice's achievements and successes. He had responded kindly to her; she answered with more letters and presents, which seemed to embarrass him. The files contain no letters from the father.

Terman was convinced that Beatrice should go to Stanford despite her shortcomings, although by interfering in her life he was violating professional standards. How could he scientifically measure the success or failure of his subjects if he intervened in their fates? What would Beatrice's life be like if she did not go to Stanford at fourteen? He wrote a thoughtful letter to the admissions office pointing out that the role of a university is primarily intellectual and that they ought not to discount applicants for reasons that were largely social.

"If Beatrice is admitted to Stanford," he added, "the worst thing that could happen would be for her parents to move to Palo Alto and keep her at home."

"I have talked with two members of the admissions committee about Beatrice," Terman wrote Gladys, "and will talk with the other three members before the choices are made May the first."

Beatrice was admitted. "Dear Dr. Terman," she wrote. "I am *so* happy! With love. Beatrice."

Gladys stayed in Belmont. But every once in a while, she would take a room at the Cardinal Hotel in Palo Alto for a week at a time to be near Beatrice — and her professors.

Barbara Ramsperger, in a report for the files, wrote that Beatrice went to sorority rush soon after her arrival at Stanford, visiting the Delta Delta Delta house several times, but did not get a bid. Somehow, the word got out that Beatrice was not really interested in a sorority and therefore was not asked. The information was apparently wrong; Beatrice wanted very badly to be asked to join. Gladys roared down from Belmont to straighten out the matter, but in the end Beatrice did not get into a sorority. Gladys, however, had set a precedent for her response to events in Beatrice's college life.

Beatrice had two disadvantages: she was younger than the other women and still lacked anything resembling social grace. She had some friends, Ramsperger wrote, and they valued her friendship, but the other women in the dorm found her unfriendly, "a complete nonentity." One woman said that if Beatrice had tried to be friendly "it would be different, but she responds to advances by saying things the girls resent." Another woman said, "She has a haughty, super-cilious way of saying hello when she sees you."

"Poor Beatrice," Ramsperger wrote. "Even her gait, the expression on her face, and the way she holds her head are self-conscious. As she drives to and fro in the little Star coupe which her parents bought her to keep her out of the rain, her face is a study. Her head is liable to droop a bit to one side, and a peculiar little smile hovers over her lips."

One of Terman's field-workers went to her home for the second study and reported back: "Almost too much parental supervision. Probably better now that she is in Stanford and at home less."

The field-worker described her as "very attractive and pretty in appearance. Looks two or three years older than she is. Somewhat 'ritzy' in manner, however. Tries to appear older than she is. The effect is somewhat ludicrous at times. . . . Tries — consciously or unconsciously — just a bit to impress you with what she knows. Has some mannerisms which seem a bit overdrawn. . . . Chuckles, asides, remarks to herself while working, etc., may be spontaneous, but give the effect of being forced for effect. She probably is a bit ill at ease."

Despite these problems Beatrice did surprisingly well at Stanford socially. She had something of a social life, particularly with young foreign students, and she was active in the Unitarian Church organization on campus.

Beatrice did remarkably well academically. The only course in which she seemed to have trouble was physical education, and Gladys soon found herself in a feud with the physical education teacher.

Gladys felt it necessary to consult with most of Beatrice's professors, traveling down the peninsula on a regular basis and camping out at the Cardinal Hotel to be within walking distance of Beatrice and the faculty offices. Many of the professors were furious at the intervention. Terman, who felt responsible for Gladys's presence because he had gotten Beatrice into Stanford, was often caught in the middle. He tried to get Gladys to leave Beatrice alone, but to no avail.

"I sincerely hope you won't be offended if I urge upon you once more the questionable wisdom of your going to Beatrice's teachers with her difficulties. The fact that you have done so so often is already a matter of considerable comment, and cannot help in the long run to make things harder for Beatrice than easier. This is likely to be the effect even in the elementary grades and in the high school. In college it is still worse as the college student is expected to handle his own difficulties." He added that her interference would give Stanford second thoughts about admitting another student below the normal college age.

It did him no good. Gladys wrote back:

"There is another fallacy which has been called to my attention during the last few days. The interference of parents. I taught large classes in music for twenty-five years. In all that time I did not have one really successful pupil whose parents didn't take a direct interest in their progress and whom I was not delighted to consult with. When a teacher is putting love and interest in his work, he is glad for any cooperation that leads to progress. Beatrice has never had an unhappy moment with her men professors, or an unkind word from one of them, nor the great teachers among the women. . . ."

The dean of women demanded Terman do something about

Gladys. Again, Terman tried, but Gladys wrote back, with years of resentment erupting, that she too was gifted, but her mother never had a chance to "interfere" because her father was bedridden from arthritis for fifteen years. By the time her teachers were "through with their repression and suppression, I became the nobody I am today. It's so much happier to be average, isn't it?"

Sara Ann

WHEN SARA ANN McKINLEY was tested for the Terman study in her school in suburban Los Angeles, she tried to slip her examiner a little bribe. Terman's field-worker found a gumdrop under the record booklet in the middle of the test.

"Do you suppose the fairies brought this?" the field-worker asked the giggling six-year-old.

"A little girl gave me two," Sara Ann explained. "But I believe two would be bad for my digestion because I am just well from the flu now."

The researcher was charmed. The little blonde girl with the gap between her teeth and the thick eyeglasses affected an old-fashioned manner of speech. She had, the researcher reported, "a remarkable memory, a good logical mind." She also had an IQ nearly off the chart: 192.

And she had parents who worried about her. In many ways they were the ideal family for a gifted child, sensible and moderately prosperous. (Her father was an engineer.) They doted a little, but the child was not spoiled, the field-workers reported. When the Terman office at Stanford told the McKinleys that Sara Ann was at least as bright as they thought she was, they rejoiced. The report, her father wrote Terman, was a "most happy cause for Christmas gratitude. We only hope that we may not fail in providing that discipline of mind and character, not less than necessary material aids which shall permit her to realize most completely her widest possibilities."

Recognizing that they were now firmly connected to an expert in the field of gifted children, the McKinleys did not hesitate to ask

Terman's advice about bringing up Sara Ann. Should they allow her to be advanced in school beyond her age group? She was already in the fourth grade at the age of seven, so Terman advised against skipping more grades, suggesting the girl do directed outside reading to keep her mind sharp.

She was clearly not having an easy time, both her parents and Terman's field-workers knew. She procrastinated and seemed to have a limited attention span. Attempts to get her to do routine chores almost always failed. She seemed unfocused.

"Sara Ann seems to be ill at ease in any social situation which does not offer an opportunity for her to display the particular mental qualities which have, in the past, brought her success and commendation," a field-worker wrote.

"She welcomed any test situation which presented her a problem for solution," another wrote. "She was interested in her task but not absorbed until towards the end of the test series. It seemed to offer her the kind of social situation which gave her the greatest amount of self-confidence and control to her sense of power and importance."

She was a very earnest little girl, very slow and deliberate in almost anything she did. She also was a dreamer. Her parents had trouble motivating her, and so did her teachers.

"We are quite seriously disturbed over two things," James McKinley wrote Terman. "One, the child's chronic time wasting and procrastination. Her mother has put her onto definite time schedules — dressing, toilet, breakfast, making own bed and so on to her departure for school with a star on her record for fulfillment within time. This works fine for a little while, then it is a constant battle again to keep her anywhere near up.

"Two, periods of utter listless inattention in school, resulting in a majority of '2' marks and some '3s' where she is perfectly capable of getting practically all '1s' and does so when she makes up her mind and attends to business. We have for two years refused to let her skip grades recommended or acquiesced by her teachers for fear of the social consequences. Can you recommend a procedure for the present difficulties?"

Terman thought she was not being challenged enough and changed his mind about advancing her a grade. That only slightly solved the problem. The next year she changed schools because her parents moved and that seemed to end her academic problems. It was less the grade than the school.

Sara Ann still had social problems. She didn't mix well with other children, but wanted to, her parents reported, and was succeeding to the point of having close friends. She was a small girl; as she grew toward adolescence, she became a bit homely, her face hidden behind her thick glasses. Sara Ann was clearly having the troubles very bright children have when surrounded by people — children and adults — who are not nearly as bright.

When Terman's office tested her for the second study, Sara Ann's IQ had fallen off some. Her father was worried. Her parents worried too much, Terman's field-worker remarked, and Terman wrote back saying the decline, about ten points, could be ascribed to any number of variables, none of which was cause for concern.

She continued to have the kind of support she needed, and Terman's researchers were full of praise for her family. "A very devoted family with plenty of family life," one reported back to Stanford. Her parents were "pleasant and intelligent appearing," wrote another. Their home was large and attractive and full of books. If they had a flaw, it was that they worried too much about Sara Ann, especially about her grades in school. Her mother felt it was bad study habits that kept down her grades, too much attention to detail, losing sight of the subject as a whole. This affected Sara Ann, who was heard to pray for good grades before going to sleep at night.

By 1928 the McKinleys were having financial difficulties, largely due to their obligations to older parents. Betty McKinley had to take a job as a substitute teacher to supplement the family income. Sara Ann was going to LaMesa, a private school in a wealthy area, and felt the economic squeeze in the way children can. She "has not been able to have as many clothes and luxuries as the wealthy class of girls which attend LaMesa have, with the result she feels inferior socially," the home report said. A teacher said that the family's financial circumstances made Sara Ann aloof and distant.

When her mother came to teach in her school, however, much of Sara Ann's unhappiness seemed to fade; perhaps having a mother who was now important to her peers made the difference.

By the time she was a teenager, she had announced she wanted to become a physicist. She went to the University of California at Los

Angeles and finally earned a master's in physics there. In 1938 she married Jeffrey Albright, another graduate student at UCLA. They announced their engagement in a telegram to the rest of the physics department in a hilarious satire of the kind of wire one scientist sends another upon making a profound discovery. They had discovered the special gravity of love. She wrote the wedding ceremony herself, New Age before its time, full of quotations from Gibran, Browning's *Sonnets from the Portuguese*, the Bible, and the Reverend A. A. Hunter's *Radiant Possibilities of Marriage*. All the parts were scripted; every participant in the ceremony knew what to say and when. The guests sang lyrics on love and marriage that Sara Ann had set to Sibelius's *Finlandia,* while family members accompanied them on three violins and a piano. The word *obey* appeared nowhere in the marriage vows.

Sara Ann was active in the kind of benign, if naive left-wing politics of the day, considering herself a socialist. She attended a camp in New York sponsored by the Fellowship of Reconciliation, dedicated to solving the world's problems through nonviolence. However, the world did not want to solve its problems nonviolently, and in 1940 Sara Ann and Jeffrey Albright moved to Aberdeen, Maryland, where he worked in the army ordnance laboratory at the Aberdeen Proving Grounds to prepare the country for war. There, she transformed herself into a woman who amazed those who knew her.

The Tadashi Family: Delores

DELORES TADASHI was the smallest of the family of Emily and Akio Tadashi, the least healthy, the most artistic, and perhaps, except for her brother Ronald, the most sensitive. She was born July 28, 1911, their third child. "I love to draw," she wrote Terman when she was ten. "It is my favorite occupation, and I draw in practically all my spare time, from two to three and sometimes four hours a day. I am tremendously anxious to go on with my art work and make it my life work because it is what I love to do above all else." She hoped to be an illustrator and to design women's clothes. She also wrote poetry and produced a weekly family newspaper, full of the activities of the swarming family.

Her health kept her out of school for several years, a chronic and threatening pulmonary tuberculosis for which Terman no doubt felt great sympathy. She had "unhealthy eyes that twitch when she is nervous or excited," Terman's field-worker noted. She had also been born a bit knock-kneed and had persistent digestive "disturbances." She was not given the right kind of body for her mind or her heart.

Her closest friend was her younger sister Sophie. Before Sophie went to school for the first time, Delores taught her to print and write letters to some of the pen pal clubs advertised by a local newspaper. She taught Sophie to draw and did several sketches of Sophie herself. Delores kept a scrapbook of Sophie's first attempts at writing stories and her sketches. "A nice little girl," wrote Terman after he met Delores for the first time in 1923, "whose inner life and ambitions have more personality than her personality."

In high school she was elected president of the press club and was a prime mover in the drama club. This prominence must have been difficult for her; Delores was high-strung, and when she got nervous, she tended to chatter incessantly. She tried to teach herself some control, but her mother said she was handicapped by her sensitivity and fear of ridicule. "She is just now beginning to be able to laugh at herself and pass over a teasing remark," her mother wrote during the first follow-up survey in 1924.

"Delores makes friends readily, is vivacious and demonstrative, but more inclined to egotism and self-consciousness than the others," her mother wrote Terman. "It is difficult for her to admit a mistake. She is inclined to self-justification. She has a good deal of perseverance and generally attains her objective. She is very fond of acting and does it well. She responds to love and can be influenced by an appeal to her heart rather than her head."

"She is a ladylike young person," Terman wrote of her, "who meets strangers with a quiet reserve, without embarrassment."

Of all the Tadashi children, only she showed any emotional instability in her tests.

She never finished her education, blaming her health, and moved to San Francisco to live with her maternal grandmother. She made her living as a fortune-teller — her family said she half believed what she was saying — and died of tuberculosis at the age of twenty-two years, one month, and twenty-one days.

The Tadashi Family: Ronald Talbot

RONALD, of all Emily and Akio's children, suffered perhaps the most alienation because of his family's mixed heritage, the domestic confusion, and poverty. Yet he began, as his mother described him, a gay and humorous child, full of "air castle optimism," and ended life a contented man.

He was the youngest, born in June 1913. He was tested at the age of eight. The field-workers remarked at his excellent rote memory, but also found him the least social of the Tadashi children. "A charming little fellow, quite Japanese in appearance except for rather large, brown eyes. Very friendly in a rather serious old-fashioned way."

"Ronald's fund of outside information is remarkable," wrote a teacher. "Much of this is due to the careful and intelligent training of his mother, I believe." Emily wrote that he hated confinement, got poor grades in penmanship and drawing, and was interested in civil engineering. She also added in her 1924 report to Terman that she found him "rather annoyingly self-willed, but I imagine that to be a characteristic of his age. He plays chess better than any of the others. He plays all games well, but *hates* to lose; he's not a good loser.

"He is inclined to be lazy, and his temper is not always well controlled. He cannot endure to be teased or ridiculed by the others. On the other hand, he is affectionate, loyal, and tenderhearted. He will work his head off when it is something *he wants to do.*"

"One notes a heartiness, gaiety, and friendliness about him that are most appealing," Terman wrote. "Life has not yet become a serious matter for him." It would become so.

When the family lived in San Francisco, Ronald was part of a coterie at school. His friends paid little if any attention to his parentage. But in Placerville things changed abruptly. For the first time he met people who were violently racist, and he felt their prejudice intensely. He had few friends, his mother wrote, and she believed racism was the reason.

His life was changed by a chance event. One of his sisters, knowing how well he liked games, brought home a magazine containing an article on whist. His mother wouldn't let him play card games until he was seven, but once he began he proved to be a genius at the game. He moved from whist to its nearest cousin, bridge, and by the time Ronald was in his late teens, he was a champion bridge player. He was otherwise not doing very well.

"All of them [Termites] seem to be making a place for themselves in society," he wrote Terman in the late 1930s, "and appear to have relatively little difficulty in overcoming their problems. This has not been the case with me." He had graduated from high school with a B− average, but managed to get into Berkeley. However, he found himself completely uninterested in his studies. "Mother thought ego had led me to take too many difficult courses. The truth is that the courses would have been very easy for me if I could have made myself study."

The story was actually more complicated than that. Ronald had found the wrong woman. His brother Alfred wrote to Terman: "Ronald decided to develop his own personality and went to great extremes to do it. He adopted a standard of living entirely different from that of his family. When he was a sophomore at college, he met an older woman who has had a very bad influence on him. He neglected his studies, did not bother to take final examinations and never made any effort to be reinstated. Spent his time playing bridge. The girl has enough money to provide shelter, food and clothing and has made every effort to discourage all ambition in Ronald. She prefers to have them both live off her money."

Alfred urged Ronald to get a job. "Ronald seems to be realizing his mistakes and the relationship between brothers has been more sympathetic during the last few months," Terman noted for the files. "Ronald is working now and is trying to get a better job. Does statistical work. Alfred was doing some statistical work which he has given over to Ronald. Ronald complains that there is no use in doing anything because the cards are already stacked against him. Alfred does not believe this is so. [Alfred] believes you are liked for what you are."

He left Berkeley without graduating and began isolating himself from his family. Feeling that his last name would be a permanent handicap, he changed it to his mother's maiden name of Talbot. Of course, he still looked exotic enough to make people wonder at his parentage. "My nationality is a handicap," he wrote. "It has an unfortunate way of coming into light at inopportune moments." He refused any help from his family and drifted through a series of jobs. One was at a chemical plant for pay ranging from twenty cents an hour to perhaps two dollars. At one time he asked Terman for help in finding a job; Terman wrote a letter of recommendation.

But he had his games. By 1937 Ronald had won sufficient championships to become well known in the bridge circuit. Three years later, bothered by the notion that this was not a serious way to spend one's life, he quit bridge. He took up farming in a small community in the Sierra foothills, where he could be left alone.

When the war broke out, he learned that all Americans of Japanese ancestry would be interned, an idea that infuriated him. Terman wrote a letter to the immigration service testifying to Ronald's loyalty, but the issue never came up; the authorities never found Ronald in his remote ranch — if they were in fact looking for him — and neither he nor his siblings were interned. Terman wrote him, expressing his horror at the discrimination he was facing: "As an American citizen I feel greatly humiliated that any of my fellow citizens should show the racial intolerance that you and many others have suffered."

Ronald became a devout Christian in 1949, which seemed to help him find some peace. He remained isolated, even from his family. A woman who knew him reported to Terman he had bought a ranch and incurred $20,000 debt doing so. He had by this time married a white woman, a divorcée. He and his wife kept themselves from their neighbors, sure of their intolerance. "He is very anxious," the woman told Terman, "that none of his friends or relatives be given his address." She arranged for Terman to communicate with Ronald indirectly. Terman could write a letter in a blank envelope, she would pass it on to mutual friends, the friends would put the address on the envelope, and they would mail it to him. His isolation was so complete that he had almost no correspondence with his siblings and he did not know when his father or mother died.

When his ranch failed, he reverted to the only thing he knew how to do well: play bridge. He began playing professionally, started a newspaper column, and wrote several books on the game. He became the highest-ranking bridge player in the country, so ethical in his playing he was called "the gentleman of the bridge table."

He and his wife had two sons. His wife traveled with him to bridge tournaments when she could, but he made it a point never to play bridge at home.

He semiretired in his early fifties, spending two months of every year traveling with his family, playing bridge less, and discontinuing his column. He moved to San Francisco and became active in charitable causes. In his middle age, he reported to Terman that he had become a happy man. "I have had excellent fortune in all areas of life," he wrote in 1972. "Our sons are apparently good boys, reasonably well-balanced for their ages, neither 'hippies' or 'squares,' not afraid to talk back, and both doing well in school without undue parental pressure. . . . Neither my wife nor I have any very bad recognizable hang-ups left. What more can you ask?"

His health began to fail in 1980. He suffered from cancer and heart disease. He died of prostate cancer in 1983 at the age of 60.

Ancel

ANCEL KEYS* became one of the most famous of Terman's kids, the only one to make the cover of *Time* and *Life* magazines and the only one to add a word to the English language. The effects of his scientific research are still very much part of our lives forty years later. In many ways he is the paradigm Terman sought.

He was one of the oldest of Terman's subjects, tested at the age of eighteen as part of Terman's high school group, which was counted separately from the main experimental group. He was then a senior at Berkeley High School. Born in Colorado, his family moved to Berkeley when he was still a child. He was the nephew of the character actor Lon Chaney on his mother's side. Her maiden name was Carrie, or Caroline Chaney.

Ancel's somewhat unusual interest in food began in childhood. At an age when most children crave sweets, he loved fresh fruit, loved it enough to steal it from a neighboring orchard once to satisfy a yen.

"Mother was reputed to be a great cook," he said often, but he admitted that was second-hand knowledge as he was rarely home. He could usually be found camping with his friends in the hills north and east of Berkeley. He surely preferred camping to school. "We just hiked and ate," he told *Time*. "Three breakfasts a day: Aunt Jemima pancakes, dried prunes, and bacon. Not too bad a diet. You can eat anything for a few days."

He was five foot seven by the age of thirteen, fairly tall for that age,

* His real name is used with his permission.

but then he stopped growing. The halt in his growth certainly had nothing to do with his appetite. "I was always ready to eat. Chinatown was wonderful: an egg roll and two bowls of chow mein for forty cents. A little concentrated on the calories, perhaps."

Ancel would do anything to avoid school. He even dropped out one spring to shovel bat guano in an Arizona cave. "Great fun," he said decades later. "I slept out in the desert with the other desert rats. I'd hate to think what we ate. Stews and sourdough bread, I guess." He finally returned to Berkeley with seventy-five dollars in savings and stayed long enough to graduate high school. His truancy did not deter one of his teachers from recommending him to the Terman study. He had no trouble passing the tests.

Ancel majored in chemistry at the nearby University of California campus, taking an awesome array of science courses, studying thirty hours a week in the library, and earning loose change by beating his classmates at bridge. He kept a constant supply of dried apricots by his bed. But Ancel's tendency toward impatience caused something of a detour in his scientific career.

"There was a scholarship prize offered in the Department of Chemistry, which at that time was considered one of the very best in the United States, and a big department it was," he could remember almost sixty years later. "I took a very heavy program in chemistry and physics and Chinese and German and mathematics. I had A grades in everything except physics, and I had a B in that. So that was seventeen credits, perhaps a little more than I should have taken. There was another youngster who had sixteen credits, all A's, and he got the prize. I was resentful about that."

He did the only thing that seemed logical to him at the time. His father got him a job as an oiler on a ship sailing to China. The engine room where he worked was extremely hot and he drank six to eight liters of water on each of his four-hour shifts. He could not remember anything he ate.

Ancel finally went back to Berkeley and as an act of spite — it's not clear whom he was spiting — changed his major to economics. He graduated in two years, moved to Sacramento, and took a job at Woolworth's as a management trainee. "He has worked very hard," his mother wrote Terman in the home visit form in 1925, "but is so interested in his work that he didn't mind." Wrong. He was bored silly.

"Only a few weeks after I began at Woolworth's I decided that this was not the way I was going to spend the rest of my life," he said. "I went back to the university and talked to one of the deans that had been friendly with me, and he immediately picked up the telephone and called the head of biology and made an appointment. After I talked for a little while, I said this was for me."

He finished a major in biology in six months. He also got married at the age of nineteen.

By the age of twenty-four, Ancel was a research assistant at the University of California's Scripps Institute in La Jolla. He was very unhappy about it. Like many of Terman's kids, he sought advice from his mentor. Unfortunately, Terman was ill when he called, but his assistant Barbara Ramsperger was in the office.

"Keys is small, but well-set up, rather mild in appearance and bearing, and wears a mustache which is carefully trimmed," she reported to Terman. "He is in a quandary about how to get out of a situation which sounds quite impossible as he describes it. He . . . is supposed to be working up some research for a Ph.D. dissertation on the side. He . . . has been in La Jolla about a year and a half. His trouble is that there is no one there that is doing any research at all akin to his, no one to give him advice or direction. There is a total lack of cooperation among the members of the staff — each goes to his own laboratory, seals himself up so to speak, and has nothing to do with anyone the whole day long. The people of La Jolla speak of the experimental station as the 'bug house,' and it seems to be one. There is a member of the staff who has intermittent attacks of insanity and comes to work there in between times. There is a terrible paucity of equipment. When Ancel needs so simple a thing as a rubber stopper, he has to requisition it and wait for six weeks. No courses are given there, but Ancel has a great need for course work in physiology and biology and zoology before he takes his degree."

In short, Ancel wanted out. He particularly wanted a job at Stanford's Hopkins Marine Station near Monterey where his wife had once worked as a secretary. That wasn't possible, Ramsperger wrote, because Hopkins and Scripps were collaborating, and Hopkins did not want to appear to be stealing staff.

Ancel somehow straightened out what he wanted and needed and got his Ph.D. from Berkeley in 1928.

His first marriage ended in divorce in 1936. The same year, Terman's field-worker noted: "He has more worldly experience than the average boy [sic] of his age. Strong influence on companions. Led a wild life but settled down."

Ancel went to Europe as a National Research Council Fellow and there wrote his first scientific papers. He went on to Cambridge University as a Fellow of the Rockefeller Foundation to work under Joseph Barcroft, head of the physiology department in the medical school. Barcroft wanted him to stay in Cambridge and arranged for him to get a second Ph.D., saying that in Cambridge it would be better to be "a Cambridge doctor." The degree was awarded in 1936 with no examination, no thesis, no cost.

Ancel decided to return to the United States, taking a job at the Harvard Fatigue Laboratory. The founder and head of the laboratory said that physiology should not be limited to caring for the sick. Keys was not particularly interested in the work at the laboratory, but decided he did want to study the effects of high altitude on the human body. The best way to do that was to go someplace high. When plans to visit the mountain K-2 in the Himalayas failed to materialize, he launched an expedition in 1937 to the Andes with a colleague from Cambridge, Bryan Matthews. Neither he nor Matthews had any climbing experience, but they soon enlisted some men who did. Eleven men, and Ancel, went to Chile.

"We took off for the Andes, but it was mid-winter, and that was kind of a rough deal," he remembered. "We spent two or three months in Chile. Had headquarters at big copper mining camp, near Chuquicamata. After getting somewhat adjusted and making our plans from 9,000 feet, we found that there was a copper mine up on the slopes of this high mountain, and we decided that that would be the place for us to go if it was possible to get up there. Very rough. Seventeen thousand feet." He, Ryan, and a couple of Indian mine workers eventually set up a camp at the 20,000-foot level. The scientists did various blood and lung tests and measured body temperature and pulse rate.

"There was snow, not deep snow, but we managed to make some kind of snow shelter, crawl in with blankets, and then we worked for a week. We did not suffer from the altitude. The thing which bothered the most was that it was 50 degrees below zero outside, and if you spend ten hours in a place like that you have to go out and urinate, and that was a big problem. That was the worst thing in the whole trip.

"During the day it wasn't bad, walking around slowly. You got a wonderful view down below almost 10,000 feet at a 45 degree angle. John Talbot — he was from Harvard, too — took an arterial puncture on me, did it very beautifully, and a few minutes later he collapsed. He was blue and we were very worried about him. The Indians managed to carry him down to 17,000 feet and he managed to revive in a few hours. He was desperately sick." (Talbot recovered and later became the editor of the *Journal of the American Medical Association*.)

When Ancel came down to the 17,000-foot level, his heartbeat was thirty-six beats a minute and very irregular. It returned to normal a few days later.

In 1940 Ancel took a battery of vocational interest tests for Terman, who assured him he was going to be much happier as a scientist than as a manager at Woolworth's.

Chapter Eight

THE GIFTED GROW UP

ALMOST A QUARTER CENTURY had passed since Terman began his study of gifted children. While comparing his gifted subjects to other people was problematic because of all the flaws in the study, Terman could now see what had happened to his kids over a generation and could begin to make comparisons *within* the group that would be both far more valid and in many cases more interesting than comparisons with other groups. His sample was ideal for this kind of comparison for two reasons. First, he had an amazing amount of data, two walls of file cabinets full of information, the likes of which had never been gathered over time on any other group of people. Second, the only thing that made his subjects unique, the only criterion for being one of Terman's kids, was intelligence, at least as most scientists were then willing to measure it. That was the subjects' great equalizer — they were all extremely smart.

Some had succeeded in every way Terman could wish, others were by most definitions failures in life, and the majority were somewhere in between. Why? What made some succeed and others fail once intelligence was eliminated as a factor? What other factors come into play?

Twenty years actually was not enough time to find definitive answers to those questions; the Termites were young adults and many had not yet reached their prime. Some careers require time to develop. Some people are late bloomers. Terman, in fact, considered himself only halfway through the study. But he felt that now he could formulate new questions, he had clues to answers to some of the questions he had asked before, and he could begin to draw some tentative conclusions.

He certainly had a right to be proud of his kids. By 1947 he could report that nearly 90 percent of the Termites had gone to college and 70 percent were college graduates, a rate ten times greater than would be found in the population of California. They went to graduate school at a rate eight times higher than the average of California college graduates. Seventy-three had earned doctorates or their equivalent, and seventeen others were working on them. There were fifty-two doctors and eighty-two lawyers. "It is doubtful whether 1,500 school children picked at random would contribute one-twentieth as many doctors and lawyers," he wrote.

They earned far more money than the general population. They had published ninety books and monographs and approximately fifteen hundred articles in scientific, scholarly, and literary journals, including eight college textbooks, fourteen volumes of fiction, three collections of poems, two books on popular science, five books on social science, and several children's books. More than a hundred patents had been awarded to Termites (nearly half to two men, a radio engineer and a chemist, and two to a female metallurgist). "Many of the patents have been sold to industrial firms, but so far as we know, none of them is of epoch-making importance." And the record would have been much better but for the fact that the lives of many of his kids were interrupted by World War II.

The Termites included nuclear physicist Norris Bradbury of Los Alamos; physiologist Ancel Keys; psychiatrist Douglas McGlashan Kelley, who headed the medical corps efforts in Europe during the war and served as psychiatrist at the prison in Nuremberg after the war; and playwright Lilith James, who wrote the Broadway show *Bloomer Girl*. Some were unknown but no less remarkable, such as the lawyer whose hobby was learning languages and who had learned fifteen — Japanese, French, Spanish, Russian, Croatian, Norwegian, Danish, Hawaiian, Greek, Latin, and several Celtic languages — for the hell of it.

That the group contains no one who shows promise of matching the eminence of Shakespeare, Goethe, Tolstoy, da Vinci, Newton, Galileo, Darwin, or Napoleon is not surprising in view of the fact that the entire population of America since the Jamestown settlement has not produced the like of one of these. Such eminence in a given field is usually

possible only at a given stage of cultural progress and can never be very
closely paralleled in a different era. For one thing, science and scholarship are growing so highly specialized that eminence is becoming progressively more difficult to obtain. Conceivably, if Darwin were living
today he might be just another specialist in a restricted field of biology. . . .[1]

And proudly he could announce not only were they succeeding, at
least most of them, but they had found contentment in life, at least
most of them.

The volume Terman and his colleagues published in 1947 was the
result of three separate studies, beginning in 1936. For about eight
years after the first follow-up in 1928, Terman's office in the heart of
the Stanford campus was relatively quiet. No attempt was made to do
organized research on the subjects, but informal contact was maintained. From the beginning it was clear that Terman was building a
sodality out of his Termites.

Many of the subjects, and even more of their parents, sent a steady
flow of information, clippings, and letters into the office. Some of the
letters ran to more than half a dozen typewritten or handwritten
pages. Everyone got an answer from Terman or, if he was sick, one of
his assistants. Many of the subjects dropped by. Many who had
moved from California visited the Stanford office routinely whenever
they were on the West Coast to talk to Terman or whoever was there.
When they were in a quandary, they sometimes brought it to their
paterfamilias and sat at his knees as he gave advice. He loved it. Every
visit was followed by a memo in the file, many quite personal and
revealing. Terman clearly had favorites and clearly disliked some of
his kids; he considered one of his most famous to be a pompous ass.
The Termites brought in their children and their spouses for
blessing — and testing. Terman wanted to see what kind of person
they married and what kind of children they produced. He pried into
their private lives when he thought it necessary or interesting. When a
San Francisco columnist wrote that Carl and Shelley Mydans had
separated, Terman shot off a letter to a mutual friend for confirmation. When assured it wasn't so, he wrote Shelley Mydans to express
his relief.[2]

Terman continued to meddle in their lives, skewing his own data.

He would write a letter of recommendation for anyone in the group, if nothing else, stating that the person was in the Terman study of the gifted. He gave them free vocational testing and sent them letters of explanation and advice with the results. He would intervene on their behalf to get them into graduate school or to get them a job. Sometimes they did not even ask; he intervened covertly, leaving the Termites wondering what role he played. Rodney Beard, for instance, thinks his mother may have asked Terman to help get him into Stanford's medical school, but he does not know for sure; Terman did write a letter. He probably helped pay for many of his kids' education by contributing to scholarships, always anonymously.

In 1936 Terman began laying plans for a formal follow-up to be undertaken as soon as he could get funding. This was in the nadir of the depression, and even he was having money troubles. Contact with his subjects since the previous study had been ad hoc and unstructured, and Terman needed to set the stage for more formal contact. When his office last had any connection with most of the subjects, they were children who were doing what they were told by their parents in relation to the study and had no concept of what was happening. Now they were adults and had to be educated about the importance of the research.

Terman needed to get his mailing list up to date and wanted to prime his subjects for the next battery of questionnaires. Letters went out to every address in the files, usually to the parents since the subjects were children in 1927 and lived at home. When he got an answer, Terman mailed a four-page form to the kids and a four-page form to their parents with a letter expressing his belief in the scientific value of the study. After about a year, his staff had tracked down as many subjects as they could. The information was filed, but it was not analyzed then because Terman had a more elaborate study in mind that would supersede this one. What he had been trying to do was to demonstrate his ability to contact his sample. It turned out that almost all of the subjects were quite willing to participate and were curious about the outcome. Even those who were less successful in life helped, Terman said.

In the winter of 1939 the money came, this time mainly from the Carnegie Corporation of New York, the National Research Council Committee for Research on Problems of Sex, the Columbia Foundation of San Francisco, and an anonymous donor. Additionally, Stanford contributed some, and Terman turned all the royalties from his previous published reports back into the office. They had been published by Stanford University Press and had sold well. With $40,000 in hand, he began hiring assistants again, and the Terman project geared up for action.

No thought was given to further medical examinations because of the expense and logistics, but everything about the subjects that could be probed through questionnaires, tests, and interviews, including deeply personal questions about their sex lives, was considered. Huge packets of forms and tests were printed. Some of the questionnaires could be filled out by the subjects at their convenience; some had to be done in the presence of field-workers to ensure validity. Only those living in the accessible parts of California were visited and given tests that required supervision. Data on people who had moved elsewhere were less complete. Since most of the subjects worked, the staff worked odd hours to be able to arrange appointments.

One thing made this study different from Terman's previous work: it was mechanized. For the first time Terman used "Hollerith cards," punch cards that could be mechanically sorted.* This permitted Terman to tabulate and cross-tabulate his growing mountain of data. He put his two previous studies on punch cards, an enormous task led by his assistant Melita Oden. Seven cards were used just for the basic information about each subject in the 1922 study, and thirty of the eighty holes on every card were taken up just by bookkeeping information. The result, however, was considerable depth and versatility in analyzing the data.

Terman decided to send questionnaires to everyone on his list, the main experimental group and the other groups, in order to broaden the data base. Of a total 1,528 subjects, 35 men and 26 women had died, leaving 1,467 living Termites. Terman contacted 1,434 of them, or 97.7 percent; of those, 1,409, or 96.04 percent, gave full cooperation. More than 1,000 sat for interviews; 364 of their children and more than 600 of their spouses took the Stanford-Binet test.

Two things stand out clearly. First, the almost incredible amount of cooperation that was secured. No other comparably large group of any kind — superior, average, or inferior — has been tested and followed

* Hollerith was Herman Hollerith who had automated the 1890 U.S. Census by using punch cards and who had invented machines that sorted and tabulated the cards, a mechanical computer.

up over so long a period. The resulting data provide, if not a final
answer, at least a better answer than has hitherto been available to the
age-old question regarding the later careers of superior children. The
second fact to be noted is the enormous amount of data which had to be
statisticized [sic] in connection with the present follow-up. Information
included not only the numerous test scores and case-history material
secured in 1940, but also the most important data secured in 1921–22,
1927–28, and 1936.[3]

Only one subject flatly refused to cooperate (the questionnaire was
returned with a curt "This subject does not wish to be studied").
Terman could not locate twenty-eight subjects, eleven men and
seventeen women (ten from the main experimental group). Terman
suspected that these "lost" families had simply moved and the for-
warding addresses had expired. He hoped to find them and kept
looking. One subject, previously lost to the mailing list, turned up
when someone spotted a letter to the editor the subject had written to
a newspaper.

The average age of his sample in 1940 was twenty-nine and a half.
Ten were still under twenty (siblings of subjects), and none was over
forty.

Terman's office analyzed the data throughout the war. In 1945,
curious to see how the Termites were faring, he sent a two-page
questionnaire to them and got responses from 98 percent, even
though more than half had been returned the first time for incorrect
addresses. The war had dislocated many of these young adults. The
replies came from all over the world, including Britain, France, Germany, Italy, North Africa, China, India, Japan, and islands across the
Pacific. Terman gleefully reported getting questionnaires filled out
aboard ship, in army camps and hospitals, and even in foxholes in
combat zones. That survey ran into the next year, giving Terman a
snapshot of how his kids did in the war.

Sixty-one were dead by the end of the war, thirty-five men and
twenty-six women. Five men died in the war. The mortality rate was
4.07 percent. Actuarial tables showed that for the white population in
the United States, the mortality should have been 5.02. Considering
that those tables did not reflect war casualties, it was safe to say
Terman's subjects had a lower death rate.

CAUSES OF DEATH FOR TERMAN'S SUBJECTS TO 1941

	MALES		FEMALES		TOTAL	
	Subjects	Percent	Subjects	Percent	Subjects	Percent
Natural causes	18	2.13	21	3.21	39	2.60
Accidents	12	1.42	3	0.46	15	1.0
Suicides	5	0.59	1	0.15	6	0.40
Unknown	—	—	1	0.15	1	0.07
All deaths	35	4.14	26	3.98	61	4.07

Terman pointed out that the suicide rate was likely to increase considerably because his subjects were just reaching the age at which suicides get more common in the general population.

Besides the five killed in the war, two men died of injuries indirectly caused by the hostilities. One was exposed to a deadly dose of radiation while he was working on the atomic bomb. Another was overcome by fumes in a war materials plant.

The deaths were few enough for Terman to list them all. Tuberculosis, his nemesis, accounted for eight of the deaths; appendicitis, nephritis, and polio each took three Termites; and the other natural deaths came from a variety of causes. One young woman, a senior in college, died of a brain tumor. One man suffered a heart attack at the age of twenty-six just after he had gotten his dream job as a sportswriter for a major newspaper. One young man, who had finished the eighth grade before he was eleven, graduated cum laude from college at nineteen, received his doctorate in physics at twenty-two, became an assistant professor at a major university at twenty-nine, and was listed in *American Men of Science*, contracted tuberculosis, finished writing a popular science book from his sickbed, and died at thirty-five. A woman whom Terman described as giving "promise of being one of our most outstanding women" and who had won several scholarships and awards as well as her doctorate, died at twenty-nine from pneumonia. She was a research fellow in linguistics at Yale at her death. A male scientist died in a car crash at twenty-two; another (listed by Terman as having an IQ of 173) was killed in a car accident at the age of twenty while still in college. Some of the suicides were people with obvious mental and emotional problems, such as "Ira," but Terman noted that others seemed to show no signs of disorder or reasons for bringing on their own death.

He could take some pride in those who died in the war. One man, who had shown serious behavior problems as a teenager, straightened himself out before joining the air corps, rose to the rank of staff sergeant, became a tail gunner on a bomber, and won two presidential citations and a Purple Heart. He was killed in action. A former journalist joined the Royal Air Force, became a squadron leader, and was killed in a plane crash in India. A lieutenant colonel was shot down while piloting a paratroop plane in North Africa. An army corpsman stationed in the Philippines was captured by the Japanese and died when his prison ship was accidentally sunk by an allied vessel.

Because of Terman's paternal bond to his subjects, he must have felt deeply about the ending of these young lives.

Otherwise, he found that his Termites were a healthy lot. He found that 90 percent of the men and 83 percent of the women listed their health as either "very good" or "good." Less than 1 percent of either reported "very poor" health. Women seemed to be doing not quite as well, but Terman said other researchers found that to be true in the general population as well.

Eight subjects had hearing losses, four of them severe enough to require hearing aids. Eleven had what he called "orthopedic handicaps of more or less serious nature," three of which resulted from polio. In no case were the handicaps an impediment to success, he noted proudly.

The average height of the men was 70.65 inches and of the women 64.69 inches. The average American male at that time was 67.5 inches and the average woman 63.5 inches, so his subjects were taller than average. They were even taller than the average college student, based on measurements taken at Stanford and the University of Minnesota, although these studies were made during the freshman year and some of these young people were still growing.

The average weight of the male Termites was 162.81 pounds and of the females 126.62 pounds. The men were more than twelve pounds heavier than the national average, the women one or two pounds heavier, depending on whose statistics one used.*

* Terman gave figures for the average height and weight for American males with more precision than for females, probably because of the draft and military examinations. Apparently, the data on women were not as good.

How was their mental health? The Terman office had collected considerable data about the subjects by 1940, ranging from field-worker reports to letters from the Termites and their parents. Terman used this data to determine the mental and emotional states of his subjects. He assigned his kids to one of three categories: "satisfactory adjustment," "some maladjustment," and "serious maladjustment." The last category was further broken down into psychotic and non-psychotic. He had enough data to rate 760 men and 603 women. He reported that 79.6 percent of the men and 81.76 percent of the women were satisfactorily adjusted. Of those with serious maladjustments, less than 1 percent of both the men and the women could be described as psychotic.* There were six psychotic men, two diagnosed as schizophrenic, two as manic depressive, and two as epileptic.† All but the epileptics had recovered. Two of the five psychotic women were in mental hospitals, one diagnosed as depressive, the other as suffering from dementia praecox, or schizophrenia.

Comparing the mental health of his gifted to the general population was difficult, but using the available data, Terman concluded that his group had slightly fewer psychotics than would be found in the population. There would be, he was sure, more cases of mental break-down in the future, but he felt that "it is doubtful whether the incidence will continue to parallel that for the general population." His subjects had already passed the age when many people suffer break-downs.

Then, no doubt using his mechanical computer, Terman decided to cross-tabulate the mental health of the gifted with such variables as IQ and education. College graduates (both male and female) seemed to be slightly better adjusted than nongraduates, but the difference was not statistically reliable, he reported. Terman found that the adult IQ of his subjects, as determined by data collected in 1940 from an IQ test he devised called the Concept Mastery test (see page 147), showed a much clearer relationship to "adjustment" than did childhood IQ. The most maladjusted men and women tended to have higher scores as adults. On the other hand, he pointed out, "many of the most

---

* Those listed as seriously maladjusted or psychotic were people who at any time had suffered these experiences, not just those who were that way at the time of the study in 1940.
† Terman's inclusion of epileptics in this category reflects his time. Epilepsy is *not* a mental disease, and epileptics are *not* psychotics.

successful men of the entire group also scored high on this test."
Perhaps that simply meant that having an unusually high IQ provided
some added risk to one's mental stability.

Ten men and five women listed themselves as alcoholics in 1940.
Two men and one woman had sought help by then. One of the men
died in the war. Four more had sought help by 1945.

Terman reported that the rate of delinquency in his subjects was
half that of the general population.

Four of Terman's males were imprisoned, three as juvenile delinquents and one as an adult offender for forgery. The forger was
apparently a habitual gambler. Terman seemed to note with a touch
of pride that "he became an exemplary prisoner and was soon the
editor of the institutional publication." The gifted succeed even in jail.
Several others had brushes with the law, but none did anything serious enough to be incarcerated.

Two women got in trouble, one for vagrancy and one for prostitu-
tion. The prostitute had been arrested several times but never jailed.

> These two cases, with almost identical IQ's (152 and 153), present a
> striking contrast in background. The former [the vagrant] was brought
> up in an atmosphere of wealth and luxury, the latter [the prostitute]
> was orphaned in her early teens and lived with relatives under difficult
> economic circumstances. To avoid the possibility of identification, the
> case histories of these subjects must be withheld, but we are able to
> report that by 1940 both had apparently made normal behavioral
> adjustments.[4]

One woman in the study was raped as a teenager and had an
illegitimate child. A few others also had illegitimate children.

Terman also reported on homosexuality among the Termites. He
found that eleven men and six women had a history of homosexual
behavior, by which he apparently meant that they had had homosexual experiences. Three women reported the experiences themselves;
information on the other three "was received from other sources," he
said. He suspected there were more homosexual men, but believed he
had counted all the women. The totals came to 1 percent of his
sample. He had no data on the general population to compare this
with. Kinsey's data was too vague, he felt, listing too many degrees of
behavior (see page 83). Four of the eleven men were married, all of

them after their homosexual experiences, and Terman reported that the marriages constituted the "final step in a definite program to attain sexual normality. All but one of these four men appear to have made reasonably normal adjustments." Four of the eleven male homosexuals "have been so outstanding in their achievement as to be rated among the 150 most successful men of the gifted group," Terman reported.

All but one of the six women who had had homosexual experiences were married. Two of the marriages took place after the experiences, and again Terman interpreted the marriages as moves back to "normality." One woman had a lesbian affair while she was married, but it ended swiftly and did not harm the marriage, he said. Two were married and divorced before becoming active homosexuals. One of those was in a mental hospital. The other, "a brilliant and highly successful professional woman, was married for a year and did not assume her homosexual relationship until sometime after her divorce."

> The highly confidential nature of the information on homosexuality prevents the inclusion of case histories of the subjects involved. Most of the histories, particularly those of the men, follow the classical patterns in respect to masculinity or femininity of interests, strong attachment to the opposite-sex parent, and (in several cases) hatred of the same-sex parent. The histories of the women in this group follow a less definite pattern than those of the men.[5]

Using his sample as his universe, Terman then began the fascinating process of making comparisons among the gifted. One thing he wanted to find out was whether there was a relationship between the intelligence of his subjects and their success in life. The Stanford-Binet was of little value in adults; the only test that offered any data he considered valid was his Concept Mastery test, which actually was a mélange of several tests, some previously published and some put together in Terman's office.

Terman tested the Concept Mastery test on 136 Stanford sophomores. The test filled a four-page booklet printed on eight and a half-by eleven-inch paper. It consisted of synonyms and antonyms and analogies ("Shoe is to foot as glove is to: 1, arm; 2, elbow; 3, hand"). "It should go without saying," he admitted, "that neither this nor any other test of intelligence measures native ability uninfluenced by schooling and other environmental factors." This represents something of a change in attitude for Terman; he never made such a bold admission about his Stanford-Binet.

> Like any other group intelligence tests of the verbal type, its scores are probably more influenced by such factors than are scores on the Stanford-Binet. Although no amount of educational effort can furnish the naturally dull mind with a rich store of abstract ideas, it is obvious that one's wealth of concepts must inevitably reflect in some degree the extent of his formal education, the breadth of his reading, and the cultural level of his environment.[6]

But, he said, those among the gifted who never went to college were capable of scoring just as high as those with graduate degrees.

The mean Concept Mastery score for 527 men in 1940 was 98.10. This figure is not comparable to an IQ score from the Stanford-Binet, where 100 is considered the average for the general population. The mean score for 427 women was 93.94. The range among the gifted ran from 10 to 179, and three spouses scored below zero (whatever that meant). The mean for husbands of gifted women was 64.32 and for wives of gifted men 58.93.

The average for the gifted, male and female, was about 96, which came out forty-one points higher than the mean of freshman girls at one college and thirty-eight points higher than the mean of Stanford sophomores. The spouses of the gifted tested slightly higher than undergraduate college students. He compared the numbers in the Concept Mastery and the Stanford-Binet, as shown in the table below.

C-M SCORES AND S-B IQS

	MEAN C-M SCORES	
S-B IQ	Men	Women
135–139	84.5	68.5
140–149	89.17	87.79
150–159	101.07	93.74
160–169	105.31	104.16
170 and up	118.14	115.09

He did not try to explain the difference between men and women whose IQs as children were in the 135–139 group, although it could have been just a function of having too few subjects in that category.

Now, Terman needed to see what the numbers from the Concept Mastery and the Stanford-Binet revealed about how the intelligence of his subjects changed. Unfortunately, this gets to be a complicated statistical problem akin to the proverbial apples and oranges. For one thing, the two tests did not measure exactly the same thing, although if Terman was correct about IQ they did measure different aspects of the same thing. Second, he could not really test the correlation with a large population; he did not have the money. Maybe Gallup could do it, he lamented, but he couldn't. Third, as Terman explained:

> The reader should understand that when a group of subjects is selected on the basis of very high scores on any test with less than perfect reliability (which includes all psychological tests), and these subjects are later retested by the same test or any other test, the retest scores will show some regression toward the mean of the general population. . . . This amount of regression would be due to errors of measurement and would have no bearing on the question of change in mental status.[7]

In other words, because of the nature of what they were doing, Terman could expect that the scores would go down. And they did. They dropped seventeen or eighteen points in IQ, according to the statistical calculations of Quinn McNemar, who served as Terman's numbers expert. Terman gave three reasons: errors in the testing, differences between the two tests, and "maturational changes, environment, and education." By including the last reason, Terman was not giving up his theory of genetic intelligence; he never said environment and aging had no effect.

Something had to be at work. A number of the gifted scored below 50 on the Concept Mastery test, which put them about average for college students in general. Maybe they just didn't try hard, he speculated. "Especially suspicious are the low C-M scores of subjects who have nevertheless graduated with honors from leading universities or who have attained outstanding success as lawyers, physicians, or engineers." The notion that there might have been something wrong with the tests was simply not discussed.

By the time McNemar was done explaining the statistics in a complicated chapter of Terman's book, Terman felt obliged to explain in English in a footnote that when errors and such arcanum as the regression toward the mean are discounted, the gifted group lost nine or ten points in IQ due to their just being alive longer.

Terman's hopes for their education were certainly fulfilled. By any standards the gifted in his study far exceeded the general population or even the college-educated population in academic accomplishments: 87.3 percent of the men and 84 percent of the women went to college; 68 percent of the men and 60 percent of the women went on to graduate school; and 51.2 percent of the men and 29.3 percent of the women earned graduate degrees. Most of the graduate degrees were in law. Besides Ph.D.s and degrees in law and medicine, the Termites earned twenty-one M.B.A.s and sixteen graduate engineering degrees. One woman got an M.A., a Ph.D., and an M.D. Ancel Keys had one Ph.D. from Berkeley and another from Cambridge.*

The social sciences were the most popular fields of study (39.6 percent of the men, 36.9 percent of the women). The men also favored the physical sciences (17.4 percent) and engineering (15.1 percent). The women favored the liberal arts (35.6 percent) and education (9 percent).

Their grades were moderately high (13.09 percent of the men and 11.67 percent of the women who graduated college had A averages), but he conceded that they were not as high as he expected. Most came out with a B average. Terman found several reasons: "idleness, unwillingness to do routine assigned tasks, excessive amount of work for self support, or the deliberate choice to give preference to social and extracurricular activities." Some Termites were socially maladjusted; some were immature. Many glided through high school without opening a book and overestimated their ability to get through college that way. Some of those who had suffered socially in high school from being younger than their classmates tried to appear more normal in college and concentrated on social matters. "Some of these cultivated an adult swagger, lied about their ages, and affected complete indifference to scholastic marks."

On the other hand, 17.2 percent of the men and 19.4 percent of the women made Phi Beta Kappa and almost 33 percent of each graduated with honors.

Most of the subjects were in school during the worst of the depression. Fully 20 percent received some kind of financial aid even though

---

* Terman did not identify him by name, of course, but that is who it was.

they came from upper- and upper-middle-class families. More than 50 percent of the men and 30 percent of the women earned some of their expenses. The men earned $586,318.86 toward their college educations, the women $85,645.08.

Terman found, perhaps not to his surprise, that the people who graduated college had higher childhood IQs than those who did not graduate, and both had higher IQs than those who did not go to college at all, although the difference was not great. He also found that the higher the education of the parent, the more education the subjects were likely to get. The relationship in this case was quite strong.

Terman asked about hobbies in his questionnaires because he felt that such interests gave some indication of how well rounded his gifted were. He was not studying idiot savants, but people with "spontaneous interests in many fields." Only 11 percent of the men and 15 percent of the women said they had no avocations. Most said they had more than one. For the men, sports, photography, and music led the list. For the women, sports, music, and gardening.

As to their reading habits, 77 percent of the men and 91 percent of the women read what Terman categorized as "literature." More women than men read "history" (which included current affairs, travel, and biography). Only 4.3 percent of the men said they did very little reading; 5.3 percent read nothing at all or didn't report reading. Of the women, 0.2 percent reported very little reading; 3.2 percent reported none or didn't report. The favorite magazine for men was *Time*, the favorite for women was *Reader's Digest*. *Esquire*, then considered somewhat racy, came in tenth on the list of men's magazines. The women probably read fewer "women's magazines" than the average woman. More read *Life* than *Time*.

The gifted were not a particularly religious lot. Asked to rate interest on a scale of 1 to 5 (1 being "very interested," 5 being "no interest whatsoever"), the men rated religion at 3.7, the women at 3.5. For men, that was the lowest score of twelve fields; for women it was also near the bottom of the list.

The gifted were not a radical lot. Only one called himself a communist. Those who labeled themselves either "radical" or "socialist" were 4.6 percent of the men, 5.4 percent of the women. Those classifying themselves as "Republican" or "conservative" numbered 45.2 percent of the men and 41.3 percent of the women. Those on the left

("Democrats," "New Dealers," or "liberals") came to 40 percent of the men and 41.6 percent of the women. Terman noted that there were more registered Republicans in California than Democrats, so his group seemed by no means odd.

The only way in which they appeared to differ ideologically or politically from the general population was in comparisons based on occupation. The professionals were slightly less conservative than professionals in the general population. Men in the trades, skilled, semiskilled, and clerical, came out the same as the general population in the upper echelons of business.

Eighty-one percent of the gifted voted, men and women about equally.

Writers tended to think of themselves as far more radical than did other subjects. Doctors and lawyers were the most conservative. Those who listed themselves as more interested in religion than the average person leaned toward the conservative. Those interested in science rated themselves as less conservative. Those who thought of themselves as more radical also thought of themselves as more interested in politics than the others. Jewish women tended to consider themselves more radical than did non-Jewish women, but the men were just the reverse. Jews, who Terman noted had a reputation for political radicalism, were actually no more radical than teachers as a group (5 percent of whom were Jewish) and much less radical than the authors-journalists (less than 20 percent Jewish). One quarter of the doctors and lawyers, the most conservative group, were Jewish. Those with the highest IQs as children, 170 or higher, tended to rate themselves slightly left of center.

Terman could find no relation between marital happiness and political inclination.

By 1940, 70 percent of his gifted (slightly more for women, slightly less for men) had been married at least once. The average age for men when they first married was twenty-five, for women twenty-three. More gifted men got married than did men in the general population, slightly fewer women. But the gifted were married at a much higher percentage than college graduates in general, particularly women.

By 1946 the percentage who had been married increased to 84 percent, a fraction higher for the men than the women. The percentage of married men was a fourth higher than men in the general U.S. population or the California population. The percentage of women who had married was higher than the general U.S. population but exactly the same as the California population.

By 1940, 10.25 percent of the men (fifty-seven men) had been divorced at least once. Six had been divorced more than once. Five others were separated. Almost 12 percent of the women had been divorced at least once. Five had been divorced more than once, and four other women were separated.* By 1945, 12.94 percent of the men and 14.42 percent of the women had been divorced once. Eight men and eight women had been divorced twice, and two men had been divorced three or more times, a total of 14.41 percent of the men, 16.32 percent of the women.

Terman said he could not compare this record with the general population because the studies either disagreed or were based on different criteria.

Gifted men ranged from seventeen years older to nine years younger than their wives. The average difference was 1.4 years older. Twenty percent of the men were younger than their wives. Gifted wives ranged from twenty-six years younger to nine years older, with an average difference of 4.0 years younger.

To test what he called "marital adjustment," Terman gave questionnaires to 636 of the gifted and their spouses. The questionnaires contained a list of fifteen categories, or aspects of marriage, such as "number of outside interests in common," "choice of spouse if life were to be lived over," and "gaiety and happiness when spouses are alone together." He also asked them to give a "happiness score," from 1 to 100, to their marriages. Another scale, 1 to 30, tested "sexual adjustment."

On the happiness score, the average rating of the men was 63.15, the women 66.34. On sexual adjustment the men reported about 15, the women a little more than 20. He generally found that couples had a fairly good idea of one another's needs and happiness: the men's sexual adjustment scores matched the happiness of their wives and the women's scores matched the happiness of their husbands. He had no way of matching these scores with a randomly chosen population, he admitted, but on the basis of the literature he said his gifted scored slightly better than the average.

He said there was no doubt that happiness in marriage was gener-

---

* Terman estimated that he had information on 93 percent of all the marriages and divorces within his group.

ally related to happiness in life, and that was certainly true of his now-maturing kids.

By 1940 the gifted had produced 783 children, 412 boys and 371 girls, a higher than average ratio of boys to girls. Here, however, the difference probably could not be blamed on Terman's methodology. He offers no explanation why his gifted group produced far more boys than girls. By 1945 the number of children had jumped to 1,551 — 817 boys and 734 girls, a ratio of 111.31 boys to 100 girls. (These were not the final numbers for the progeny of the group.)

Terman finally had a chance perhaps to see if the native intelligence of the original group had been passed on to the offspring. He had made it a point to test every child of every gifted subject he could get to, sometimes testing children at the age of three. He tested 384 of the offspring in 1940 using a revised edition of the Stanford-Binet.

What he found had to please him. The average IQ of the Terman kids was 127.70, with 127.23 for the boys and 128.17 for the girls. While that was below his 135 or 140 cutoff for genius in the original study, he pointed to a law first devised by Francis Galton: the law of filial regression. Only one-half of one's total heredity comes from that person's two parents as individuals. Half the genes come from a long line of remote ancestry of undetermined and unknown attributes. That's why very tall parents frequently have children much shorter than they. To score as high as the children did was, to Terman, good news. More than 16 percent of the boys and 14.6 percent of the girls had IQs over 150, about twenty-eight times higher than that found in the general population.

Perhaps the most asked question from the parents of the original group of gifted had been whether to accelerate their children in school, so Terman was anxious to see how many did skip grades and what effect that might have had on their lives. He acknowledged that skipping grades was controversial. The bright kid in a class operating below his or her intellectual level is apt to be bored, perhaps even to the point of developing behavioral problems. Accelerating them to grades more in line with their mental abilities might keep them interested. In addition, it gets them out into the world sooner, even permits earlier marriage, if either of those is considered a benefit. On the other hand, many parents and educators felt it stunted a child's social adaptability and could even be physically harmful. Terman had an ideal group of subjects to use to test the question of whether it was good to accelerate. Using his mechanical computer, he was able to break out a number of variables and match them among his subjects who were accelerated and those who remained on a normal timetable.

- There was a solid relationship between the intelligence of the subjects and their chances of having been accelerated in school, demonstrated in both childhood IQ and the scores from the Concept Mastery test.
- The more grades skipped, the more likely the gifted were to get a college degree and go on to graduate school. Also, the better their grades were in college even though they were younger than their classmates.
- Those who accelerated were more likely to end up in the professions or the higher reaches of the business world.
- Getting into the somewhat murky business of quantifying social adjustment, Terman reported that fears about the social adjustment of children who skipped grades were exaggerated. "There is no doubt that maladjustment does result in individual cases," somewhat more for men than for women, he wrote, "but our data indicate that in a majority of subjects the maladjustment consists of a temporary feeling of inferiority which is later overcome."
- He could not demonstrate any statistical difference in marriage rates for those who accelerated and those who did not.
- He found no evidence that skipping grades had any deleterious effect on either the physical or the mental health of his kids.

Not skipping grades, he concluded, may not be harmful to the development of the gifted; many of his subjects who did not skip grades were doing splendidly. But many of his subjects languished in school and failed "to develop the ambition or habits of work necessary to make them successful in college. The gains of acceleration, he believed, outweighed the dangers.

It is our opinion that children of 135 IQ or higher should be promoted sufficiently to permit college entrance by the age of seventeen at latest, and that a majority in this group would be better off to enter at sixteen. Acceleration to this extent is especially desirable for those who plan to complete two or more years of graduate study in preparation for a professional career.[8]

Terman would have liked to see if he could find any racial or ethnic differences among his kids. The only group large enough to provide meaningful statistics were the Jews. He had Stanford-Binet scores for seventy-one Jewish boys and fifty-one Jewish girls. The mean of those scores differed in no significant way from the gentiles in the study. He gave the Concept Mastery test to fifty-six Jewish men and forty-five Jewish women. The women came out almost exactly the same as the non-Jewish women in the study; the men came out somewhat higher, but not enough to be significant.

He then compared the occupational status of the Jewish men against non-Jewish men in the study (there were not enough working women to do anything useful with the results) and found that Jews did tend toward some professions at a higher rate than gentiles. For instance, 57.5 percent of Jewish men were in the professions, compared to 43.9 percent of non-Jewish men. This also was true among businessmen; 27.5 percent of the Jewish men and 25.4 percent of the gentiles were in business. On the other hand, 30.6 percent of gentile men were in jobs classified as lower on the success ladder, compared to only 15 percent of Jewish men. Looking at the data for particular professions, he found the same thing: among physicians more than twice the percentage were Jews than non-Jews; among lawyers, the percentage was almost double that of gentiles. Non-Jewish men were much more likely to be engineers or college professors.

In 1940 Jewish men earned 25 percent more money than non-Jewish men; by 1944 it was 42 percent higher.* "The Jewish element among the 150 most successful men in the gifted group is considerably greater than in the gifted group as a whole," he added.

He found that Jewish men, far more often than non-Jewish men, rose above their fathers' occupational classification. He didn't say so, but most of the Jews he studied were first- or second-generation Americans and they were living the immigrant's dream.

Seventy-five percent of Jewish men graduated from college; about

---

* By 1944 the number of subjects reporting was smaller (only forty Jewish men reported), but Terman found the results met the statistical tests. He counted only those in civilian work.

70 percent of non-Jewish men did so. Jewish men were less likely to end their education at high school and more likely to go to graduate school. Jewish women also had a higher college graduation rate.

Terman's Jewish kids were more likely to be married and somewhat less likely to be divorced; indeed they tended to do better at marriage than their parents. The husbands of Jewish women tended to score a bit higher in the Concept Mastery test than the husbands of non-Jewish women, but similar results for the wives of Jewish men in the study were not statistically reliable, Terman reported. The wives of Jewish husbands tended to be slightly happier than the wives of non-Jewish husbands.

"It is a common belief that people of Jewish descent are especially prone to nervous and mental maladjustment," Terman wrote, but he could find no differences.*

Politically, the Jews tended to be less conservative than the non-Jews, but they did not dominate the group who had declared themselves "radical."

Terman wrote: "The conclusion suggested by these detailed comparisons is that the Jewish subjects in this group differ little from the non-Jewish except in their greater drive for vocational success, their somewhat greater tendency toward liberalism in political attitudes, and somewhat lower divorce rate."9

Terman then asked his field-workers to take a look at the subjects and their spouses to score their impressions of the couples' physical attractiveness. Why he needed to know this he didn't say. More than 50 percent of the gifted men and 60 percent of the gifted women were rated by the field-workers as good-looking and attractive. The field-workers rated 56 percent of the husbands of gifted women as attractive and 61.5 percent of the wives of gifted men as so blessed, prompting Terman to remark, "Certainly, far from the least of the achievements of the gifted group has been their choice of spouses."

* Two of the eight suicides at that point were Jews.

Chapter Nine

HOW TO MEASURE SUCCESS

ALTHOUGH WORLD WAR II and the Great Depression were defining periods in the lives of all Americans, Terman seemed almost oblivious to the meaning of these events for his subjects. It seems as though to him in his lovely, relatively isolated campus, the war existed only in newspapers and newsreels. He paid attention only when one of his kids was killed or when events obviously interfered with their careers. Some of his subjects were astonished at the absence of questions in his forms about these experiences; some even noted the lack of attention angrily in the margins of their questionnaires. It remained for other, later researchers to probe his data base to find how the war and the depression altered his subjects' lives.

Terman's blindness to these calamitous events mirrored a similar blindness in the field. Glen H. Elder, Jr., of the Carolina Population Center at the University of North Carolina at Chapel Hill, who went back to study the consequences of the war and the depression, said that Terman's reaction was typical. "Psychologists at this time didn't have the slightest clue how to deal with that stuff. It was sort of noise in their world. They didn't know how to make it into a set of variables or incorporate it into their analytical framework." Researchers across the bay at Berkeley, who were doing longitudinal studies of mostly middle-class families, collected information on how the depression affected their lives and then did nothing with it. "They just had trouble coming up with an adequate way to represent environment and think about it in terms of developmental processes."*

---

* Elder also said that psychologists are still having trouble with this aspect of their research.

In Terman's case, this seemed especially ironic to Elder. "He came out of the First World War and he was keenly interested in setting up this study to try to place people, the bright, talented people, in appropriate positions in society. This whole notion of meritocracy and training the best and the brightest for positions of responsibility came out of his experience in the war," Elder said. "But he had a very strange micro-view of the institutions that were impinging on his people."[1]

For Terman the 1930s were golden years professionally. No one needed to measure his success: he was one of the most famous and powerful psychologists in the United States. Even his family life was happy.

Fred had been hired by Stanford's electrical engineering department and wrote what was to become the standard textbook in the field. He was on his way to a career as distinguished as that of his father. Helen, now divorced, returned to Stanford and took a minor administrative job. Terman had five grandchildren to spoil, which he did with great love and pleasure. Terman and Anna made peace and settled into mellow happy years.

His health and that of his family still plagued him, however. X-rays taken of Terman in 1925, while Fred was bedridden with tuberculosis, showed Terman's lungs filled with scar tissue from his bouts with tuberculosis. In 1936 Terman had to spend six weeks in a sanitorium. He began developing cataracts a few years later. Anna became progressively deaf.

None of this interfered greatly with his work. In 1931 Terman began the first major revision of the Stanford-Binet. By that time the test not only was the standard IQ test in this country, but had been translated into various languages and was used throughout the western world. Terman felt the 1916 version could be vastly improved, particularly the standardization of test scores; he wanted a score to mean the same thing for everyone taking the test everywhere. He also wanted some protection from test coaching and came up with the idea of two versions of the test of equal difficulty. The person administering the test and the person being tested would have no idea which of the forms he or she was getting until they opened the envelope to begin the testing. He hired Maud Merrill as his assistant and by 1930 she had become his partner in this and subsequent revisions.

The new version of the Stanford-Binet was published in 1937. It relied less on rote memory and more on nonverbal material for younger children than the earlier tests. Terman's test, as it had always been, was used generally for children.* Indeed, in 1939 the Wechsler-Bellevue Intelligence scale was published, taking over the adult testing market.† In 1941 Terman revised his group test for older subjects, basically high school students. His Stanford Achievement Test had gone through several revisions; the 1940 version was largely the work of Giles M. Ruch and his wife, Verness. Terman was too busy to make a major effort.

Terman became politically active, leading a group of Stanford faculty who opposed America's isolationism, a stand that put him in direct, unhappy conflict with Stanford trustee and alumnus Herbert Hoover and Stanford President Ray Lyman Wilbur. He opposed the state loyalty oath imposed on students and faculty at the University of California's campuses in 1950.‡

Terman had cut his work load considerably in the 1930s as retirement neared. He supervised only seven graduate students in the last twelve years. He had developed a cadre of protégés who took over most of his research. He continued to serve as department chairman, known for his lack of bureaucracy and a minimum of supervision. He continued to teach, mainly his course on educational psychology (required for all his graduate students) and another on the psychology of biography. The education course was not a lecture class. Students picked a topic from a given list of topics; they were given four months to prepare a written report and then another four months to develop an oral version of the report. Terman continued the weekly seminars at his home, the legacy of Hall and Clark University. The seminars were on data collection and methodologies, not theory; they were "nuts and bolts sessions" for students and faculty doing research and preparing books, dissertations, or grant proposals. He also drove his students crazy with his insistence that even social scientists ought to

---

* One of the problems with the Stanford-Binet was that the toys it employed to test small children were made in Germany, and as war approached, it became harder to get the materials from Germany and harder to sell the test because of an informal boycott of German goods.
† In 1949 a children's version of the Wechsler test for adults became the Stanford-Binet's main competition. It has now become the standard, replacing the Stanford-Binet.
‡ Loyalty oaths are still required at all the University of California campuses before anyone can get a job as faculty or staff. Graduate students acting as teaching assistants also must sign the oath.

write well, although he found writing to be an extremely difficult chore himself.

He coauthored several books, including *Sex and Personality* in 1936 with Catharine Cox Miles, who had done her dissertation on geniuses of the past (see page 68). He continued his close relationships with his students, meddling in their lives and helping with their careers, sometimes years after they left Stanford. In one case, he even named one. Harry Harlow's real surname was Israel; he was one–sixty-fourth Jewish. Terman felt that having a Jewish name would harm Harry's career and recommended that he change it. Harry agreed and chose one of Terman's name suggestions, becoming Harry Harlow, who went on to a distinguished career in psychology. Any number of his former students owed their jobs to Terman. Even promising Stanford undergraduates could count on Terman to help them get into good psychology departments elsewhere.

Under Terman, Stanford's psychology department had become one of the top-ranked departments in the country. Five of the twenty presidents of the American Psychological Association between 1922 and 1944 were either Stanford faculty members (including Terman) or people who had been nominated for faculty positions. All five were elected to the National Academy of Science. Three of his students, Harlow, Kelly, and McNemar, also became presidents of the APA. Terman helped choose his successor, Ernest Hilgard, whom he had recruited for the department.

Deciding that Stanford's library was already rich with material and needed little further help, Terman donated his vast collection of psychology and education books to a consortium in Nashville, Tennessee, so it could be used by students at several nearby schools, including Vanderbilt University.

His later years were marred by poor health and a series of accidents. Several months before he was to retire, a fire broke out in his campus home. He was a chain-smoker despite his tuberculosis and accidentally set the fire while smoking in bed. The house was seriously damaged and Terman suffered extensive second-degree burns. He was disabled for eight months, confined to bed for six of them. The skin grafts he had to undergo were so painful he could not wear any clothing except light cotton pajamas. He also developed arthritis in his right arm, making him unable to write for a while. His cataracts worsened; he had to give up movies until he underwent surgery. An accident in 1946 sent him to the hospital with a broken leg; he had tripped over a wastebasket. He underwent repeated surgery.

He formally retired on January 15, 1942, at the age of sixty-five. His retirement present from his students was a book called *Studies in Personality,* a collection of articles by them with an introduction by a Columbia University psychologist. It was all original work in Terman's field by the people he loved most.

But retirement from teaching and his increasingly poor health in no way meant an end to his research, his lectures, or his writing. Terman had all his kids out there, and he wanted to know how they were doing. He moved into a new office and went to work on another follow-up on the gifted.

He wanted to know how successful his Termites had become. His obvious first question then was: how do you measure success? Terman's goal was to compare his most successful subjects with his least noteworthy, but that required both a definition of what he was measuring and a way to quantify it. He acknowledged quickly that his survey of success included only men "because of the lack of a yardstick by which to estimate the success of women. By means of rating techniques, it is possible to identify fairly accurately outstanding chemists, astronomers, mathematicians, or psychologists, but no one has yet devised a method for identifying the best housewives and mothers, and this is what the vast majority of women aspire to be."[2] It remained for others to attempt to measure the lives of Terman's women (see Chapter Eleven).

Terman had many yardsticks by which to measure success in men, perhaps too many. Occupation, income, education, moral character, marriage, social adjustment, and health were some, he said, but that list didn't cover all possibilities. Think of the great artists who starved in garrets and "were guilty of moral transgressions," who failed in marriage and narrowly escaped insanity. Some people did not complete all the education they might have wished for because of financial problems or because they had to make sacrifices for others. And is a wealthy and imaginative entrepreneur more successful than Napoléon or Newton?

In order to determine relationships between his subjects and their occupation, he had to find some way to quantify a person's job. Using something called the Minnesota Occupational scale, he divided possible occupations into seven categories (see table below).

Using data from the U.S. Department of Labor, he went about trying to put all the Termites' jobs into one of those categories. None of the Termites fell into the seventh category. Life does not necessarily match the classifications of social scientists, so he had to cram some square pegs into decidedly round holes. Many of the Termites were still young enough to be considered interns or "trainees," and where should they be put? He finally decided on entering them in group III, but suggested that their earning powers would almost certainly move them up to group II.

Since 83 percent of the gifted men attended at least one year of college, much higher than the average in the general population, the results of the comparison between the gifted men and men of California were not surprising:

OCCUPATIONS OF THE GIFTED MEN AND
MEN OF CALIFORNIA

Occupational Group	Gifted (Percent)	California (Percent)
I. Professional	45.4	5.7
II. Semiprofessional and managerial business	25.7	8.1
III. Clerical, skilled trades, and retail business	20.7	24.3
IV. Farming and other agricultural pursuits	1.2	12.4
V. Semiskilled trades, minor clerical, and minor business	6.2	31.6
VI. Slightly skilled trades and other occupations requiring little training or ability	0.7	17.8*
VII. Day labor	0	

*Groups VI and VII in state data were combined because of ambiguities in the way the state reported the data.

The largest single occupation was law (9.53 percent) in Group I. Clerical workers, which included junior accountants, in group III came in second (8.97 percent). Twenty-six men were listed as authors or journalists. Two had already reached some degree of fame: the science fiction writer L. Sprague de Camp and William A. P. White, who wrote novels and essays and edited under the nom de plume Anthony Boucher. Nine were in film, seven in radio. Twelve were in the military as a career.

But how did the gifted compare to college graduates, not just the general population? He found they did better, although the data he used were not completely compatible. In the general population 45.8 percent of male college graduates fit into classifications roughly analogous to groups I and II. In Terman's group 71 percent fit into those groups.

Keeping in mind that the 1940 study was done while the country was still in the depression, the figures on unemployment were startling. While 11 percent of experienced male workers of a similar age group in the general U.S. population were out of work, less than 1 percent of Terman's men were unemployed. Nationally, 2.1 percent of college graduates were idle, more than twice the percentage for Terman's kids. What Terman did not note in his conclusions was that this apparent immunity to the depression was not universal. Other researchers would find that the older Termites did less well than the younger ones (see page 178).

Terman had no problem spotting the upward mobility of his gifted compared to their parents. Far more of the gifted were in the professions than were their fathers, and far fewer went into business.

Also not surprisingly, the higher the childhood IQ or the adult Concept Mastery score, the likelier the man was to be classified in group I than in other groups. The situation was different for gifted women: the higher childhood Stanford-Binet scorers were not the women who ended up in the highest categories, but were those women who were social workers, nurses, writers, and librarians. Their mean IQ was two points higher than the women in the professions. The women who had the highest scores as adults taking the Concept Mastery test tended toward the professions. Terman said the differences, however, were too small to be statistically significant.

The highest-paying jobs for the men were not in group I (in most cases the men were just starting out and would eventually earn much more), but in group II, the semiprofessional and higher business or managerial group, where the peaks came earlier. Physicians earned the most, but writers beat out lawyers for second place, a temporary situation to be sure.

College graduates earned far more than those who did not graduate from college by substantial margins for both men and women.

Terman did the occupational and income survey again in 1945. The war made its mark. More than 42 percent of his men were in the service. Those not in service found their careers greatly accelerated, moving upward into groups I and II. Perhaps their competitors were in the military or they were in professions in great demand in wartime. No one was in group VI, and only 1.9 percent were in group V. Nineteen men had been discharged from the military by 1944. Two were incapacitated by ill health; one received a discharge for mental reasons. Of those men working, almost half were in group I, another 32 percent were in group II. In other words, fully 80 percent were in the top two occupational classifications.

Terman's data base for income shrank because many of the men were in the military and he had statistics only for the 445 men and 199 women who were earning civilian salaries. The median income for men rose to $392.77 per month or $4,713 a year, an increase of 98.6 percent. More than 3 percent were earning better than $25,000 a year, a great deal of money in 1944. One man (he wouldn't say who) was earning $84,000 a year. The lowest annual salary reported was $1,500 (he wouldn't say who that was either).

Using the available data, which because of wartime constraints were not exactly comparable, Terman concluded that the proportion of gifted men with incomes more than $7,500 in 1944 was eight times higher than the 1946 *family* incomes of the population in general.

The next step was to try to see if he could discover what made some men wonderfully successful and others not. He admitted that the best he could do was provide subjective judgment. He, Melita Oden, and Barbara Mayer, one of his former students and later supervisor of counseling at the San Francisco office of the U.S. Employment Service, went through the data on 730 men who were twenty-five years or older in 1940 with the goal of dividing the men into three groups: the 150 most successful (called the A group), the 150 least successful (the C group), and everyone else (the B group). He wanted to find the difference between the A's and the C's. Terman decided the only general definition of success that would do was "the extent to which a subject had made use of his superior intellectual ability." If the subject went to college, how good were his grades? If someone entered a profession, what was his standing in the profession? The judges went out of their way not to use income as a criterion or even as a major variable. Although it was impossible to keep income out of their deliberations, they tried; for example, young lawyers with brilliant records who were not yet making much money were not penalized in the accounting.

Each of the three judges made an independent judgment on each of the 730 subjects. They thrashed out their disagreements in what must have been fascinating debates. They started with those subjects whom all three agreed were successful and worked down until they filled the quota for A's. Then they went to the files of those all three agreed were the least successful and worked their way up until they had 150. These 300 were the core of the study.

The A group included everyone in the study who was in *Who's Who* or *American Men of Science*. It included professors at prestigious universities or colleges, outstanding lawyers, physicians, and artists. Of the C group Terman wrote:

> The reader must not assume that the C group is composed almost entirely of failures. It does include a half-dozen who have been more or less chronically unemployed, and many others who are in occupations that do not make heavy demands on general intelligence, such as skilled or semiskilled trades, clerical or minor business positions, and civil service jobs in police or fire departments. But it also includes twenty-five men in occupations classified as professional, semiprofessional, and managerial whose records of accomplishment were among the least impressive found among our gifted subjects in such occupations.[3]

Being a talented carpenter or a good cop was not considered making the most use of one's intellect to Terman, Oden, and Mayer, all elitists to the core. Terman acknowledged that some of the people in C were there because they deliberately chose to march to their own drummer. Perhaps they liked working with their hands. Some, he said, were hiding from responsibility, including a few still in school beyond their thirtieth birthday. A few were crackpot scientists and inventors, although they were not particularly socially maladjusted. "Often the difference between a C and an A is little more than a difference in level of aspiration," Terman commented.

He also acknowledged that the study was cross-sectional; it was a snapshot of these people's lives. Some now deemed highly successful could later fail; some deemed failures might eventually get their lives in order. But the three judges said that the gap between the A's and the C's was wide, and while someone might slip from A to B or raise themselves from C to B, it was not likely that A's would become C's or C's A's.

The A's were successes indeed.

Terman did find a control group with which he could compare his best and brightest, a study done in 1945 by Frank Aydelotte, director of the American Rhodes scholars organization of men (and they were only men) who had studied at Oxford as Rhodes scholars between 1927 and 1937. These men would be about the same age as the Terman men and, by every measurement, at least as smart. Aydelotte had data on 309 men. Terman compared their occupational classifications to those of all of the gifted men and to the A group.

OCCUPATIONAL CLASSIFICATION OF RHODES SCHOLARS
AND GIFTED

Occupational Group	Rhodes Scholars (Percent)	All Gifted (Percent)	Gifted A's (Percent)
I. Professionals	79.3	48.3	69.3
II. Semiprofessional and managerial	20.7	32.0	30.7
III. Clerical, skilled, and retail	—	15.7	—
IV. Agriculture	—	4.0	—

The Rhodes scholars greatly exceeded the gifted men in general and were slightly superior to the A's in Terman's 1945 study. Terman pointed out, correctly and somewhat defensively, that the average age of his kids when selected for the study was eleven, while the Rhodes group was selected for excellence and brilliance when they graduated college and that the Rhodes group had, almost by definition, more education. All were college graduates, and all did at least three years of graduate work at one of the world's great universities. Comparing them to all the Termites was unfair; matching them to the A's was closer to the point, he felt.

More Rhodes scholars (41 percent) went into education than did A's (18 percent), and a greater percentage went into the liberal arts.

The A's had a higher percentage of men who attained the rank of professor or associate professor (41.4 to 28.6 percent). More A's went into journalism or other forms of writing (7.3 to 5.8 percent). An equal percentage went into law, but more A's went into medicine. The A's had a slightly better percentage of men who made *Who's Who* or *American Men of Science*.

Terman was tickled with the results; the best of his people matched the best and brightest of any group in America, just as he hoped they would.

With his categories straight and his definitions as clear as he could get them, he began tearing apart the two groups to see what made them different.

OCCUPATIONAL CLASSIFICATION OF GROUP A AND GROUP C, 1940

Occupational Group	GROUP A		GROUP C	
	Number	Percent	Number	Percent
I. Professional	103	68.67	14	9.33
II. Semiprofessional and managerial	46	30.67	11	7.33
III. Clerical, skilled, and retail	—	—	73	48.67
IV. Agriculture	—	—	2	1.33
V. Semiskilled	—	—	33	22.0
VI. Slightly skilled	—	—	6	4.0
Students	1	0.67	3	2.0
Unemployed	—	—	6	4.0
Incapacitated	—	—	1	0.67

Their average age was almost the same, about thirty and a half years. More than two-thirds of the A's were in the professions (group I), and except for one student, everyone else was a semiprofessional or a manager (group II). Of course, they were selected for that, but Terman played it straight, as if that was a discovery. Only 17 percent of the C's were in the top two categories; most were in group III (clerical, skilled trades, and retail). The A's in group I included the usual: doctors (sixteen), lawyers (twenty-four), professors (twenty-seven), engineers (eleven), and writers or journalists (ten). The fourteen C's who made the top grouping included three writers, two teachers, three engineers, three chemists, a clergyman, a lawyer, and an artist, who were, at least by Terman's standards, not very good at what they were doing. The biggest cluster of A's in group II were economists, investment brokers, and banking executives (twelve). Three musicians made up the biggest occupational subgroup among the C's in group II. Most of the men in group III did clerical work. The seven policemen and firemen, whom the judges did not consider successful, were classified as group V. One naval officer made the A's.

The six men who were unemployed had been that way for years or had been underemployed (one man ran his father's estate and apparently didn't have to work full time). The man listed as incapacitated was a hypochondriac who considered himself too sick to work.

Terman said he went out of his way not to judge the men by their incomes, but obviously it was a factor in their lives and he collected all the data he could. He found that the average monthly income of the A's was $387.81 and that of the C's $144.25. He said even he was surprised at the difference. Seventy-three of his A's earned more than $300 a month; none of the C's did.

The difference in some regard was educational. Sixty-five percent of the A's but only 5 percent of the C's had graduate degrees. Ninety percent of the A's finished college; only 37.2 percent of the C's had degrees of any kind. None of the A's ended their education with high school, but 16.7 percent of the C's did. Here, as much as anywhere, Terman was caught in a methodological trap. Since education was one of the variables he used in determining success, it would have been astonishing had there not been a great difference between the two groups. He simply said that "we believe that the procedure of classification used is on the whole defensible."

Why did some get out of school as soon as they could, while others spent another decade doing graduate work? Using data going back to the original 1922 study, he found that generally the A's and C's had about the same record of educational achievement before high school, although the C's were slightly older at graduation. The A's did slightly better, but not much, not enough to account for how they turned out. In high school, however, the two groups began to diverge dramatically. Using achievement tests as the ruler, he found that by the time they graduated from high school the A's were substantially ahead of the C's; 95 percent of the A's had passed all the units they should have passed, while only 67 percent of the C's had done as well. By

college — at least for those C's who went on to college — the difference was even greater, as measured in grades. Of college graduates,
more than 33 percent of the A's, but less than 2 percent of the C's were
elected to Phi Beta Kappa. The A's won more scholarships and more
graduate fellowships. A's and C's seemed to earn an equal proportion
of their college expenses by working, so there was no obvious financial factor accounting for the differences. The two groups also studied
essentially the same kinds of courses. Yet at every turn the men in the
successful group got through high school and college and graduate
school faster and more easily. Why?

Terman looked at the IQs of both groups to see if that made a
difference; all his subjects were smart and quick, but some were
smarter and quicker. The intelligence scores of the A's were higher,
but not by very much. Counting almost every test his kids had been
subjected to, Terman found that the difference between the two
groups' scores was statistically significant (the mean score for the A's
in the 1922 Stanford-Binet was 155, for the C's 150), but the difference did not appear great enough to account for the vast difference in
their lives. Using the Concept Mastery test results of 1940, he found
that the C's still scored in the top 15 percent of students at superior
universities. The A's matched Ph.D. students at the same schools. He
commented, "Notwithstanding the reliable difference between mean
C-M scores, it can hardly be claimed that this accounts for the striking
contrast between the groups in adult achievement. Where all are so
intelligent, it follows necessarily that differences in success must be
due largely to non-intellectual factors."[4]

The results of vocational interest tests gave him a clue. He found
that far more A's scored higher in the fields they eventually entered
than did C's; in other words, more A's were doing what they liked for
a living than were C's. One of the problems appeared to be that C's
had more generalized interests, that is, had interests that were less well
focused, than interests of A's. In general terms, the interests of the C's
more closely matched the interests of unskilled workers, not professionals. Test results might reflect this tendency of C's to be working in
fields that did not especially interest them, but, Terman correctly
warned, the results could just as easily reflect the fact they were not
doing well in their fields.

Terman found no material difference between the groups in the results of the masculinity-femininity test, although there was a "slight tendency for C's to be more masculine in their interests." He thought this could be explained by the greater interest of A's in cultural matters, which, in his wisdom, he classified as a feminine attribute.

There were no clues when he looked at hobbies.

Leaving absolutely no stone unturned, Terman then went back to the records to see if there was anything in the early child development of the two groups that gave any indication of what was to follow. Did the achievers walk, talk, reach puberty before the non-achievers?

WALKING, TALKING, AND PUBERTY

	Group A	Group C
Age at walking (in months)	13.6	12.8*
Age at talking (in months)	17.3	16.8
Age at puberty (in years)	14.5	14.9*

* Statistically significant.

The results puzzled Terman greatly, if for no other reason than they appeared contradictory. The C's seemed to mature faster at an earlier age; they walked and talked more than a month earlier than the A's, but reached puberty about five weeks later. He cautioned that the results must be taken with some suspicion, in part because he apparently had trouble believing this finding. He said the data are suspect because of "both errors of observation and of memory and are notorious for their low reliability." Since the parents of the A's had higher educational and cultural status than that of the C's, the results for the C's were to be particularly distrusted as the source wasn't as good. He might have added — but didn't — that the test for pubescence was when the pubic hair of the boys curled, a somewhat careless definition since puberty in boys is a process, not an event.

The A's tended to read a bit earlier than the C's, but the difference wasn't enough to satisfy a statistical test. The C's actually seemed to have read more than their chums and seemed to have had a greater interest in reference books, such as dictionaries. According to the reports filled in by the parents, there was no difference in interests such as music, science, or art. The A's tended to collect things (such as stamps and seashells) more than the C's.

If data on early development were no help, looking back at how the boys played provided no insight either.

Terman looked at family background. First, he eliminated the stuff of folklore. He found no evidence that the age of parents when the child was born made any difference. Neither did such things as the size of the family and birth order. He did find that almost double the number of C's were only children. On the other hand, the families of C's had slightly more children than did the families of A's (2.79 children versus 2.83).

When he looked at siblings, he found that two-thirds of the brothers of A subjects were in occupational groups I and II, while only 37.9 percent of the C brothers were so employed. There was even some tendency for this to be true of sisters, although the data were not convincing.

Terman found an impressive difference in the education of the siblings. Twice the percentage of brothers of A's graduated from college and more than twice the percentage of sisters. Thirty-five percent of A brothers did graduate work compared to only 7.8 percent of C brothers.

Brothers of C's tended to have a higher divorce rate, but there was no difference between A and C sisters.

The greatest difference in the families remained the education and occupations of the parents. The C parents had less education and lower status jobs, and it seemed to run in the family. Then, in a line reminiscent of the debates over IQ testing a generation before, Terman added: "Our data does not enable us to appraise the relative influence of heredity and environment in causing these parallels, but the lower IQ of the C siblings indicates that heredity may enter into the picture."

Terman found a vast difference in the occupational classification of the parents of his two groups of subjects. Thirty-eight percent of the fathers of A's, but only 18.5 percent of the fathers of C's were in the professional class in 1922.

Many of those in the C group came from broken homes, but Terman found no compelling evidence that a broken home stunted their social growth. He theorized that unstable marriages of either the parents or the children were symptoms of "ineffective social adjustment," not the cause.

Terman looked to see if the C's came from families with a higher percentage of people he called "abnormal" than did the A's. He found no appreciable difference.

When he investigated the mental health of his subjects, he found a large difference between the two groups: the C's had far more adjustment problems throughout the period of the study. From childhood C's were far more likely than A's to have "some" or "marked" nervous symptoms. In the 1922 reports teachers and parents were far more likely to rate children who eventually became A's as having attributes such as self-confidence, willpower, and prudence. Similar evaluations were found in the 1928 reports. By 1940 the pattern was clear. Only 16 percent of the 150 A's who reported said they had suffered from either "some maladjustment" or "serious maladjustment," but more than 37 percent of the C's reported these conditions. "The group differences here are extremely significant; there can be no doubt that serious difficulties of mental adjustment have been far more prevalent among the C's," Terman wrote. Five C's reported drinking problems, but A's, and, oddly, far more C's reported they were teetotalers than did A's.

In the original study and the 1928 follow-up Terman found that a higher percentage of A's than C's were described by parents and teachers as being satisfactorily socially adjusted. In the 1928 questionnaires A's showed more preference than C's for friends older than they. A's also tended to have more extracurricular activities than C's both in secondary school and college.

C's tended to classify themselves as Democrats more than A's, but Terman could find no real political differences between the two groups, which somewhat surprised him. He thought there would be more political radicalism among the less successful C's, but in the 1940 sample, even after almost a decade of depression, he found no statistically reliable difference.

He checked other possible factors differentiating the A and C groups. He found A's were almost an inch taller than C's and weighed almost four pounds more.* He suggested that, if it meant anything, the difference might be a matter of better diet attributable to the better education of the A parents.

---

* Terman warned that these figures were based on self-reports and might not be correct, so he did not make much of them except to note they were interesting.

More of the A's were married in 1940 (80.7 to 66.7 percent), but both groups apparently got married at about the same age, twenty-five. "If the larger average income of the A's has influenced the proportion of marriages, it does not seem to have influenced the age at marriage."

The A's had a lower divorce rate than the C's, which Terman attributed to the C's tendency to maladjustment.* He also considered the possibility that the A rate was lower because the A's married better, or at least by his standards. He found that 53.8 percent of A wives were college graduates as against 24.4 percent of C wives. More than 50 percent of C wives had high school educations or less, compared to 14.6 percent of A wives. He could find a familial correlation here as well: 40 percent of A wives, but only 14.5 percent of C wives, were the daughters of professional men. In fact, most of the C wives came from the working class. Terman gave the Concept Mastery test to as many wives as he could and found that the A wives matched the IQs of Stanford students and the C wives' IQs weren't close. He also found that fewer C wives were happy in their marriages. How much of that was ascribable to being married to men who were not, by conventional standards, great successes in life was not discussed.

Terman went through his gigantic amount of personality data to see what attributes, such as "integration toward goals," "freedom from sensitiveness," "freedom from emotionality," might be responsible for the relative success or failure of the Termites. He used data from self-ratings, ratings of wives, and past ratings of parents and teachers. He found three attributes were significant: "integration toward goals," "perseverance," and "self-confidence." "The members of this triad of traits undoubtedly have much in common," Terman admitted, "and it would have been surprising if they had not shown clear differences between the A and C groups." "Absence of inferiority feelings" came in fourth. It would be hard to succeed in life without these traits.

Some of the self-ratings were interesting. The C men described themselves as more conformist than the A men. The two groups were about equal in terms of freedom from emotionality (which meant,

* He reported that 14 percent of C's and 6.7 percent of A's were divorced or separated, but because he was dealing with a very small data base (121 A's and 100 C's), the conclusion was not entirely reliable.

apparently, just the ability to keep cool) in self-ratings and in their wives' ratings, but there was a difference in ratings of teachers when the men were boys; the C's were cooler. "A difference in this direction was not expected, and may have been due to the fact that the lack of emotionality was defined in such a way that it could have been interpreted as meaning emotional coldness or hardness," Terman explained. The two groups were about equal in ego and sensitivity. The A's appeared to have had more common sense as children, at least as rated by their parents.

In 1940 Terman's field-workers interviewed eighty-one A's and 115 C's. The field-workers' judgments were entirely subjective, but they apparently did not know how the subjects had been categorized. They found the A's better looking (listing "appearance" and "attractiveness" as separate categories); better spoken and more poised; more alert, attentive, and friendly, more curious and original. The only category in which the C's won out was "freedom from vanity," which prompted Terman to wonder if vanity is an undesirable trait. He wouldn't think so.

How did the two groups do in the war years? Three A's and four C's died during the war; one A and three C's were killed in action, and the others died from causes not related to the war. A fourth A died after filling in his form in 1946. Terman heard from all but one of the 147 A's still alive and all but ten of the 146 living C's.* The A's, Terman reported with satisfaction, continued their distinguished careers, with one exception, a man who "suffered an emotional upset which caused him to throw overboard his whole way of life." The man was starting a new career, but Terman did not reveal if he was demoted from the A group. Two A's of Japanese ancestry were interned and relocated; a third entered the army as a private and ended the war a major.

The C's improved their lot in the war, Terman reported, but the gap between the two groups remained wide and deep. A few men did improve themselves considerably, and at least one, who finally found his niche in life, was promoted out of the C group to the B group. Terman said it was too early to know if he'd ever reach the A group.

Terman found a marked improvement in the job classification of

* The one A not reporting was located eventually and found to be "a successful radio engineer."

those C's who stayed in civilian life. The A's were already doing well and continued so during the war. Two of the C's were unemployed in 1944, which was not an easy thing to be in those years of manpower shortages; one had been discharged from the military as a "psycho-neurotic." Both groups of civilians showed income increases; the annual median income for the A's was $7,187.50, an increase of 90 percent since 1940, and the C's was $3,571.43, an increase of 108.7 percent.

Terman did not probe in depth how the war affected their careers, but he looked at how the men did in the military. Of the two groups, 40.5 percent of the A's and 36.4 of the C's served. A larger percentage of the C's went into the army. Three men went into the marines, a private first class and two lieutenants.* If Terman needed any further confirmation that the A's were success-oriented people and the C's were not, the military provided it. More than 61 percent of the A's in the military went in as commissioned officers, while only 19.4 percent of the C's had commissions at the beginning of their service. By the end of the war, 82.4 percent of the A's in the army and 88.5 percent of the A's in the navy were commissioned. Among the C's only 33 percent in the army and 13.3 percent in the navy were officers.

A's ranked from second lieutenant to brigadier general in the army and from ensign to captain in the navy. A fair percentage of the officers were physicians; 71 percent of the physicians in the A group were in the military.

Three men were taken prisoner. Two captured by the Germans survived; one captured by the Japanese at Corregidor did not (see page 144).

Terman's data showed a total of ninety medals, including four Legion of Merits, two Silver Stars, eight Bronze Stars, and fifteen Purple Hearts. One flying Termite won nine medals from the United States, Canada, Great Britain, and Yugoslavia.

The self-reports from 1945 showed the health of the two groups remained about the same, although the C's reported feeling not quite as healthy as they had before.

The percentage married from both groups went up; the rate of divorce for the C's was double that of the A's.

---

* Twelve Termite women were in the service, and two worked overseas with the American Red Cross.

In his several studies Terman had found only hints of what might have made the difference between success and failure, and he always was faced with the conundrum of cause and effect. Were the traits he found in the C's the cause of their relative failure in life or the result or both? After his death, one of his disciples would try again.

Terman could note that the Termites were beginning their careers just as the depression drowned the economy of the country and still not think of looking for ways to determine its effect on them in anything but a superficial way. He could get a letter from a subject written in a foxhole proclaiming the idiocy of filling out a form while people were shooting at him or lose a subject who was a prisoner of war and still not think of the war as a major event in the lives of his subjects. He also missed one basic point: one group in his subject was more affected by these two events — the most traumatic of the twentieth century — than was another.

Terman also suffered from an inability to compare his subjects to other groups. He did not use even obvious opportunities. For instance, researchers at the University of California began a study of about 200 families in Berkeley at about the same time as Terman began his study, but there is no evidence Terman even telephoned across the bay to see what they found. Another study of about the same size was done in Oakland; again, Terman made no effort to see if he could find any comparisons. The two East Bay studies were more representative of the general population, and it might have been interesting to see how these people compared to Terman's subjects. The groups of researchers might even have coordinated their efforts, but they did not. A study done of Harvard University graduates might have proven useful; again, no use was made of this resource.

Glen Elder, somewhat amazed at these weaknesses in the Terman studies, went back into Terman's files in the late 1980s to see what he could find. To his chagrin he discovered that one of the reasons Terman ignored the war and the depression was the poor state of his data. Much of what had been converted to computer tape, the resource used by most people mining the Terman data, contained errors. Elder and his graduate students, on various trips to California, had to go back into the basic forms and recode the data. "We could not take the scores and the values that were on those sheets for real, and much of the [computer] coding, we felt, we had to redo. It's been a long haul."

What Elder found out was that if one broke the Terman men into two groups by age, the older of the cohorts, those whose careers began with the depression, suffered greatly from that economic disaster and suffered again when the military derailed them. The younger group suffered less in both instances.

> Their economic trajectories were flat across the 30's. If you look at their earnings, for example, they just don't go anywhere much. Then they hit the war years and so many of them were mobilized on the home front because of their skills and sent all over the place. They couldn't really get their careers together and off the ground until '46, '47. The one group that shows long-lasting negative effects are the professionals in the older group who were well-established when the war came and they just never made up their earnings. They were out there four or five years, and never really caught up.[5]

Elder quotes one depression veteran as saying, "The essence of being in your twenties in the Thirties was that no matter how well tuned up you were, you stayed on the ground. Many of us stayed on the ground, or just above it, for ten years." Elder noted, "The older cohort of men also encountered World War II at an age that placed them at greater risk of life-course disruption and disadvantage. They were in their thirties when the United States entered the war, a time when most had assumed substantial responsibilities in family and work roles."[6] The older men suffered more marital disruption, family strain, and "substantial lifetime earnings losses."

Elder found that the older men also were more likely to wind up in Terman's group C than were the average Termites, and age was a much stronger determining factor than family background. Despite all his cross-tabulation, Terman apparently missed that. The war and the depression did not seem to have much effect on the younger group.

Overall, the war had less impact than the depression. "Men who were mobilized into the service did not differ on career achievement when compared to the non-mobilized," Elder wrote. The war actually advanced the careers of one group of professionals, the physicians. The war seemed to have no effect on the careers of Terman's lawyers.

The Termites as a whole seemed to have some advantages, Elder found. They were better able to cope with the exigencies of the depression than were people not as gifted or as well endowed mentally.

They had more options. In the 30's, because they were so well educated and skilled, the economic disruptions were things they could overcome. The work that I've done on the 30's, and in the Berkeley and Oakland studies, shows very clearly that the economic downswing was certainly shorter. It might have been very pronounced and very powerful, but [it was] shorter for the middle class, and they came out of it very nicely.[7]

Terman himself lamented some of the shortcomings of his study, mostly because of lack of adequate funding. But he thought the 1940 and 1946 surveys could not have been better. He was not a man to see his flaws easily.

ADULTHOOD

Beatrice

BEATRICE did four years of college in three, graduating from Stanford at the age of seventeen. During that time she continued to write poetry and began a novel. One poem, inspired by the stained glass windows at Stanford's Memorial Church, was one of Terman's favorites.

> There stood the angel suddenly
> In sunlight at the door.
> And Mary, grave with reverence,
> Knelt, till he spoke no more.
>
> Mary knelt down for reverence.
> And more were crouched for fear,
> And many did not move, for awe
> To know an angel near.
>
> The air was still as after storm;
> But of them one was there
> Who marked she bent as flowers bend
> And worshipped her gold hair.

A San Francisco newspaper did a feature story: "Stanford Girl Genius Takes Degree Today: Entire Curricula Gleaned in Three Years." It reported that she was the youngest woman ever to graduate from Stanford and that she now had a total of only six years of schooling. The newspaper paraphrased Terman as calling her "the most extraordinary example of genitative genius he had ever seen." It went on to say, "Good times, pretty clothes, youthful friendship share

Beatrice's enthusiasm along with science, music, art, and literature. She is no highbrow or bluestocking despite the intelligence quotient of 188 that places her in the genius class." A picture taken for the article shows a pretty woman in cap and gown, looking her age, her head tilted toward the right, her long, graceful fingers holding a Stanford diploma.

Beatrice decided to be a writer and was accepted at the University of Pennsylvania for graduate work. Terman decided it was time to free her from her mother. He wrote to Gladys: "There is something that has been weighing on my mind for some time that I think is important for Beatrice's development, and after a great deal of consideration I have decided to present to you my views on the matter rather fully and frankly.

"Here is the problem. In my judgment Beatrice's life has always been and still is of the too sheltered kind. The fact that Beatrice is your only child and that she is so extraordinarily gifted makes it only natural that as parents you should want to lavish every possible measure of devotion on her. However, while nothing is more beautiful than such devotion, I know as a psychologist that it often has certain unfortunate effects on the recipient. . . . Beatrice is now eighteen years old and no longer a child. If her literary development is to proceed as it should, it is imperative that she learn to know people better and that her general horizon of experience be broadened. It is of particular importance, I think, that she should spend a year or two entirely away from the family . . . however much it may hurt you both to give her up even temporarily. Here is my recommendation which I sincerely hope you will be able to bring yourselves to adopt: that Beatrice be allowed to enter the University of Pennsylvania as a graduate student of English next September, and that she be allowed to go absolutely alone. She will then be nearing the age of nineteen and I am sure that she can be depended upon absolutely for the right kind of behavior."

It didn't work. Gladys moved Beatrice to Philadelphia and stayed for months.

Meanwhile, the news services had picked up the story of Beatrice's graduation from Stanford and the fact that she was working on a novel about love entitled *The Fifth Story*. Several publishers expressed an interest in the novel, and several magazines offered to buy serial rights. Unable to reach Beatrice, they wired Terman, who now became her literary agent. He notified the first publisher that the novel wasn't finished, but Beatrice would send him the manuscript as soon as it was. He sent copies of Beatrice's poems and an introduction he had written at Gladys's urging to Clifton Fadiman at Simon & Schuster, who also had expressed an interest in the novel. Fadiman wrote back that the poems were "not sufficiently distinguished," but he would still like to look at the novel. When he finally saw *The Fifth Story*, he suggested that Beatrice let it percolate a bit longer and try again.

Beatrice and Gladys went to England in 1930 after her year at Penn. A year later, she finished her rewrite and sent it to another publisher. "A week has gone by since I finished *The Fifth Story* and sent it back to Dutton," she wrote Terman from England, "thoughtfully, one day before my nineteenth birthday. Stylistically, it is much better now, but I left the fundamentals as they were. The great criticism to be made against it is that it isn't sufficiently subjective; and I had made that so much a part of it. It would be a bloodless thing if I altered it. I am not concerned about its fate because I have a new novel in my head now, one of which I am becoming absurdly fond. (*The Fifth Story*, by the way, was read and approved by several English literati I have met.)"

Dutton rejected the manuscript. The book was never published.

In 1934 Henry Carter was found with his throat slashed in a bathtub in a San Francisco hotel, a suicide. After his death Gladys and Beatrice returned to Europe for several months, and Beatrice wrote to Terman that she had abandoned her new novel. The reason she gave was that another like it was published during the time she was coping with her father's suicide and there was no longer a market for it. She had taken up sculpture instead.

Gladys returned to Belmont a few months later and reported to Terman that "the greatest sculptor in Germany saw her work and begged her to stay a short time longer and work under his direction. He refused all compensation, so doubtless he felt she was gifted. Of course it will never take the place of her writing but it will give her an avocation that she loves."

Beatrice stayed longer, falling in love with a German engineer, a member of the Nazi party. She stayed through the rise of Hitler, finally leaving her lover and fleeing Berlin on the last train out before the invasion of Poland and the true beginning of the war.

"Just before the train started there was a wild surge of people who threw themselves madly against the train," she told a reporter. "They broke every window and packed into the aisles, staterooms and on the tiny platform. The police were powerless. The next day the porter told me that the Germans were taken off the train on the German side of the border."

She made it back to San Francisco where one of her statues, a male nude, was being exhibited at the World's Fair.

Then a strange transformation came over Beatrice. Perhaps tired of being a prodigy (certainly no longer qualified to be a child prodigy), perhaps weary of trying to fulfill her mother's aspirations, she seemed to unplug her mind from the complexities of high intellect. She did a few more statues, including a bust of Terman in plaster, and in April 1943 she married a private in the army, Leon Johnson. In a move generations ahead of her time, she became Beatrice Carter-Johnson, and her husband, after leaving the army, became Leon Johnson-Carter. He later became an investment banker and a relatively wealthy man in the San Fernando Valley.

Shortly after her engagement, she stayed with the Termans for a few days at their Stanford home. "She has unquestionably improved in personality since she left college, though now and then, when strangers came in she dropped back into the somewhat conceited or supercilious type of mannerisms," Terman wrote for the files. "Even Mrs. Terman developed a marked liking for her."

Shortly after the war Beatrice had a daughter, Ingrid. Terman, who kept in touch with her, noticed an increasing distance about Beatrice. She left it to her husband to teach Ingrid how to read. Her conversation became an unending chain of clichés with no sign of the bright, burning intellect of the young "genius." Terman found Leon infinitely more interesting.

Warfare with her mother continued. Gladys moved to Los Angeles and into the apartment next to her daughter. The stress became too much for Beatrice, who became ill. Her doctor recommended she go away with Ingrid for two weeks and make sure she left her mother behind. When Beatrice returned, the warfare resumed, and the doctor ordered her off on another vacation. The doctor then told Gladys that

Beatrice would not get better unless Gladys finally left her alone. Beatrice told Terman the doctor had been quite cruel, but it worked.

In 1955 Beatrice visited Terman at Stanford. "She evidently made the trip to convince me that she is developing new abilities she didn't know about in addition to sculpturing," Terman noted for the files. "One of the new talents she has discovered is her ability to influence people. She took a leading part in . . . getting a foundation set up for the better educational uses of radio and TV. Quite a number of stations over the country from coast to coast (the nature of which I could not get through my head because of her vagueness) have joined this foundation.

"Ingrid . . . is the pet of all her teachers in the school and the most favored playmate of children for two or three blocks around who attend the same school. . . . In other words, although she didn't exactly use them, she is the perfect girl. . . .

"Then, out of the clear sky she told me that she was never in love with [Leon] and that he knew it from the start, but that she is fond of him and he is fond of her and a perfect father."

She talked to Terman about the German engineer. "He was not a Nazi at heart," she said, merely a patriot.

"Beatrice thinks she is envied by the parents in the school PTA because of her charming and brilliant daughter and because she has such an attractive husband," Terman added.

"Beatrice is better dressed than on past visits and obviously came up alone in order to impress me with her development. Fewer clichés than usual but too much pose and mysterious hints about her accomplishments that I could not very well clear up."

During the next ten years Beatrice and her husband dabbled in real estate. Then in 1965 Beatrice and Leon divorced. She lived with Ingrid, who became a lawyer like her grandfather. Beatrice stopped sculpting. She died of breast cancer in 1985. Her death certificate listed her profession as "landlady."

Sara Ann

THE WAR was about to break out, and Sara Ann Albright and her husband decided the faster they made babies the quicker he would get a draft deferment, so they began immediately. During the next ten years she had eight children, four boys and four girls. When Terman tested the children, he discovered that six of the eight had IQs that met the requirement for his gifted study and the other two were close.

She wrote long letters about her life to Terman, whom she had not seen since she was six. He was highly amused by her fecundity, writing that she was tied with two other women in the study with her eight children, but was the winner as far as how little time it took to produce that many children.

Sara Ann was much too busy with her family to do physics; indeed, she never worked as a physicist. She said later that her interests had changed. She had a house full of children, the family required two cars to go anywhere, and nothing the Albrights did was done without noise. "We hope to bring our children to adulthood without burning off fingers," she remarked.

Jeffrey was constantly bringing home guests for a few days or a few weeks, usually foreign visitors from the laboratory.

She always felt, she said, as though things were hanging over her head, as though she had unfinished projects. Some of this, she knew, was normal in a tumultuous household, but she felt there was more tension than was normal. She feared high blood pressure and said she suffered from more stress than was good for her. She was totally absorbed by her family, but sensed something was missing. She blamed it in part on how her remarkable mind worked.

Sara Ann felt she had suffered because of her intellect, particularly the advancement through school which put her at a social disadvantage, perhaps suppressing her social development. Her parents, she felt, concentrated too much on grades, not nearly enough on her relations with other people.

She moved too slowly, she wrote Terman. She was incapable of quick action unless she concentrated "continuously on the motions being performed, a process which generally became rapidly too uninteresting to hold to. . . . In addition, I seem to have a very short span of attention in regard to mechanical performance. Housework I find exceedingly boring and often the prospect of the necessary hour and a half of a morning looming ahead of me proves less enticing than reading. As a consequence, housework doesn't get done and I then don't get to other, more interesting things. My husband suggests that I get a job and get a maid."

But she did not want to do that, because she feared she would be running away from her disquietude and because "vague ideas and questionings of the past two years have been crystallizing recently into the conviction that I have the ability to make a definite contribution, creative in nature and possibly through writing — and if so, with it the great responsibility to see that it is made. Time and energy not being unlimited, I feel that I cannot waste time on just any job, merely to be working, but should bend all the effort toward discovering the special nature of that ability. . . ."

Terman, ever ready to advise his kids, wrote back: "I don't feel that solving [your personal problems] by work is really running away from them. Work is a good thing for anyone, and the combination of domestic duties and outside work should keep you happy."

She did not get a job at that time.

In 1948 Sara Ann and Jeffrey carted the family west to visit their families in Southern California. They drove north to see Terman at Stanford and to have their offspring tested. Later she wrote: "It has been so long since I last saw you previously, and then through child's eyes, that it was a happy experience for me to be able to finally associate a physical entity with the personality that has always accompanied the impersonal record blanks."

Terman was just as pleased.

"Sara Ann," he wrote, "is of average or superior appearance as compared with other members of the group and very interesting in her conversation. For personal attractiveness, however, I would rate her husband perhaps a little higher. The marriage seems to be happy despite the moderately low happiness scores they made on the last test in 1940. . . . A highly enjoyable visit."

"It was one of the most delightful visits I have had in many a day," Terman wrote after another visit in 1952. "Not once was there any squabble among the children in the two hours they were here. . . . Sara Ann looks well and seems quite calm in temperament — much more so than the biographical blank led me to expect. In fact she seemed perfectly adjusted."

She was not.

When Sara Ann returned again in 1956, he wrote: "This is an extraordinarily interesting family, all of them so attractive and so bright." She finally got a housekeeper two days a week.

With the children mostly grown, Sara Ann McKinley Albright left home. The Albrights were divorced two years later.

She explained in her questionnaire from Terman's office that she had suffered from depression, "intermittent or chronic," with an inability to keep her household going. A part-time job did not help. Group and individual therapy did not help. Only leaving home seemed to make a difference. She got a full-time job with a religious service organization in Washington.

She lived with friends or moved from home to home "house-sitting." For several years she lived in an "intentional community," but left because it was not "egalitarian enough." She lived for a while, now in her late 50s, in a commune. She reported several intimate relationships but gave no details. One relationship ended badly.

"I think I was made, as a child, to be far too self-conscious of my status as a 'Termite,' " she wrote, "and of being smart and young for my grade (all passive), and given far too little to actually *do* with this mental endowment (so I'd stop thinking about myself)."

"My great regret is that my left-brain parents, spurred on by my Terman group experience, pretty completely by-passed any encouragement, of whatever *creative* talent I might have had. I now see the latter area as of *greatest* significance, and intelligence as its handmaiden. Sorry I didn't become aware of this fifty years ago."

Sara Ann lives in San Francisco in a cooperative community for older people. All her children have done well.

Jess

JESS OPPENHEIMER became a writer for some of the most famous shows of radio's golden age, Fanny Brice's "Baby Snooks," "The Edgar Bergen Show," "The Jack Benny Show," "Screen Guild Program," and Fred Astaire's "Packard Hour." When Edgar Bergen announced his name on the air as chief writer, memos flew around the Terman office; Jess became the study's first real success in show business, and considering his somewhat ambiguous beginnings, this was something of a surprise.

"I have been doing very well since Stanford University decided that it and I had nothing in common and severed our relationship," he wrote Terman in 1940. "Very well, that is, from a financial point of view. I have, in the years and my conquest of the town Hollywood, brought my salary to a neat $500 a week. A startling figure, you will admit. In fact, my agent had to forbid my answering a producer when he asked me my salary because I could not say it without giggling. The conditioning of years of San Francisco values never bridged the gap to fanciful movieland."

He also wrote Terman in the same letter that he had an invention that would revolutionize the world and wanted some advice. He had remained, since his puttering days as a child, interested in inventions. Unfortunately, there is no record what this invention was or if Terman ever spoke to him about it. There would be others.

Jess's salary probably put him near the top of the list of Termites by the time World War II broke out. During the war he joined the Coast Guard, writing radio programs for overseas broadcasts, and freelancing on the side, earning about $200 a week.

"I didn't get out of the States," he wrote in 1948, "and was lucky enough to be able to keep writing for radio during my whole tour of duty. For the past six years I have been writing Fanny Brice's 'Baby Snooks' radio program and have now worked my salary up to $1,500 a week. I don't know when they will catch up with me, but in the meantime I am salting it away in the old bank. Also, along the way, I managed to sneak in a short story in the *Saturday Evening Post* and the *American Magazine*. These were in collaboration."

He added: "I married last August, a Jewish girl from Los Angeles named Estelle Weiss, and I'm happy to tell you I'm expecting some new Oppenheimers." They thought it would be twins. But a single daughter, Jo, was born in 1948. A son, Gregg, was born three years later.

He and Estelle did not have an easy time at first because of his mother.

"My mother-in-law wasn't the easiest person to get along with," Estelle said. "She was a tough lady. She made the first four years of dating terribly uncomfortable — she was so critical of everything he or I ever did. He finally reached a point where he didn't want to spend time with her at all. He said he just felt she had ruined his early life and he didn't want it to continue. I finally had to force him to call her again."

Meanwhile, an optometrist in Culver City solved Jess's vision problems.

"I had been like a hypochondriac," he said. "I knew there was something wrong with me and wanted to find out what it was. I got this fellow and he tested my eyes. He said, 'You have no stereopsis at all, you have no third dimension. You have a vertical and a horizontal displacement.' " Jess, who had learned to compensate for his problems, argued that could not be so. "As long as you want to pay me, I'll keep looking for other things," the optometrist said. He put a prism in Jess's glasses and suddenly the world made sense, Jess said later.

"He remarked with humor," Terman wrote after a visit, "that it was after he got three-dimensional vision that he looked around and saw Estelle as she really was. And married her."

"I must say I am earning more than I ever in my wildest dreams expected to, but such a busy schedule has its drawbacks," he wrote Terman. "I have a lovely wife and a year-old daughter (I am enclosing a picture of her), but can only find a little less than one day a week to be with them. Confidentially, I am in the process of trying to get off the Bergen show as I feel this part of my life is even more important than the breadwinning side. It won't entail any great sacrifice as my other activities insure our living in the manner in which I'm afraid we've become accustomed."

Terman remarked there were very few in his group then earning $40,000 a year.

Jess thought his unhappy childhood had helped his career. He wrote once: "Almost an essential for a comedy writer is to have a major psychological maladjustment in childhood which gives you a platform from which to observe other people that's off to one side so you see them in a different light than they see each other. If you accept the commonplace as commonplace, you have no reason to see it in any other light. But if you can't understand what everybody else is doing, then you have to be a keener observer. An offbeat slant like that is a prerequisite to the kind of sort of wild comedy writing that I've been doing in radio. . . . I'm still, what we call, holding up the mirror in my writing to show the frailties of people but it isn't as wild and it isn't as bitter as it used to be when I was young, and in a sense through my writing I was getting even with people because I disliked them because I didn't understand them." Many of his life's experiences would later be found in his most famous work.

"From whatever that moment was when I discovered that I could be accepted on the basis of making people laugh, the needle on my life's compass swung until it pointed at humor and led me steadfastly in that direction. Little by little and with increasing skill as I gained experience, my every waking moment saw my brain taking in each word or phrase I heard or read and testing it for comedy content; turning it first this way and then that to see if any other meanings or relationships would reveal themselves. . . . But I still had a lesson to learn in connection with my new-found avenue to social success, and in the thrill of succeeding where there had always been failure I almost destroyed myself before I learned it. I am speaking of course of restraint, for if nothing scores like success, nothing bores like excess. . . . To survive, the would-be humorist must be sensitive to the fine dividing line between the amused groan and the snarling growl. Without such sensitivity, he will be forever doomed to wooing, amusing, and finally repelling group after group for life."

In 1948 he was asked by a CBS executive, Harry Ackerman, to write a radio program for a Hollywood comedienne whose show

business career was running dry. He agreed, but also ended up as the
writer, producer, and director of "My Favorite Husband." The actress, with bright red hair, a wonderful dazed expression, and an
intelligence that was belied by her film roles, was Lucille Ball.

"My Favorite Husband" was a success. Ball played the ditzy wife
of a midwestern banker portrayed by Richard Denning. But Ball was
anxious and unhappy. Her film career was virtually nonexistent, her
marriage was faltering, and several miscarriages had brought tragedy
into her life. She wanted to do a television version of her radio
program, but William Paley, who ran CBS as a fiefdom, would not
agree to having her husband, the Cuban bandleader Desi Arnaz, on
the television show. "Lucy's an all-American redhead. Desi's a Latin
with a thick accent. Nobody will believe it," a network spokesman
said with assurance.

She announced that if she could not appear with her husband on
television, she would quit acting and travel with his band. CBS was
unrelenting. Using a classic ploy, she and her agent then began nego-
tiating with NBC, which got Paley's immediate attention. Harry Ackerman went to work, finding a radio program for Arnaz while he
negotiated with Ball for a television program. What it would be,
however, was still a problem.

"I didn't want to play a typical Hollywood couple," Ball wrote. "It
would have been a stereotype. Everybody thinks if you're a Hollywood couple you have no problems. . . . I didn't want my character to
be glamorous. I didn't want her to have beautiful clothes. And I didn't
want her to be a wisecracking girl who drops a line and walks out of
the room. I'd done that in pictures and I certainly didn't want to do
that over again.

"Of all the thirty or forty films I had made up to that time, I could
find only three or four scenes in those pictures that I cared anything
about. When I put them all together, I discovered they were domestic
scenes, where I portrayed a housewife."

She and Ackerman decided to call on Jess to create the show. She
trusted his instincts implicitly.

"I hit upon the idea of a middle-class working stiff who works very
hard at his job and who likes nothing better than coming home at
night and relaxing with his wife, who doesn't like staying home and
wants a career of her own," Jess recalled in an interview with the *Los
Angeles Times*.

On March 2, 1951, he registered the following "treatment" for a television program with the Screen Writers' Guild.

I LOVE LUCY
Created by Jess Oppenheimer

This is a title of an idea for a radio and/or television program incorporating characters named Lucy and Ricky Ricardo. He is a Latin-American orchestra leader and singer. She is his wife. They are happily married and very much in love. The only bone of contention between them is her desire to get into show business, and his equally strong desire to keep her out of it. To Lucy, who was brought up in the humdrum sphere of a moderate, well-to-do middle western, mercantile family, show business is the most glamourous field in the world. But Ricky, who was raised in show business, sees none of its glamour, only its deficiencies, and yearns to be an ordinary citizen, keeping regular hours and living a normal life. As show business is the only way he knows to make a living, and he makes a very good one, the closest he can get to his dream is having a wife who's out of show business and devotes herself to keeping as nearly a normal life as possible for him.

The first story concerns a TV audition for Ricky, where Pepito, the clown, due to an accident, fails to appear and Lucy takes his place for the show. Although she does a bang-up job, she forgoes the chance at a career that is offered her in order to keep Ricky happy and closer to his dream of normalcy.

Lucille Ball, five months pregnant with "Little Lucy," made a thirty-four-minute test film to distribute to advertising agencies on March 2, 1951. The program was performed live. A film camera recorded the show off a studio monitor, and that film, the kinescope, was circulated to advertising agencies. That's how things were done in the days before videotape. The tobacco giant Phillip Morris quickly bought the program. The only snag came when Lucille Ball and Jess discovered that the ad agency intended that everyone move to New York to do the show. The agency's position was that if they stayed in Los Angeles, only the West Coast would get the show live. Everyone else, 85 percent of the country, would be watching the kinescope, which had nowhere near the quality of a live broadcast or today's videotape. At that point more creativity was called for, and Jess and Harry Ackerman came through, forever changing the face of American television.

Shelley

THE JAPANESE FORCES invading from the north and the south paused on the outskirts of Manila to consolidate. They sent word through the American High Commissioner's office that all Americans were to remain indoors where they were. Carl and Shelley Mydans waited two days in their hotel before Manila's conquerors arrived. "The army used Japanese civilians who had been interned by us at the start of the war to question us," Shelley remembered. "When they came into our room they were very polite. They searched around but Carl had hidden his cameras before they got there."

The Filipino staff was ordered to leave, so the foreigners in the hotel organized themselves into a sort of commune. After two days they were told they were to be taken to "register" and were instructed to pack what they could carry and food for three days. Besides light clothing and toilet articles, almost everyone took a few books. "We had Shakespeare and Tolstoy coming out our ears at camp," Shelley said.

"When the Japanese troops had been deployed around the hotel, an officer sent the command through the hotel manager that everyone was to come into the lobby and from there we were assembled in the street outside. Japanese soldiers with fixed bayonets surrounded us, but they seemed quite placid. It was obvious we were not going to start running.

"They loaded us in trucks they had captured from the U.S. Army and took us to Santo Tomás University where we were housed in the empty school rooms — women and men in separate rooms, though we could be together during the day."

The date was January 2, 1942. Shelley learned to live with what she later described as a "constant, oozing fear." She was elected monitor of her room of thirty-five women and volunteered to work in the makeshift camp hospital where she helped in the food preparation, picking worms and weevils out of the cereal.

They had little contact with their Japanese guards and were not brutalized — a situation very different from that of military prisoners. What civilian internees suffered from, primarily, was emotional turmoil, overcrowding, and neglect, she said.

Their captors, busy with the battle on Bataan, neglected to feed them in the early months, and in the first few days — until the Philippine Red Cross delivered sacks of rice and cracked wheat to the camp — Filipinos brought food and bedding to the fence and simply threw them over for anyone in need. The Japanese commandant complained that this made his prisoners look like monkeys in a zoo, so these acts of spontaneous charity were organized into a daily delivery through the gate.

Early in internment three men escaped and were quickly recaptured. They were brought back to camp, beaten, taken out to the cemetery where they dug their own graves, and shot. Their room monitors were forced to watch, and the commandant announced that if any more prisoners escaped, their room monitors also would be shot. A very Asian and effective way of controlling groups of people, Shelley thought.

After eight months the internees were told there was a ship prepared to take 150 of them to Shanghai. This was in response to a request of Shanghai residents who had been at sea and were off-loaded in Manila when the war broke out. Now, these months later, many of these mostly women and children were afraid to make the move, so the commandant had several slots to fill. Carl and Shelley volunteered themselves. For one thing, Shelley was going blind in her right eye and the American missionary doctors in camp had no means of treatment. For another, Carl and Shelley thought they might have a better chance of repatriation or escape from Shanghai than from Manila, which was, after all, on an island.

The Mydanses and three other correspondents were among the 120 internees from Santo Tomás who were taken to the port area where the ship was docked. It turned out to be a small, aging freighter, the *Maya Maru*, that had been converted to a troop transport.

"What a voyage!" Shelley said. "There were about a thousand Japanese soldiers going home on leave with a group of twenty Formosan prostitutes who travelled with them and kept them happy, as well as 120 of us rather gaunt and ragged prisoners. A young Spaniard and a couple of men from Hollywood who called themselves Lithuanians, being neutrals, had booked passage as though on an ordinary ship and were dismayed to find themselves in the hold with the rest of us.

"As we stood on the truck beds on the dock we watched those before us climb up the flimsy, swaying gangplank, lugging 'what they could carry' as they had when they went into camp, cross a stretch of deck and then plunge down.

"There were long shelves built against the bulkheads all around the holds, a bottom shelf which was really on the deck, and another about three feet above it. On them were the remains of what would have been Japanese mats, I guess, and the soldiers, the little Formosan girls and we prisoners all lay on these and watched the small seagoing cockroaches race back and forth above us.

"It all had a certain comic aspect, it was so strange. But when we started out through Manila Bay they closed the hatch cover above us. It was pitch black and the air was thick and the decks seemed to throb all around us. 'Some people will not survive this,' I thought. 'But I will.'

"Then, as soon as we cleared the harbor they rolled back the hatch cover and allowed us to go up on deck. It was lovely weather, September 1942. There were bales of hay for the horses that we could sit on. And we were moving. Moving! After eight months of sitting still. Suddenly, it was a very happy trip.

"The soldiers and the prisoners kept pretty much to themselves. But I got up one morning very early to try to sponge myself a little under my clothes. The only water was in a big tank on the port side with a spigot very low to the deck. I was brushing my teeth when suddenly a group of soldiers came to brush their teeth too, so we were crouched there together and I was trying to finish as quickly as I could but my mouth was filled with soapy water. Just as I spat out, one of the soldiers held out his cup and I spit right into it.

"I stood up and bowed, and oh, I was horrified, and I said I was sorry and bowed again. And he stood up too, and he bowed to me, and he said — well, I don't know exactly what he said really, I didn't know any Japanese at that time. But he said something polite and we both bowed, and boy, you know ... he could have hit me, he could have done anything. But he bowed. I don't forget him.

"On the starboard side of the deck, across from the water tank, were the latrines, so called, built out over the side of the ship. Have you ever heard of Lanny Davis, the tennis star? He was at Stanford when I was. Lanny Davis was on that ship.... At any rate, that latrine: you had to step out on a kind of plank over the water and there was a little flimsy door that you could pull after you. I got all ready on the plank and the ship pitched and the door flew open and I kept trying to drag it so that I wouldn't be exposed to the world. But what I was exposed to was Lanny Davis."

The ship first went to Taiwan, then called Formosa, where the troops and their whores disembarked, then continued to China. The trip was more dangerous than Shelley and Carl thought; on at least two occasions Allied ships sank Japanese prison ships thinking they were carrying troops.

At Shanghai they found they had made the right choice. American, British, and other Allied civilians were free within the city bounds, which the Japanese patrolled. Shelley and Carl checked into the Palace Hotel where they lived in luxury and regained their lost weight. They were able to borrow money from the Swiss consulate on the strength of their passports. Shelley found a German eye doctor who diagnosed and treated her for tuberculin retinitis next to the optic nerve.

There were few restrictions at first, but soon the Allied civilians, or "enemy nationals," were issued red arm bands stamped with their nationality and a number. They were ordered to wear the bands at all times. Early the following year, 1943, the Japanese began rounding up all enemy nationals and putting them into camps; the American families were interned in the war-battered buildings of Chapei University, the British in Lunghwa, the single men in abandoned tobacco warehouses in Pootung. In February Carl was put into Chapei, but Shelley's doctor sent her to a Japanese ophthalmologist who asked her how long she wanted to stay out of camp and arranged a pass for her.

"I had a fascinating time," she said, "because there were only a very few of us 'red arm bands' free on the streets and everyone except the Japanese was sympathetic to my side of the war." She moved to a French boardinghouse, explored all corners of Shanghai, and had friends among the refugees who were not interned. She enjoyed it but felt guilty, and after a few months she decided to join Carl in camp.

Shelley and Carl were finally repatriated in September 1943, along with fifteen hundred other Americans and Canadians in exchange for an equal number of Japanese civilians in the United States. The exchange took place in Goa, then a Portuguese colony on India's west coast. Carl borrowed a camera from a State Department official and he and Shelley began covering their own exchange.

While in Goa they gave an article they had written based on their observations of the Japanese at war to a correspondent to send to New York. When they got home, they discovered their editor had altered the copy. He explained he had to cut it for length and then, using a phrase that makes writers actively nauseous, he "ran it through the typewriter." In that process he added the words "The only good Jap is a dead Jap." When, white-faced with anger, they confronted him later, he said that he thought everyone felt that way. The Mydanses did not. "It still lives with us," Shelley said more than forty years later.

The Mydanses spent several weeks at home in New York writing letters to the families of fellow prisoners. Carl got a draft deferment as a war correspondent and went to Europe for the battle of Rome and the landings in southern France. Shelley took a six-month leave of absence and went home to her mother's house at Stanford to write a novel about Santo Tomás, *The Open City,* which got good reviews and sold well.

Her eye got worse. American doctors seemed amused at the diagnosis of "tuberculosis" made by the German doctor in Shanghai. "All I know is that when it was treated by that German doctor it got better and since then I have totally lost the sight in that eye. I don't want to exaggerate; I can get light through the periphery, so it's not entirely black but I can't see with the eye."

Then she and Carl were sent back to the Pacific, where they hoped to cover the recapturing of the Philippines. MacArthur had a rule against female correspondents in his "theater," so while Carl was attached to MacArthur, Shelley got a position with the less conservative navy, attached to Admiral Chester Nimitz. Carl was at Leyte Gulf when MacArthur, true to his promise, returned to the Philippines.

Carl took the famous photo of the general, pipe clenched in firm jaw, wading ashore through the surf. The photo was staged for propaganda; MacArthur had already come ashore in the Philippines, but there were no photographers around so he staged another "landing."

Shelley went to Hawaii and then Guam and joined Carl in the South Pacific for a story. She was welcomed back publicly. "Shelley Smith Mydans, the Pacific's first gorgeous war correspondent is here," wrote an editor of a GI newspaper. "[She] cannot be summed up in a sentence, but a sentence can report that she's an able newspaperwoman who has been more places than a globe-trotter, has had more adventures than a soldier of fortune, knows more about the Japs than most military commanders, and, at twenty-nine, is better to look at than 75 percent of the movie stars. . . . She's as cool as a Tom Collins."

At the end of the war she covered the Japanese surrender in the Philippines while Carl flew to Japan to cover the surrender on the U.S.S. *Missouri,* his famous photographs recording one of the twentieth century's most important moments for history.

After the surrender Shelley joined Carl in ravaged Tokyo. "The Japanese themselves were splendid; they kept their dignity, but they didn't moan and groan. They all started right away to plant a little garden, or people who had been captain of industries began to twist two pieces of wire together to make a bicycle or something. They were exhausted, but if they wept, they didn't show us. Defeat became them far better than success."

They spent three years in Tokyo following the war, reporting on the occupation, then returned to New York.

"[Time-Life] asked me to take over a radio program for Time Inc. The announcer on the "March of Time" had been Westbrook Van Vorhees, who had a very dramatic delivery. With peace they wanted a gentler tone, and because there were more women than men readers at that time, they decided they wanted a woman's voice. Why did they think that women necessarily want to listen to a woman? They asked me to 'voice' that program and write some segments for it. I guess it might be called an anchor today but we didn't use that term. The program was called "Time for Women." It was broadcast out of New York on a national network for half an hour every afternoon. It didn't last too long."

For one thing, she was pregnant. The producers thought it would be wonderful to chronicle the pregnancy and birth on the radio, something Shelley found embarrassing. Carl's assignment, however, saved her from public pregnancy. A little adrift in postwar New York, Carl was asked by Time-Life to return to Tokyo as bureau chief. "This was a very important job and a very good chance for him," Shelley said, "so I gave up the radio program which might have been a jump-off point on a new career for me. But I have to soften this a bit because I'm not sure I wanted that sort of a career. But I'm aware I definitely took a back seat then and it still rankles me a little."

The Time-Life Tokyo bureau needed a "man and a half" and Shelley became that half-time reporter. "I was that half man and half mother in Tokyo," she said, "until our second child was born and I went on maternity leave — and never went back." The two children were Seth, born in New York, and Shelley, born in Japan.

When the Korean War broke out, they were in California on their way to New York. Carl turned around immediately and flew to Seoul. Shelley, who said her heart had always remained on the Stanford campus, stayed with the children at her mother's house until she could buy an acre on the edge of the campus and build a home. She was done being a war correspondent.

"I guess I've had enough of covering war," she said at the time. "The fact is, I am not one to enjoy the smoke and sound of battle. It's no use pretending I don't care about leaky planes and all the other hazards that go with front-line reporting. I do care. I used not to worry about them consciously but looking back on it, I just wouldn't want to do it again."

She was, she said, busy with the "heavy work load that is the daily lot of the average American mother. Frankly, I've lost pounds since I've been back."

When Carl returned from Korea, they had less than a year in their California house before they were sent to London for four years. Shelley did not have a work permit so she started the research for a novel. And on their return to New York Shelley and Carl collaborated on *The Violent Peace*, a picture book with text on the small wars of the "peacetime" era after World War II. "The roots of war are deep in man's heart, lodged in fear, ambition, a thirst for vengeance, hate," they wrote.

The Tadashi Family: Alfred

ALFRED, THE FIRST CHILD of Emily and Akio Tadashi, bore the burdens of their love and their separation. He was relied on as the man in the Tadashi family, his mother wrote, and much of his early life was sidetracked because of his family responsibilities.

Field-workers described him as a young man with great intellectual curiosity and independence of thought, a strong sense of justice and honor, and a strong sense of responsibility.

"Alfred, I think, more than any of the other children, feels his mixed heritage to be a handicap," Emily wrote Terman. "He cannot yet understand that his own attitude is the only permanent handicap. He loves friends and their approbation, but he is also keenly critical of them. He is sensitive to many shades of meaning in people's intercourse with him which by others might be passed unnoticed. He lacks Ronald's gay and humorous attitude toward life, his air castle optimism. Life is a serious business to Alfred. He has had too much responsibility. He is a splendid fellow but I am afraid he is going to suffer a great deal."

Emily wrote to Terman that Alfred "can not bear to hear of injustice, and becomes angry through and through if he hears of any weak thing being mistreated."

He wanted to go to college, but placed his duty to the family first. He was needed to run the ranch, so when he graduated from high school at the age of fifteen and a half, he stayed home. This freed his sister Sophie to go to college, a sacrifice he seemed not unhappy to make. "He is frank, competent and ambitious," his mother wrote Terman. By May 1930 he had built a fifteen-cow dairy on the property. Like his brother Ronald, he also changed his name to Talbot, his mother's maiden name. It would, he felt, simply make life easier.

In 1932, ten years after the initial test, he finally met Terman. "Is not exceptionally attractive appearing," Terman wrote. "Is perhaps a little introverted and dreamy. . . . I should expect to see Alfred make a wholly satisfactory adaptation."

"Fortunately, Alfred is a tall, well-set boy, and a tower of strength, for he feels his responsibilities very keenly and has discharged his heavy duties like a man," Terman noted for the files. "His younger brother has now reached the age that Alfred was when he graduated from high school, and is taking increasing responsibility. It is quite possible that if an opportunity came for Alfred to secure further schooling, the family could arrange to let him go.

"Alfred makes a very favorable impression personally. He is frank, manly, competent, and ambitious. In appearance, he is just what his parentage would suggest — half Japanese and half American. His complexion has a light brown cast and his hair is straight and black like that of a Japanese, but his features tend to be Caucasian rather than Oriental in type."

Alfred managed to get into the University of California at Berkeley. He found when he arrived that he had received a scholarship from an anonymous donor at Stanford and suspected the money came from Terman. He asked, but Terman refused to answer. It is likely he was correct; Alfred would not be the only one of Terman's kids to be helped monetarily and always anonymously. When he was at Berkeley, Alfred held a paid position as chairman and secretary of the Institute for Pacific Relations, a reflection, probably, of his heritage. He edited the institute's newsletter, which was dedicated to serious, intellectual analyses of foreign affairs.

At Terman's suggestion Alfred transferred to Deep Springs College, a tiny, eccentric, but altogether serious college-ranch community in a remote section of the California desert, but family pressures forced him to leave. A Deep Springs official wrote Terman:

"Alfred came in May 1930 to take charge of and operate a . . . dairy during the summer. This he did well until the majority of the students returned in September. From then until Christmas vacation he did excellent work on the general ranch jobs for the four hour daily period. At that time the increasing pressure from home reached its culmination, causing him to remain in Berkeley as head of the family once more.

"He reentered the University of California as a part time student, all the while helping the morale and budget of the family. Again in May he returned to Deep Springs and is operating the dairy with the hope of staying on. Academically, he did good work — not exceptional in comparison with the best here, but yet above the average of our group. . . . It has taken much effort on his part to overcome a shyness and suspicion of those about him. However, he has grown and overcome in a large measure these somewhat unsocial tendencies, with the result that he is better liked, more open-minded, and has a much broader outlook on life."

His experiences at Deep Springs were more complicated than that, Alfred told Barbara Burks, the field-worker assigned to the family. "From time to time there had been trouble with homosexual instructors," Burks reported. "The dairy which Alfred had charge of was a pest spot of filth and corruption until he got it straightened out, not without a royal battle. He left the school after one term, but later came back as a paid employee, ranch foreman or something of the sort, and might still be there if the school had not practically collapsed from the Depression. At present, the school has only one teacher."

Alfred returned to Berkeley to graduate with honors in the field of philosophy. He told Terman that being one of the Termites, particularly one who received some publicity, was a serious disadvantage in college. "Because of your published account of your early work with us, our reputations preceded us to U.C. People constantly looked to us for exceptional work, poverty or no poverty, and I for one rebelled. When professors say, 'If any other student had written this paper, I would have given him an A, but you can do so much better that I am going to give you a B to stimulate you,' it is time to call a halt. . . .

"I fell madly in love with a lovely girl about two years ago. I had to withdraw from school that year and earn the money to bury Delores and support Patience [another sister]." Later, in 1936, he married his love, a Caucasian.

When Alfred was considering going to medical school, Terman suggested he take the usual battery of vocational interest tests. Alfred scored a B in several areas, but no A; nothing registered strongly enough. On the basis of Alfred's past experience, Terman suggested farm management, ignoring the C Alfred had scored in that area.

"I don't want to be a doctor or a lawyer or a linguist or what; I want to be myself," he wrote Terman, "and that seems impossible. . . . I don't want to be anything, and yet custom keeps up its everlasting cry, demanding that I place a label on my back, stay in one place and govern my actions by the clock."

He considered every profession, even using his better-than-average voice to learn opera. Nothing stuck. The opera career option ended when chain smoking destroyed his voice.

By 1942 Alfred had bought a 630-acre ranch in the Sierra foothills. San Francisco columnist Herb Caen, who knew Alfred because of his work with the Pacific institute, noted that Alfred and several of his siblings had disappeared at the beginning of World War II. Their Japanese ancestry had apparently caught up with them. Alfred had fled to his chicken ranch. Two of his three children looked very Japanese. He asked Terman to help keep his family from being interned. "I tried hard to get an exception made in your case when the American-Japanese were being relocated," Terman wrote back, "but the military authorities were adamant." Indeed, he had written the immigration service attesting to the loyalty of all the Tadashis, but had not received any assurances they would be spared. As it turned out, they were spared, either because they had all chosen to live in remote parts of the state or because Terman had vouched for them. Alfred simply ignored the orders to turn himself in and was never caught. "I am delighted to know that your family has been able to live in relative peace and comfort during the critical years," Terman wrote Alfred.

But the unity of the four surviving Tadashi children had exploded. Ronald and his sister Patience moved without telling any of their siblings where they were. "I don't have addresses for Patty or Ronald," Alfred wrote when the Terman office asked for assistance in tracking down his brothers and sisters. "They have chosen to isolate themselves from the rest of us." Terman, in fact, never found Patience, and to this day no one in the Terman office knows what happened to her.

Alfred and his family lived on their ranch, tending a dozen head of cattle and cultivating their orchard. One year, after failing to return a questionnaire from the Terman office on time, he apologized saying the farming was taking up all his time. That struck a chord with Terman, who wrote back describing his early life on an Indiana farm and comparing Alfred and Terman's father, both men eking out a living from the land while keeping their respect and dignity.

Alfred Talbot became a community leader in his town, organizing the citizens to establish their own regional high school district. He served on the school board, resigning after a tax revolt cut funding to the schools. He was elected by the weekly community newspaper as the citizen of the year in 1951, the paper citing his "tireless work . . . his calm and masterful manner of conducting a meeting, his cool adherence to logic, his convincing arguments, and his willingness to listen to arguments. . . ."

Alfred (Tadashi) Talbot died in 1963.

Chapter Ten

TERMAN'S LAST REPORT

BY 1950 Terman's kids were at or near the height of their success and power. Most were in their mid-forties and had carved their places in the world. Now Terman could find out what had indeed happened to his "superior" children. Had they lived up to their promise? He and Melita Oden launched the fourth mass survey of the Termites. It would be the last in which Terman participated.

His office again mailed out envelopes stuffed with forms and tests. Field-workers visited most of the Termites still living in California (82 percent) and when possible administered the Concept Mastery test to measure their intellect once again. In 1955 the office sent out a two-page form asking for personal data so that Terman could include the most up-to-date demographic information in his published results. Again, cooperation was astonishing. The Termites, addressed by Terman in all his correspondence as "my gifted 'children,'" sat themselves down and took hours to fill out all the forms to help their paterfamilias with his life's work. In 1950, 1,437 of Terman's kids were still known to be alive and 95 percent of the living subjects responded: 93 percent of them actively cooperated in the 1955 follow-up. Additional information was obtained on several others, giving Terman and Oden data on 97.5 percent of the living Termites. In addition, Terman's field-workers tested 1,525 of the subjects' children. This level of cooperation — and the results of his survey — must have pleased him enormously. Some of those located near his office gave less than complete cooperation, and Terman could not give those outside the state the full battery of tests, but the data he accumulated and the indulgence he received were still extraordinary.

Few scientists have been indebted to their subjects for as long or as deeply as Terman was to his Termites, and few scientists have had the kind of loving relationship Terman enjoyed with them.

Terman once again had foundation money to fund the survey,* but he was his own best contributor, providing a fifth of the cost out of his own pocket and donating even more from test royalties.

By 1955 Terman's office had recorded 104 deaths among the subjects and had lost track of twenty-eight (eleven men and seventeen women). Terman could not tell if the missing were still alive and had just moved away or, in the case of some women, had changed their names and would therefore be hard to find. Nonetheless, he and his office tried to track down each one. There were 759 men and 629 women left in his sample. Their average age was forty-four.

Of those deceased, the average age at death was 28.4 years. Most died of natural causes, with heart disease, cancer, and tuberculosis the leading killers. Accidents, mostly motor vehicle, accounted for the second largest number of deaths. Fifteen of his subjects had committed suicide. Ever impressed by degrees as a measure of attainment, Terman reported that the dead included three Ph.D.s, three M.D.s, three LL.B.s and five people with master's degrees. Several others had been on the verge of getting graduate degrees when they died. The mortality rate for his subjects was lower than that for the general population for both men and for women.

Terman seemed somewhat surprised at the fifteen suicides. Going back to whatever data were available on the general population, he found that the rate was indeed somewhat higher for his kids, particularly the women. And, more interestingly, while far more men commit suicide than women in the general population, that was not true among his gifted. Although the numbers of suicides in his group was small, the women accounted for a much greater percentage of suicides. It was another small clue — which he never had a chance to pursue — that his gifted women were somehow different.†

The surviving subjects remained fairly healthy, although Terman had no way of comparing their physical state with that of the general

---

* This time the money came from the Rockefeller Corporation.

† Many researchers believe the suicide rate for Terman's women is even higher. Several women may have committed suicide, but made their deaths look like accidents. One woman, reputedly a fine swimmer, walked into the ocean and drowned, but her death was listed as accidental.

population. With the bulk of his sample sliding into middle age, those reporting their health as "very good" declined slightly, but there was not much change among those in "poor" or "very poor" health. Again, women reported their general health to be not as good as men's overall, but Terman noted that was true in the general population; women have a higher morbidity (disease) rate than do men even if they do live longer. Again he found that his gifted tended to be slightly taller than the general population size, and he still could make nothing of that.

He asked the subjects to rate their mental state, dividing the sample into those reporting "satisfactory mental health," those reporting "some maladjustment," and those reporting "serious maladjustment." The last were divided into those "without mental disease," by which he meant those who had never been hospitalized, and those "with mental disease," or those who had been hospitalized. Two-thirds of the men and slightly fewer of the women reported themselves in satisfactory mental health. Nine percent of both sexes reported serious problems, about 3 percent of the total having been institutionalized at least once. Some of those who had been institutionalized reported they had recovered; a few said they were worse. The mental problems ran the gamut from simple nervous breakdown to serious derangement. Ten men and three women were classified as alcoholics, seven men and eight women as manic-depressives. The others suffered from a variety of disorders including schizophrenia (no longer called dementia praecox) and "psychoneurosis."*

He found that the rate of mental disease among his men was slightly lower than what was to be expected in the general population; the rate among his women was slightly higher.

The rates of alcoholism and criminality among his gifted remained far lower than in the general population. Men seemed to have a more difficult time with alcohol than did women. No more of his Termites got into trouble with the law than had been previously reported.

Most of his kids (78 percent of the men, 77 percent of the women) said they had no sexual problems. The biggest problem reported was difficulty with sexual adjustment in marriage. Four percent of the

---

* This information was self-reported, but where he could, Terman obtained independent confirmation of what he was told. Again, he erroneously included those suffering from epilepsy among the mentally ill.

women and 1 percent of the men reported frigidity or impotence; 2 percent of both sexes said they were concerned about being over-sexed. The issue of homosexuality was something else. Oden wrote:

> The sex problems so far discussed, though presenting difficulty for the individual, have not been of the dimensions to constitute an aberration or an insuperable obstacle to adjustment for the individual. Homosex-uality, on the other hand, is a deviation of such serious proportions involving both personal and social adjustment that its incidence in the gifted group has been reserved for separate discussion. Our concern here is with subjects who have had homosexual experiences and for whom heterosexual adjustment has been difficult or impossible. Homosexuality, thus defined, has been reported for seventeen men (2 percent) and eleven women (1.7 percent). Undoubtedly, there are, in addition, instances of latent homosexuality in which there has been no overt expression or even recognition of the tendency.[1]

Using Kinsey's data (which reported 25 percent of all males had at least one homosexual incident and 4 percent of white males were exclusively homosexual), Terman concluded that the rate of homo-sexuality in his sample was well below that of the general population. Only ten of the seventeen self-defined homosexual men were exclu-sively so, nine of them overtly so and one still in "the closet." All but one of the eleven self-defined lesbians were married, six of them successfully. One woman was married three times before she finally moved in with another woman. One unmarried woman was bisexual. "There is no doubt," reported Oden, "that homosexuality has inter-fered with the personal and social adjustment of these persons."

Terman went back to see if he could find any relationship between education and mental disease (including epilepsy and homosexuality). Surprisingly, he found none among the men, but did find that "there is evidence that the present status of those [women] who did not go to college or who entered but did not complete college is less satisfactory with respect to general adjustment than that of the college graduates." He also found that those women with the highest IQ scores as children had a greater tendency toward maladjustment as adults, the reverse of what was so with men. Brighter women seemed to have a more difficult time.

Terman was, of course, determined to find out how his Termites did intellectually. He had found a drop in IQ in some of his subjects earlier. Using a revised version of the Concept Mastery test, which he believed accurately measured adults, he tested 1,004 subjects and 690 of their spouses. He managed to find several control groups with which he could compare scores, something he did all too infrequently. The Concept Mastery test was given to several groups, ranging from graduate students at Berkeley to applicants for Ford Foundation fellowships to captains in the U.S. Air Force.

The average score for his gifted was far higher than the average score for any other group. The average Concept Mastery score for the Termites was 137.* The next highest average score was 119, reached by the Berkeley graduate students. The air force captains scored the lowest, 60. The greater the education of the subject, the higher the score was likely to be. He found that was true of every group, including the air force officers. There were no scores for the general population, but Terman said that one could assume the air force captains, who were chosen for intelligence and were either college graduates or had at least attended some college, were smarter than the average American. Since the average Concept Mastery score for the gifted was 77 points higher than the average for the captains, he felt pretty confident that the Termites were still among America's intellectual elite.

He could not accurately compare the Concept Mastery scores with the Stanford-Binet scores the gifted had achieved in childhood, but he did have Concept Mastery scores from the 1939–1940 battery of tests when the Termites were generally in their thirties, so he could see what changes had occurred in the twelve years between tests with the Termites having moved into middle age. "The data show that the scores of both the gifted and the spouse groups were consistently higher at the second testing when the subjects were approximately twelve years older." The increase was "highly significant statistically." The gifted men went up 16.3 points on average, the women 15.5. Even the spouses went up in the final calculation; the wives of gifted men increased 11.4 points, the husbands of gifted women went up 14.9 on average.† Although the average went up, not everyone had

---

* Remember that these numbers are Concept Mastery scores. They are not IQ scores.

† Terman vehemently fought the notion, propounded by Iowa researchers, that IQ could be increased by education (see Chapter Four). The increase in scores could be attributed to the subjects' increased familiarity with the test, having seen versions of it before, but Terman discounted familiarity as a factor.

a higher score; 6 percent of the subjects lost 5 points or more, and two people dropped more than twenty. The test performance of one of those who dropped more than twenty was dismissed as a fluke. He had a Ph.D. and was teaching at the college level at the time, so Terman mused that perhaps he had had a bad day when he took the test. The other twenty-point loser was described as a housewife who had "intellectually unplugged" from life.

Oden, who wrote that section of the report, felt the results showed that people can continue to increase test scores (she did not say intelligence) at least through the age of fifty.

Much was made of the educational attainments again. Several more subjects had earned college degrees. Some had been in college at the time of the last survey and had since graduated; others went back to school. One man earned his high school diploma at the age of forty-five and was attending university extension classes. Terman and Oden pointed out that 70 percent of the Termites were college graduates at a time when only 8 percent of all Americans had college degrees. What Terman neglected to attend to, of course, was that his sample was drawn largely from the middle and upper classes. Had he compared his sample to those social classes rather than to the general population, the difference might have been considerably less. However, even in a more rigorous comparison his subjects would still have been remarkable. Two-thirds of the men and almost three-fifths of the women had graduate degrees. Now there were ninety lawyers (up from eighty-two) and fifty-five doctors (up from fifty-two). Ninety-three had doctorates. According to another study, only one-quarter of those Americans receiving undergraduate degrees went on to graduate school, so the Termites' record was vastly superior.

Terman was puzzled by what he considered failures in their records. Seventy-eight percent of the men and 83 percent of the women graduated with a B average or better, but he thought that since all his subjects were gifted, all should have done superior work. Moreover, fifty-three men and ten women flunked out of college. Late blooming explained some of those early failures, since twenty-four of the men who had failed went back to college and graduated; fifteen got advanced degrees, including four doctorates, three law degrees, two medical degrees, and one engineering degree. Only one woman went back and she graduated cum laude. As we've seen, at least two of those who flunked out did just fine in life, but this still puzzled Terman and Oden. They found no pattern to explain this "failure," but said that many commented they had had an easy time in high school and had trouble adjusting to the work load in college. Many, Terman and Oden felt, had been the victims of incompetent guidance.

Most of his subjects said they were satisfied with the education they received and had as much as they needed or wanted. Most credited their parents with encouraging them to stay in school and to succeed.

Terman again probed the question of whether the gifted should be accelerated in school. His data confirmed his first conclusion that gifted children should be accelerated so that they entered college no later than the age of seventeen and that the advantages of acceleration outweighed the disadvantages.

Terman and Oden went back to the Minnesota Occupational scale and found considerable upward mobility (see page 163). Now 45.6 percent were in the professional group, 40.7 in the semiprofessional classification. Only 10.9 percent of the men were in clerical, skilled trades, and retail business. Almost four-fifths of the men classified in the bottom three groupings (agriculture, semiskilled, and slightly skilled) moved upward on the scale.

OCCUPATIONAL CLASSIFICATION OF GIFTED, 1940–1955

Occupational Group	PERCENT OF EMPLOYED MEN		
	1940	1950	1955
I. Professional	45.4	45.6	45.6
II. Semiprofessional and managerial	25.7	39.4	40.7
III. Clerical, skilled, and retail	20.7	12.0	10.9
IV. Agricultural	1.2	1.8	1.6
V. Semiskilled	6.2	1.2	1.2
VI. Slightly skilled	0.7	—	—

The most frequent single occupation was business executive (seventy-nine men). The most frequent profession again was law, with 10 percent (seventy-eight) of the gifted men either practicing law or serving as judges (nine people with law degrees were in other professions). Teaching at a university and engineering came next. Twenty men were unemployed because they were ill, retired, independently wealthy, or temporarily out of work.

Twenty-seven men had gone into show business in one form or another, including

a motion picture director who has made some of the most outstanding pictures of the last ten years. His pictures made in England and on the Continent as well as those made in the United States have won him an international reputation. He has received a number of citations and awards, including a special award at the International Film Festival. Other honors include several "Oscar" awards by the Academy of Motion Picture Arts and Sciences won either by his pictures or by actors under his direction.[2]

They did not say who he was.

One man was a police chief, the only law enforcement officer Terman and Oden bothered to note. He was chief in a small city and had "developed a coordinated communications system, which is considered a model. A special interest in the prevention of juvenile delinquency has brought him frequent invitations to lecture on this and other aspects of his work."

In the agricultural group eleven men were farm owners and operators, and one was a nurseryman. Two were listed as semiskilled tradesmen. Terman and Oden noted one bartender, a truck driver, a warehouseman, two clerks (both suffering from alcoholism), and one sandwich shop operator. They also noted one man who rose to a managerial position but found himself philosophically alienated by the corporate culture. He left his job after the war and had been working for ten years as a laborer and union activist. Terman and Oden seemed puzzled by this, but admitted he seemed to be happy.

The total family income of the Terman men averaged $9,640 a year, with a range of $4,000 to $400,000. More than 10 percent earned $25,000 a year or more, which in the mid-1950s was an excellent income. The six men with the highest incomes each averaged $100,000 a year or more for the last three years. As would be expected, income varied with education; the more education, the more money someone was likely to earn, not counting the Ph.D.s. Practicing physicians made the most money, $23,500 a year on average. Business executives earned $17,680. Show business executives (nonperformers) came in a close third with $17,500. The lawyers were fourth with just under $16,000, followed by architects and economists. Musicians and actors ranked tenth ($10,830), college professors seventeenth ($8,167), and writers and journalists eighteenth ($8,000). Clergymen came in last, earning an average of $4,500 a year. In every case, the Termites outperformed their colleagues in the same general occupational classification.

Half of the men and more than half of the working women reported to Terman that they had "deep satisfaction and interest" in their vocations; 5 percent of the men and 2.6 percent of the women were unhappy with their jobs but would stick it out; and 1 percent of both men and women hated what they did and wanted a fast change. The men in the lowest job classifications were least likely to love their jobs. Physicians tended to be more satisfied than any other group of men. There was a solid correlation among the men between how much money they earned and job satisfaction.

Terman had noted that his gifted had many, varied hobbies and activities when they were children. He could report that they remained catholic in their interests in middle age. Four-fifths of them had two or more hobbies and more than a half reported having three or more. Many of them continued the activities that had interested them as children, and if they had special talents then (music or writing, for instance), they retained them in mid-life. They enjoyed membership in a variety of organizations and in service clubs.

What they appeared not to be particularly interested in was religion. Only 10 percent of the men and 18 percent of the women expressed a strong interest in religion. Terman lumped "strong" with "moderate" interests in his report and could say that 38 percent of the men and 53 percent of the women had strong or moderate interest in religion, but the lack of strong faith is still apparent. Another way to look at it — and Terman did not, despite his own lack of religious faith — was that 62 percent of the men and 47 percent of the women had little or no religious faith, which surely distinguished them from the general population. The Termites reported that most were members of religious congregations, however. Apparently, they felt obliged somehow to go to church or synagogue, but they were not driven there by abiding conviction. Terman said that church affiliation seemed to match the general population. He noted that the percentage of men belonging to organized congregations exceeded the percentage of women who did so, contrary to expectations. Perhaps that was further evidence that something social not spiritual was at work.

As might be expected, the gifted became more conservative as they got older. The percentage of men who considered themselves radicals dropped by half from 1940 to 1950. The change in the women was less extreme, but fewer thought themselves radical by 1950. The percentage of Termites who considered themselves conservatives grew somewhat, but most of the motion was from the left toward the center. In 1940 eight men and four women called themselves "extremely radical," but none did ten years later. In 1940 eighteen men called themselves "extremely conservative," but only thirteen did so by 1950. The end of the depression was a decade in the past by that time. Thirty-seven percent of the men and 40 percent of the women said they hadn't changed their political philosophies in the intervening years.

Age was a factor in political attitudes, again as might be expected. The younger subjects were less conservative than their older colleagues. The cutoff was 1915; those born after 1915 were more liberal than those born before. The younger subjects would have been teenagers when the depression began and in the full bloom of young adulthood when the war broke out.

The most conservative, interestingly, among both the men and women, were those who entered college but did not graduate. College graduates were closer to the center (the women more so than the men), and those who did not go to college at all were somewhere in between.

Among men their place in the political spectrum was frequently a function of occupation. Terman did not have enough numbers to draw conclusions for the women except to say that professional women were the most liberal, businesswomen and office workers were the most conservative, and housewives were in between. The most liberal men were personnel directors or welfare workers* and journalists. The most conservative were military officers, bankers, farmers, and salesmen. Teachers were in the middle; lawyers and doctors to the right of center.

Terman felt he had evidence that intelligence had a connection to political philosophy because he had statistically significant results that

---

* That was the way Terman lumped them.

the people with the highest scores on the Concept Mastery test tended toward the liberal for both men and women. He went back and found that the pattern held in the childhood Stanford-Binet results.

Philosophy aside, about half the Termites listed themselves as Republicans (this was during the Eisenhower years). One-third of the men and two-fifths of the women said they were Democrats. Terman happily noted that no one "claimed membership in the Communist party" although there was a smattering of Socialists.

The Termites displayed their interest in politics by voting; 82 percent of the men and more than 89 percent of the women always voted in national elections and about half voted in local elections. However, only a few engaged in political activity as a vocation or an avocation. Two men were elected superior court judges (one went on to an appointment to the appellate court), and two men were elected to a state legislature. One man ran for the U.S. House of Representatives but lost. Several Termites were active in other people's political campaigns. The most politically powerful of Terman's kids was a young man who at the age of thirty-two became an administrative assistant in the White House and was on the White House executive staff for seven years. Terman, of course, did not identify him.

The family life of his kids was placid. By 1955, 93 percent of the men and approximately 90 percent of the women had married. Those figures match the census data for the U.S. population as a whole. "In other words," Terman and Oden assured everyone, "being highly intelligent apparently is not an obstacle to marriage for either sex; at least that is true for this group." Six men and nine women did not marry until they were over forty. Male college graduates in the study married at about the same rate as male college graduates in the general population, but Terman's women were more likely to marry than women college graduates in general.

The divorce rate for Termites seemed to be slightly lower than that of the general population, although the data on divorce in this country were not solid. Terman and Oden also found that college graduates tended to have fewer divorces than nongraduates; 16 percent of the graduates had been divorced, while 36 percent of those who did not go to college had a failed marriage. Other studies showed the same thing, the researchers said. Again, men who went to college but did not graduate had the highest divorce rate; for women the highest rate was among those who did not go to college at all. "One might speculate," Terman and Oden speculated, "that greater restlessness, discontent, or frustration is felt by the gifted persons who do not complete college and that this may bring about greater instability in personal relationships."

Terman and Oden did find, however, that the men who said they were the most satisfied with married life were the men who never entered college. They had no explanation for that and were amazed enough to end the sentence with an exclamation point!

Childhood IQ scores and Concept Mastery scores as adults had no relationship to divorce rate for men or women, Terman and Oden found.

Eighty-six percent of divorced Termite men and more than 66 percent of divorced Termite women remarried, and the odds of having a happy marriage the second time seemed to be in the Termites' favor.

Terman and Oden believed their data indicated that his kids were happier in their marriages than the general population. He used a shortened form of his marriage satisfaction questionnaire for both the gifted and their spouses and matched the answers with the results of the work of a number of other researchers. Fully 85 percent of his subjects reported themselves happily married; outside data showed only about 65 percent of Americans would say that. Moreover, more than 70 percent of Terman's subjects said they felt their marriage was an aspect of their lives that gave them the greatest satisfaction.

"A discussion of marriage in the gifted group would not be complete without a description of the men and women they marry," Terman and Oden wrote.

- Like the rest of the population, the gifted men tended to marry women younger than they, and the gifted women tended to marry older men.
- More than one-half of the husbands of gifted women and two-fifths of the wives of gifted men were college graduates. One-quarter of the husbands and one-tenth of the wives had graduate degrees.
- A large portion of the men that gifted women married were in the top two occupational classifications.

- The men and women the gifted subjects married were not quite as bright as the gifted were on the whole, although about one-fifth of the spouses had higher Concept Mastery scores than their gifted husbands or wives. As a group, the spouses scored better than the average college graduate.[3]

Terman found that twenty of his gifted men and women married each other. He credits the fact that most of the sample came from two metropolitan areas, Los Angeles and San Francisco, and sooner or later some of his kids would bump into each other, especially considering the large number who went to Stanford and Berkeley. The record of Termite intermarriages, however, was not splendid: three of the ten couples got divorced. Two of these marriages were over quickly and there were no children. The third marriage lasted twelve years and resulted in two children. One of the successful Termite marriages produced four children.

The Terman kids produced 2,452 children by 1955. Eighty-four of the children died and fifteen stillbirths were reported. Accidents were the most frequent causes of death. Since nearly two-thirds of the women were still under forty-five, he presumed they had not ended their childbearing. The reproduction rate was 2.4 children per woman. Since 2.8 was the rate needed to "maintain the stock," Terman and Oden worried that the gifted were not reproducing themselves.*

College graduates tended to have larger families than the other subjects, which Terman and Oden suggested was the result of their superior economic conditions.

Terman tested 1,525 of the offspring of his kids and found that the average IQ was 132.7, exactly the same for boys and girls. The girls tended to be slightly more variable, which was consistent with his earlier findings. Approximately thirty-three percent scored 140 or higher and were, by his definition, gifted. Only 2 percent were below 100. An additional thirteen children, not tested, were known to be retarded ("mentally defective" in Terman and Oden's words). The retardation rate was much lower than what would be expected in the general population. Fifty families had adopted children. Terman did not have the funds to give all the adopted children Stanford-Binet

* A reproduction rate of 2.0 is not a replacement rate because of the effect of mortality rates on population.

tests, but he did test eighteen. Their IQs ranged from 100 to 146. Six of the eighteen were gifted. Terman and Oden did not pick up on this: if heredity is the leading factor in intelligence, how did these families find so many gifted children?

Fifty of his kids had become grandparents, Terman and Oden happily reported, a total of 115 grandchildren. One woman, who had had five children, had eleven grandchildren by 1955. She was fifty-two years old.

Oden, who wrote most of the 1955 study, concluded that "the follow-up for three and one-half decades has shown that the superior child, with few exceptions, becomes the able adult, superior in nearly every aspect to the [general population]. But, as in childhood, this superiority is not equally great in all areas. The superiority of the group is greatest in intellectual ability, in scholastic accomplishment, and in vocational achievement." It was likely the Termites' accomplishments in life were not over, she said. In most cases the gifted adults were just reaching their peaks professionally and personally; in some cases recognition of their achievements might still be twenty years away, particularly for the nonscientists in the group. "And the record shows that the gifted subjects, in overwhelming numbers, have fulfilled the promise of their youth in their later life achievements," she wrote, a statement beyond dispute. In many respects that was one of the things Terman set out to prove — gifted children become gifted adults.

The final question on the forms sent to the Termites was in many ways the most important: "From your point of view, what constitutes success in life?" The answers were diverse. Oden found five that seemed to summarize the answers of the majority of the Termites.

- Realization of goals, vocational satisfaction, a sense of achievement
- A happy marriage and home life, bringing up children satisfactorily
- Adequate income*
- Contributing to knowledge or welfare of mankind; helping others, leaving the world a better place
- Peace of mind[4]

* Reported by men, she wrote, not by women.

Terman spent some time in 1953 and 1954 doing a spin-off from his survey, a study of how the scientists in the gifted group differed among themselves and from the nonscientists. The result, a monograph published in 1954, was a minor contribution, and it is a classic example of getting a government grant (in this case from the Office of Naval Research) to prove the obvious or the trite.

Terman and his son Fred, then dean of engineering at Stanford, classified 800 male subjects. They created categories such as "physical science research" and "medical-biological" for people who did science (including physicians) and "physical or biological science, non-research" for people who studied science, but did not work as scientists. There were separate categories for engineers, social scientists, people in the humanities, lawyers, and people who did not go to college or who attended for less than three years.

By 1951, he proudly announced, his men had published 46 nonfiction books, 21 novels, 1,411 scientific papers, 313 short stories, novelettes, and plays, and 55 essays and works of poetry and criticism.

The physical science group "leads all the others in scientific achievement," followed by the medical-biological contingent and the engineers. The social scientists did not do very well. He found out such things as:

- Most of the physical scientists had parents who were born in the United States.
- The social scientists tended to be less healthy during their youth than the other scientific groups.
- A large proportion of the parents of the scientists thought science was a worthwhile profession.
- The lawyers scored better in "moral traits" than the other groups, with the nonresearchers coming in last.
- The engineers were more mechanically oriented.
- The physical scientists had a higher proportion of professional fathers.
- The medical-biological group was the most sociable; the engineers were the least.
- The physical scientists had the highest work load in high school and the highest grades.

- Lawyers weighed the most.
- The nonpracticing scientists were closer to their fathers than were the practicing scientists; physical scientists and the engineers were the least closest to their fathers.
- The medical-biological group seemed the most happy with the money they were making and with their work. The humanists thought money was less important.[5]

Terman, as he got older, seemed to acquire some understanding of those of his kids who chose not to succeed in conventional, and in his, terms. In a paper he delivered to the American Psychological Association meeting just before he died, he said:

> Although failure to achieve was in certain cases the result of social maladjustment or other defect of personality, it was more often due to lack of ambition or drive to achieve. We know of several in the group who deliberately chose not to enter the usual American rat-race for material success. Nor can I find it in my heart to criticize those who made this choice; it may well be that fewer honors and lower incomes have been fully compensated by greater contentment and lower incidence of anxiety and ulcers.[6]

"If we sometimes get discouraged at the rate society progresses," Oden concluded, "we might take comfort in the thought that some of the small jobs, as well as the larger ones, are being done by gifted people."

Lewis Terman probably did take comfort in that. He did not, however, live long enough to finish the fourth survey.

Terman's later years were filled with family as much as with work. He had his grandchildren and a slew of nieces and nephews, some of whom went to Stanford or spent time in the Terman home. When his brother John, the teacher who had helped him so as a child, began suffering economic hardships, Terman supported him.

Helen, who returned to Stanford after her divorce and took a job as a switchboard operator in a dormitory, eventually became an assistant in one of the administrative departments. Still overshadowed by her father and her brother, she began to take over some of the chores of running the family.

Fred achieved a level of fame that in many ways exceeded his father's and a level of accomplishment that would have made any Termite proud. He became dean of engineering and later provost at Stanford, but his influence went far beyond the university. In 1938 Fred Terman convinced two of his graduate students, William Hewlett and David Packard, to go into business together. He not only encouraged them, but helped with some seed money. By the end of World War II Hewlett-Packard was already a major electronics firm.* Fred did the same thing with several other students and faculty members, including the Varian brothers, who invented the kylstron, a microwave transmitter that is the basis for airborne radar. Varian Associates is still a major defense contractor.

Shortly after the war, he convinced the university to set aside some of its extensive land as an industrial park and then convinced his protégés to move their companies there. This land use had two effects: the establishment of an unusually close relationship between industry and Stanford's engineers, which is still the model for industry-university relations, and the creation of the complex of electronic industries that is now known as Silicon Valley. Fred became known as the "father of Silicon Valley." Even his illustrious father couldn't match that. Lewis bragged that his son was more famous as an engineer than he was as a psychologist. They became one of the few father-son combinations ever elected to the National Academy of Science.

Terman was enormously proud of Fred, and Fred reciprocated widely and publicly. Helen had to make do. One day when she was on vacation, Fred, then university provost, volunteered her early retirement from her job without asking her. Helen returned from vacation to find she was out of work.

Helen died of a stroke in 1973 at the age of seventy. Fred died, also of a stroke, in 1982 at the age of eighty-two.

In 1953 Terman wrote:

Approaching seventy-seven now, I have lived more years than I dared hope for a half century ago and accomplished more than I ever dreamed possible, probably as much as I would have accomplished if I had never had TB. From this distance, it is possible to look back upon the threats

---

* Their first customer was Walt Disney, who needed their equipment to record the sound for *Fantasia*, the first film recorded in high-fidelity stereophonic sound.

of those earlier years without reviving the raw anxiety they caused me. Though I long ago lost my fear of death from tuberculosis (or anything else), I still find myself occasionally counting my pulse or reaching for the clinical thermometer that lies on a table by my bed — perhaps out of habit, perhaps because I want to finish another book and to watch for a while longer developments on the world scene. Besides there are my 1,400 gifted "children," now at mid-life, who were selected by mental tests in 1922; I have already followed their careers for thirty years and should like so much to follow them for another thirty![7]

As he and Oden worked on their 1955 study, his health began to fail. So did Anna's.

In 1954 Anna suffered a stroke. She was mildly paralyzed and required constant nursing. Another stroke the next year greatly affected her memory. On March 26, 1956, she died of a heart attack while her nurse was helping her into bed. Terman was in the hospital at the time, suffering from an injured vertebra, the result of a coughing fit. He was devastated. The house, he reported to a friend, seemed empty without her. They had been married almost fifty-seven years.

Many condolence letters came in. One of the saddest came from Florence Goodenough, his former graduate student and assistant, herself blind from diabetes and unable to write without typographical or spelling errors. Goodenough offered herself as Terman's companion in his loneliness and asked him to join her in New England for the summer. He was beyond traveling, and if he responded, the letter is lost.[8]

By May Terman was out of the hospital and able to work a few hours a week in the office. Oden did most of the work on the fourth report. He was able to write only the first draft of four chapters and notes on the fifth.

A law student moved into the house to keep him company. Terman bought him a television set and spent several hours in front of it himself every day. He had a stroke in September but seemed to recover fully. In November he had another stroke and was unconscious most of the time. When he was awake, his mind was still working. Biographer May Seagoe wrote that one day a colleague came into his hospital room and found Terman mumbling to himself. "You caught me," Terman said. "I can't imagine living without a decent IQ. . . . I'm trying to recall things, to be sure I can recall. . . . This really worries me terribly. So if you see me again with my mouth going, you'll know what is happening."[9]

He died December 21, 1956, three weeks before his eightieth birthday. To a large extent, the life went out of his study as well. Oden finished the fourth study. It remained for his protégés to continue his work.

Chapter Eleven

TERMAN'S WOMEN

LEWIS TERMAN was baffled by the women in his survey. While he seemed to feel he knew how to measure the success of his men (although that was not as clear as he thought it was), he admitted he could not figure out how to assess the lives of his women subjects. He was probably a man who thought he understood women; he loved some (despite the way he treated his wife and daughter), and he surrounded himself with them. But his understanding was not sufficient to help him phrase the questions that would measure how happy his women were with their lives and how successful they were in achieving the things they thought important in life.

Terman missed a good story. His women were ahead of their time.

Terman demonstrated intense loyalty and support for women he knew professionally — mainly his students who later became his colleagues and sometimes his lovers. He seemed to understand the problems women had in the professions, the sexual discrimination rampant in academe no less than in other fields, and he was a strong ally in their battles for equality. His reputation and power made him a good person for a woman to have on her side in her struggle against discrimination. But he had serious problems understanding women who had chosen not to fight those battles, and whatever understanding of women's problems he had did not extend to women in his own home. His attitudes were shared by Anna, and Helen and his granddaughters suffered.

Doris, Helen's oldest daughter and Terman's oldest grandchild, reported several incidents to Terman's biographer Henry Minton. Once during an Easter egg hunt, Anna intervened when Doris seemed to be winning so that she would not find more eggs than Fred's son. Girls didn't beat boys, particularly when the boy was Fred's son. Doris said neither she nor her sister was encouraged to find a career. Whenever Terman wrote letters, they were full of Fred's accomplishments with nary a word about his sister. Helen, of course, had fulfilled her parents' expectations by being a virtual nonentity.

Seating at the Terman dinner table was determined by intellectual rank. Terman and Fred sat at one end of the table holding court and the family women at the other end. Anna was deaf in one ear, and Doris was always seated next to her on the side of her bad ear. That's where Helen used to sit as a girl. Doris's position was handy, the older Termans felt, because she helped the maid. She had, they noted, "domestic inclinations." She majored in chemistry.

The only exception in the family to the women-to-the-back-of-the-table was Sibyl, Fred's wife. She had done some graduate work with Terman before she was married and was continuing to work part-time. She got to sit near the men. She confided to Doris that she found those dinners tedious at best.

Perhaps, Minton noted, Terman's regard for his former students was based on a regard for intellect. His young female protégées were extremely bright women and he could respect that. The women in his family were, he thought, not as bright. He also had a predilection for beauty; many of his women students were as beautiful as they were smart. No one ever suggested Helen was a beauty, and Anna did not age especially well.

But Terman was more complicated than such a simple analysis would indicate. Helen took the Stanford-Binet when she was a girl and had no trouble getting over the cutoff mark. She was gifted. Yet her father gave her no credit for intelligence and discouraged her from doing anything except marrying and reproducing. He kept a file for her in the office with the files of the other members of the gifted group, but it contained very little about her.

What Minton and Doris did not know (they did not have access to the files) was that Helen's folder was full of Doris and Doris's accomplishments. He was very proud of her. Apparently, he never succeeded in getting that across to anyone else, especially Doris.

Terman had considerable data on his female subjects' demographics, financial condition, and family status, beginning with his 1940 survey. He knew, for instance, that the average women's weekly salary then was $144.96, far below the men's. More than 2 percent of the men earned incomes of $10,000 a year or more, but less than 0.5 percent of women earned more than even $5,000 a year. Among women, the highest professional group, of course, was paid the best. Employment for his women did not reflect the increases in wartime employment found in the general population. The percent of working gifted women fell from 48.5 in 1940 to 36 in 1944. Terman suggested the reason was the increase in marriages and the increase in number of children among his women subjects. "The gifted women also did their share of war work," Terman reported, "and although their accomplishments were less spectacular than those of some of the men, they were nonetheless valuable." "Rosie the Riveter" clearly was not a role model for his gifted women, although between fifty and sixty were directly engaged in war work, some with the government and others with industry, including engineering "draftsmen," aircraft workers, a truck driver, statisticians, economists, and secretaries. Twelve enlisted in the military, including one woman marine.

The women continued to make economic progress during the war. The proportion of married women working decreased, from 31.9 percent in 1940 to 23 percent in 1944. Income for women increased. The median in 1944 went up to $2,550, an increase of 52.4 percent. Six women reported earning $6,000 a year and one woman took in $9,200, the highest reported income — slightly less than one-tenth the highest salary earned by a man. By 1955, 50 percent of all of Terman's women were not employed, 42 percent were working full time, and the rest were working part time. Less than 30 percent of the married women had a full-time career, and only 10 percent of them worked part time. Four-fifths of the divorced and widowed women were working to support themselves.

Women with advanced degrees were more likely to have careers than those with only undergraduate degrees. All but two of the women with doctorates or law degrees were working. One doctor and one lawyer had abandoned their careers temporarily to raise a family. The largest percentage of working women were schoolteachers or counselors (123 women, or 20.9 percent), followed by secretaries (106 women, or 19.8 percent). The women also included six physicians, three clinical psychologists, two lawyers, and a research metallurgist. Seven women were listed in *American Men of Science* (which was what that work was called before it was changed to *American Men and*

Women of Science). Five were biologists, two social scientists. One, Terman and Oden reported, helped develop the polio vaccine.

It was Terman and Oden's custom to present a few case studies, always anonymously, to show the scope and variety of the gifted's accomplishments. They did so for a few women, but all was not as presented. In at least one case they gave an incomplete picture, not fudging the data so much as fudging an anecdote. They describe a woman who is clearly "Beatrice." In the 1959 volume she is described in glowing terms, her many accomplishments listed for most of a page. The picture is far removed from the sad woman that Terman described for his files. How many other cases were distorted can't be determined.

Terman's subjects grew up during World War I and lived through the depression and World War II. They spanned the time from when the United States was at its most traditional to the days of feminism. By Terman's standards they were brighter than the average woman and generally came from more enlightened families than the average American family, but even so they had no alternative to traditional social ideas, no alternative philosophy to support and to be supported by. Any societal pressure they might have felt was to live within the traditional family and traditional female roles. They felt none of the pressure of modern, well-educated women to strive for other things besides hearth and family. How did they turn out?

Terman tried in the early 1950s to see how happy the women were, but his success was limited. Fifty-three percent of the housewives who reported back to him said they were deeply satisfied in their work, a lower percentage than professional women (66 percent); about 33 percent reported being fairly contented, and 1 percent wanted out.

He then asked them whether they thought they had lived up to their intellectual abilities. Less than 3 percent of the housewives said they had lived up to their potential "fully," about half said they had done "reasonably well," and all the rest said they had failed to some degree. About 6 percent of the professional women said they had lived up to their potential fully; 62.6 percent said they had done reasonably well, and 30 percent said they had fallen considerably short of what they could have done.*

---

* One would have to factor in sexual discrimination in the working world to understand these numbers in their context.

This was in the 1950s, and the Terman women were clearly ahead of their times. Terman could not rise above his times and his own attitudes. He did not pursue the matter or probe their response to their situation. It was left to Oden to write:

> As a group, the accomplishments of the gifted women do not compare with those of the men. This is not surprising since it follows the cultural pattern to which most of the gifted women as well as women in general have succumbed. Not only may job success interfere with marriage success, but women who do seek a career outside the home have to break through many more barriers and overcome many more obstacles than do men on the road to success. Although the gifted women equaled or excelled the men in school achievement from the first grade through college, after school days were over the great majority ceased to compete with men in the world's work. This characteristic appears to be due to lack of motivation and opportunity rather than to lack of ability.[1]

Sixteen years after his death, two of Terman's women disciples became the first to see if they could succeed where he failed. Pauline S. Sears, the wife of Robert Sears, Terman's successor, and Ann H. Barbee, Oden's successor, put together the first comprehensive report on "career and life satisfactions among Terman's gifted women."

In 1972, they sent out questionnaires and received answers from 64 percent (430) of the original women Termites.* The average age of the women who responded was sixty-two (born in 1910), an age from which they could look back on their lives with some wisdom and judgment.

Sears and Barbee were interested generally in work patterns and satisfaction. They defined four "work patterns" in the women's lives: (1) women who were primarily homemakers, (2) career women, (3) career women who took time off to raise a family, and (4) women who supported themselves but did not consider what they were doing a career.

In order to measure what they called "work pattern satisfaction," Sears and Barbee asked the women a series of questions, called "As It Was," about what they had thought their lives would be like when

---

* It was believed that 573 women (or 85 percent of the original group) were alive at the time.

they were girls. They also asked a series of questions, called "As I Now Would Choose," about their present thoughts about their work lives.

Sears and Barbee also created a series of questions to assess what they called "general satisfaction." They asked how important were the life goals the women made for themselves when they were young — not just work, but life in general — and how successful were they in attaining those goals.

Sears and Barbee also tried to measure an even more elusive feeling, "joy in living."

The women were divided in several subgroups such as single, married, divorced or separated, income workers, homemakers, childless (see the table below).

MARRIAGE, CHILDREN, AND WORK

Category	Percent
Current marital status	
Always single	9
Divorced or separated	11
Widowed	15
Married	65
Head-of-household status	
Head of household	19
Single	9*
Divorced	6*
Widowed	4*
Non–head of household	81
Work pattern	
Income worker	43
Homemaker	57
Children	
Childless	25
Had children	75

* Percent of subgroup.

Sears and Barbee did three other things that would have pleased their mentor and that made their study particularly intriguing. First, they went back to the 1922–1923 forms filled out by the parents and teachers of the subjects to see if anything in those comments could serve as a predictor of how the women would turn out. Second, they devised several hypotheses that seemed logical to them and tested those hypotheses against what the women told them. Third, they had some data on women outside Terman's gifted study that came close enough so they could make some comparisons. One of the virtues of Terman's study, however, also was a weakness: there was nothing like it in all of social science that could provide a control group, a group Terman and his students could use for comparison.

Comparing their data to that from the 1970 U.S. Census, Sears and Barbee found some small differences. Somewhat more of their women were divorced than women in the general population, more were employed full time, and more were professionals. Terman's women had on average 1.79 children,* slightly lower than the number for women in the general population. Total family median income for Terman's women was $18,000 a year, and 68 percent of Terman's women lived in families earning $15,000 a year. Only 27 percent of husband-wife families in the United States were above that figure, so the traditional families that included Terman's women were far more prosperous.

Sears and Barbee did not find their task a simple one. For instance, in trying to discover what they called "work pattern satisfaction," they matched what the young girls had thought their lives would be like ("As It Was") to how the women now approaching retirement age thought their lives had turned out ("As I Now Would Choose"). When the answers to the two questions matched, that is, when the women's lives turned out the way they had hoped, Sears and Barbee labeled their satisfaction high. Sixty-eight percent of the women fell into that category. "Childless women who checked 'career during most of adult life' as what they thought life would be like when they were girls, and then 'career except when raising a family' as their preference now, were coded a high satisfaction; this was only eight cases," Sears and Barbee wrote. When the answers disagreed, Sears and Barbee tried to sort the women into categories of moderate or low satisfaction.

Buried in the numbers was a shift in attitude from 1922, when these Termites were girls, to 1972, the end of their middle age. In

---

* This figure is much less than the figure reported in the 1955 study. No explanation is offered.

1922, 41 percent of the girls thought they would be "primarily a homemaker" (at least as the women remembered it), but in 1972 only 29 percent would chose that as their way of life. In 1922, 30 percent thought they would have careers; fifty years later 37 percent would choose that option. Sears and Barbee suggested that in an era in which more women were working (and they did not list homemaking as income-producing work), "possibly some of the homemaker women felt that they had missed an interesting and challenging part of life."

Using the old records, Sears and Barbee then looked at another way of measuring work pattern satisfaction. Were there harbingers in their childhood or early adulthood of later work satisfaction? They looked at such things as the education and occupation of the parents, "the girls' apparent identification with their mothers and their fathers," the attitudes of their parents, the opinions of their teachers, and the attitude of the girls toward themselves as described in the questionnaires, particularly such things as self-confidence and ambition. They thought up several additional hypotheses to test with the data.

- Women who combined marriage, children, and income-producing work and lived on a higher-than-average income would report higher satisfaction with work than those who did not lead those kinds of lives.
- Girls who came from families in which the parents were highly educated and made a good living, usually as professionals, were more likely to grow up to lead a similar life and to be more satisfied with their work than girls who came from families with less education and lower income.
- Early feelings of self-confidence, lack of inferiority feelings, and ambition would predict later work satisfaction. Girls with these attitudes would also be more likely as adults to work than to be homemakers.[2]

Sears and Barbee soon found that all these hypotheses were wrong.

The first hypothesis, that women who seemed to combine marriage, children, and career would be the happiest — a theory the researchers themselves admitted was naive — was quickly shot down when the data were analyzed. It was particularly wrong in the case of women who had no children; they tended to show a higher degree of satisfaction with what they did with their days than mothers. Women who never married and never had children were the happiest of the lot with their work, over 89 percent reporting high work pattern satisfaction. Job satisfaction also seemed to have little correlation with family income. The percentage of satisfied women below the median was not much different from the percentage above. Those women earning more seemed happy they were doing so, but the total family income seemed to have nothing to do with work satisfaction.

The occupation and education of the parents had no relation to work satisfaction either, but the occupation of the woman did; not surprisingly, professional women were happier than sales clerks or housewives.

Some relationships became apparent after simple cross-tabulation. For instance, income-producing work and vocational advancement were obviously easier for women without children. However, Sears and Barbee found no relationship between work pattern satisfaction and the ratings the parents had given their daughters as children and the children's feelings of self-confidence or any other feeling or attitude.

Sears and Barbee probed further into the lives of the women to assess their success in meeting goals they set when they were young in several areas of life, not just work: occupational success, family life, friendships, richness of cultural life, and "total service to society." They unimaginatively called this measure "general satisfaction 5" after the five factors they employed.*

In reports throughout the fifty years they found some factors that appear to predict the general satisfaction these women had with their lives.

- They found a correlation between satisfaction and what their parents thought about the women as children and what the daughters thought about their parents. Did the parents think their daughters had high self-confidence and low feelings of inferiority in the 1928 questionnaires when the girls were approaching womanhood? For most women who reported being satisfied

---

* They described the measure this way: "General Satisfaction 5 is the quotient obtained by multiplying the planned goal (early adulthood) by the reported success in attaining that goal, adding the five of these multiplied areas, and dividing by the sum of the planned goals for each area. These scores range from 0 to 5. They are continuous, not discrete. A high score means that in those areas she considered important for herself, her success was good. It also takes into account individual differences in the choice of important goals."

with life, they did. Did the women in 1950 remember their parents as being understanding and helpful? Did they admire their mothers? The answers again, for the women happiest with life, were yes.

- The happiest women were the most self-confident women. The women who claimed self-confidence in 1940 also reported high self-confidence as they matured.
- What gave the women satisfaction in the early years (1950 and 1960) still gave them satisfaction later on (1972).
- Good health, having a career instead of just a job, the educational and occupational levels of the husband, and a woman's opinion that her father had a high level of vocational success, also seemed to predict happiness ahead.
- Time devoted to volunteer work — what traditional women were supposed to do outside the home — also gave satisfaction.

Equally interesting were the things that did *not* predict satisfaction, including the number of children, income, and ambition.

Sears and Barbee measured the joy in life, the joie de vivre, by asking the women how successful they were in achieving the kind of life and life-style they sought. The researchers found the answers correlated with general satisfaction 5, and the same predictors seemed to operate, particularly the goal of excellence in work. One strange factor that appeared here, with hints in several other places, was that "teachers reported special ability in math as early as 1922 for those subjects high in joy." Sears and Barbee admitted that one puzzled them, and they offered no explanation.

Sears and Barbee then studied their subgroups separately to see what they could find.

Among single women, "not many in this group rated their parents' marriage as more happy than average, but more than in other groups reported that both father and mother encouraged independence" when the subjects were children. Not many considered their mothers very self-confident. Few of the mothers were professional women. "When we add in the fact that these single women were distinctly better educated than the other groups, a picture emerges of a woman without a strong maternal role model but encouraged to be independent by her parents, and finding her own satisfaction in work for which she has been well prepared by education." Again, there was some correlation between mathematical prowess and single women.

Many more married women than single women remembered their parents' marriages as being happier than average. The married women had less education than the single women, perhaps because marriage and family interfered. A large proportion took great satisfaction in their families, particularly the children, most especially as the children grew up and moved from the home. "Absence of older children from the home may make the heart grow fonder," Sears and Barbee wrote, "and grandmothers are notorious for their love of children." The married women generally reported that their husbands were well educated and in professional or managerial jobs and that incomes were high.

Divorced women generally reported their parents' marriages as not especially happy.* They were not encouraged to be independent. Many remembered their mothers as being very self-confident, however, and many of the mothers were professional women. They did not feel particularly close to their parents or to their families in general. Income was low. And that strange factor, mathematical talent, pops up again: few of the divorced women were particularly good in math.

Since widowhood is seldom voluntary, Sears and Barbee may have made too much of this, but some factors still stood out. Widows largely felt that their parents' marriages were happy, their parents were remembered (in 1940) for encouraging independence, and they were close to their parents. They had the least education of all the subgroups, and their incomes were the lowest. Oddly, they had the highest proportion of women who reported both excellent health and a loss of energy and vitality, as if something had — as indeed it had — been sapped from them. Sears and Barbee reported that this group was not any older than the other groups. Perhaps they were just less fortunate.

Sears and Barbee then compared homemakers and income producers, that is, women who had steady employment for most of their lives. The income workers included 89 percent of the single women,

---

* Sears and Barbee make no allowance for the possibility that a woman who had an unhappy marital experience might denigrate her parents' marriage in her memories.

65 percent of the divorced, 45 percent of the widows, and only 32 percent of the married. Combining marriage and a career was hard even for these very bright women. Most of the homemakers, of course, were married. The researchers found only a few small differences between the homemakers and the income workers in the early years. Many of the homemakers rated their parents' marriages as a little happier, and more of them felt closer to their mothers. Family income of the homemakers was higher — their husbands earned more. The two groups were equal in their assessment of their health, but the income workers reported having more energy. The income workers also were a little higher in math as children.

Next, Sears and Barbee compared childless women with those who had children. One hundred percent of the single women were childless. Women with children reported their parents' marriages happier; their mothers' self-confidence greater; their husbands' occupation, education, and income higher, and family satisfaction greater.

Sears and Barbee found one study of nongifted women they thought was close enough in methodology to be useful in comparing Terman's women with those of the general population. Angus Campbell and his team at the University of Michigan's Institute for Social Research studied 2,164 adults over the age of seventeen in 1975. Their sample was scientifically drawn — which of course was not true of Terman's study — and social scientists are confident it represents a true picture of people in the United States at that time.

Campbell was out to measure the same thing sought by Sears and Barbee, life satisfaction, but he went about it in a different way, the old apples and oranges problem. The sample included 1,249 women. The older ones were generally comparable to but somewhat younger than the women in Terman's group. Only women over the age of thirty (669) in the Campbell study were useful to Sears and Barbee. They seemed to feel the age difference did not prevent comparison, and it's hard to know if they were wrong, but they were compelled to limit some of their comparisons and express some skepticism about the ones they made. The greatest difference between the two groups was that Terman's were chosen for their intelligence and Campbell's for how well they represented the general population.

Sears and Barbee found the following differences between the two groups of women. More of the Terman women were currently married; fewer of them were widowed or divorced. The younger age of Campbell's women might affect these results.

Terman's women were far better educated (67 percent had college degrees compared to only 8 percent of Campbell's women). However, the percentage of women who had college degrees and were working was similar. "In all probability, many of Campbell's 8 percent were as 'gifted' in IQ as our sample," Sears and Barbee wrote.

The women in Terman's group who went to college but did not graduate had a higher level of employment than women in Campbell's group with similar educational experience. Women in Campbell's group who went to college but did not graduate did no better occupationally than did those who had only a high school diploma. Sears and Barbee thought that a higher level of intelligence plus family background gave the Terman women an advantage in succeeding in the work force despite the lack of a college degree. They added that here again the sample may have been skewed by the age differences.

Campbell had his women fill out a questionnaire that ranked level of satisfaction with life as a whole. In both Terman's and Campbell's groups, those most satisfied with life were women who were married, with or without children, followed by the widowed, the single, and finally, the divorced.

"All results so far show that absence of children contributes to satisfaction with work, at least in this group of sixty-year-old women," Sears and Barbee wrote. "The strain of thinking and acting on children's development ... apparently contributes to less wholehearted devotion to work and satisfaction in it." That apparently was so in the Terman women even when the children were grown. Women with children, they added, may have come late and with less preparation to the work force.

In measures of general satisfaction both groups were in agreement. Housewives were the most satisfied. "The time release from job requirements no doubt permits the housewives to gain more satisfaction from other aspects of life: friendship, cultural activities, volunteer service to the community, and perhaps children and husbands. In regard to work pattern satisfaction, the most satisfied are the employed women."

The most conspicuous difference between the women of the two studies was when education was related to satisfaction. What Sears and Barbee found was worth the effort, even if it does seem self-evident: "*College graduated housewives were lower in satisfaction than are employed married college [graduates] in every one of their measurements* [italics added]."[3]

Sears and Barbee wrote:

> Finally, disregarding the specific hypotheses, what can we say about the factors that have contributed to the joy and well-being of these gifted women over the last half-century? Clearly, there is no single path to glory. There are many women with high satisfactions, both in the general sense and with respect to their work, who belong in each of the subgroups we have distinguished.[4]

What the researchers could conclude, however, was that "happiness under various circumstances depends on one's earlier experiences."

> Married women with children are more likely to be happy if their own parents' marriage was a good one, and if there was an affectionate and warm relationship between them and their parents. But such a relationship does not guarantee happiness at average age sixty-two, if the life style followed by the gifted woman was one that led her into a single life or a childless married life.[5]

Being satisfied with life, work, and family depends on the total personality of the women, Sears and Barbee reported. What makes one woman happy does not necessarily give satisfaction to another woman whose experiences have been different. Their study of Terman's women argues compellingly that intelligence is by no means the universal key to a happy life. However, in many cases intelligence may have made the women better equipped to cope with whatever slings and arrows life threw at them. "There are various suggestions that our gifted sample in many instances identified circumstances which would allow for the possibility of a happy life on their own without a husband, took advantage of these, and were able to cope comfortably with their lives thereafter," the researchers wrote.

That the Terman women were ahead of social trends became apparent from research reported by Pauline Sears in 1980, using data collected three years earlier. The average age of the women was sixty-six. Sears found that 60 percent of Terman's gifted women had worked full time at one point or another in their lives. That was a majority not likely to be matched by any other group of women their age. "This is a rapidly growing trend in the general population of women of all ages, but the Terman women, born on average in 1910, have been in the vanguard of this movement," she said.

To find out more about this phenomenon, she divided the women who answered her questionnaire into three groups: career women, homemakers, and women who worked because they had to or wanted to for the income. The career women averaged $13,000 a year, while women who worked for income earned around $8,000. The married women had an approximate family income of $36,000, single women $20,000, widows $18,000, and divorced women $13,000.

All three groups were about equal in the state of their health, they reported. Sears felt that the gifted women were as a group probably healthier than women in the general population, in part because so few of them were poor.

The kind of work the women did was influenced by marital status, but marital status was not influenced by the kind of work. Marriage determined work patterns, not the other way around. This, Sears felt, raised an interesting question: Do bright women go to work because of a love of challenge, boredom, a need for independence, a need for money? Many women said they went to work to be with other people, especially those who worked for income (who did it also, of course, for the money). Career women tended to like the creativity, stimulation, and personal growth they received from their jobs.

Married women got much of their life satisfaction from their marriages; divorced women from cultural activities. Women without children found happy lives with friendships and relationships within their careers. Homemakers, "supported by good earning husbands, enjoyed some activities not open to more time-constrained career women." Sears wrote:

Times are changing. Our report previous to this (1972) showed that many more of the apparently comfortable homemakers wished that they had so guided their lives that they had incorporated a career after raising their children, than did career women wish for the homemaker alternative. The "always" homemakers felt, apparently, that they had missed a challenging part of living. Perhaps our times may change more in the future so that both decent child-rearing and useful career life can be done by energetic women with motivation and who have some help from others.[6]

Another researcher to go back into the 1977 Terman data to study women was Carole Holahan, now of the University of Texas.* The women were five years older than they were in the Sears and Barbee research. More were retired or considering retirement, and the oldest children had probably left home. Holahan studied 352 (about 70 percent of those believed still alive) to measure their "life satisfaction." About 25 percent of those who worked were now retired. Almost 9 percent were spinsters, 61 percent married, about 35 percent separated or divorced, and 20 percent widows.

Holahan found that the women had not changed greatly in the five years since Sears and Barbee collected their data. The women satisfied with life then remained essentially satisfied with their lot as they began to ease beyond middle age.

The median family income for the homemakers was $23,150, for the career women $21,000, and for the job holders $14,100.

The women who held jobs for the sake of working were less satisfied with life overall and liked their jobs least. It appeared to have nothing to do with the level of income. Women who were divorced or widowed, not surprisingly, reported themselves less satisfied with their lives, but the career women among them seemed to fare better emotionally. Homemakers and career women who had been widowed did better than widowed job holders.

Career women seemed to be most motivated by a pursuit or ambition for excellence, Holahan reported, a finding similar to what Terman researchers found in the A group of successful men. Even job holders were more highly motivated in that regard than housewives. Divorced job holders had more trouble finding creativity in their work, disliked competition more, and were less influenced by recognition.

Obviously, retired women had more spare time for other pursuits. Holahan found, however, that they generally chose pursuits that did not require great intellectual effort. They read less than those who had not retired. "Perhaps this reflects a greater interpersonal orientation

---

* Holahan and Robert Sears will be the authors of the next major survey of the Termites, due in 1993.

among employed women when they are retired, for which they may have not had the time when they were working," Holahan suggests.

Married women were happier overall than women who were not; divorced women were the least happy. The fact that married women had double the income would seem to help, but Holahan could find no statistical correlation. Women seemed to depend less on money for their happiness and satisfaction than did men.

Women who were working still reported slightly better health than those who had retired, she found. They were the women who seemed to enjoy competition and recognition more, although the retired women seemed more financially motivated and more determined to maintain an excellent standard of living.

Homemakers returning her questionnaires "did not show indications of unhappiness relative to the other groups."

> It is possible that, when faced with lesser opportunities and support for career attainment in their youth, these women channeled their abilities and interests into other realms. . . . In fact, as suggested by Sears and Barbee, it is possible that the preference for careers reported by homemakers in 1972 may have reflected the fact that these women were viewing their lives in the 1970s, a time of expanding aspirations and opportunities for women.[7]

Career women had several advantages over women who went to work because they were widowed or divorced, even women who suspended their careers to raise a family. They were happier as they aged and the married career women suffered fewer of the financial and psychological problems that occur when a spouse dies. Their careers acted as something of a life jacket.

By and large, Holahan found the Terman women reported high levels of life satisfaction and happiness. But since there was no way to compare them with any other group of women, she could not make any conclusions about whether intelligence had anything to do with their satisfaction.

Terman's women were in the vanguard of several current trends. Compared to women in the general population, they were quicker to join the work force, they waited longer to marry and have children, and more were childless. The career women did well and were happier. The divorced women were more likely to find happiness. The single women were happier than most working women, and that happiness came from the work, not from the money. And many of the women, knowing of their mental abilities — in part because the Terman office reminded them every decade or so — felt the frustration of their conventional roles and of a life that might have been. They were ahead of their time.

AGE

Ancel

ANCEL KEYS LEFT HARVARD just after he returned from Chile. He left, in part, because he had been unhappy with the work he was doing at the fatigue laboratory and in part because the Mayo Clinic offered to double his salary. His Harvard colleagues clucked that he was leaving the cultural center of America for a dismal hole somewhere in Minnesota. He used his first days at the clinic to write up the papers from the Chilean expedition. At the Mayo, he met his second wife, Margaret, who would become his chemical assistant and later his editor.

Ancel went from the Mayo to the University of Minnesota. He soon became one of the most prolific scientists in the United States, grinding out scientific papers at a tremendous rate. Between 1938 and 1949 his lab produced 166 scientific papers, many of them in major journals. Ancel had 183 coauthors. We know, because Terman kept count. Terman finally gave up trying to collect Ancel's papers, keeping instead a curriculum vitae that simply listed them. He did collect the numerous magazine and newspaper articles about this most prominent Termite.

Ancel was made full professor at the age of thirty-three at a salary of $6,000 a year. He seemed particularly happy with his affiliation with the medical school, doing some work on x-ray imaging of the beating human heart, a technique he traveled around the country demonstrating. Terman, in a memo dated 1939, reported "he has an almost ideal set-up in Minnesota. Teaching confined to graduate students of whom he has seven at present who are working for advanced degrees. Does little routine lecturing. . . . Gets considerable research money from the medical school. Has an extremely attractive personality. Is modest but not too reserved. Talks well and appears to have a well-balanced personality." His office was in the football stadium. Terman's only lament to Ancel was that he wished some of his more technical writings could be rewritten in lay terms.

In 1940 Ancel left the Department of Physiology in the medical school to found his own department, the Laboratory of Physiological Hygiene in the School of Public Health.

Ancel and Margaret began to study the growth and development of the heart in children, going to Mexico City to x-ray Mexican children and compare them with children x-rayed in San Francisco and Minneapolis. He was in Mexico when World War II broke out. The war would make him famous.

The U.S. War Department asked Ancel if he would work on developing emergency rations to be used by paratroopers. Ancel first tried buying various foods and testing them in various combinations and amounts at a local army base. He and Colonels Rohland Isker and Paul Logan later tested different versions at Ft. Benning in Georgia. "At the time we were trying this out, the general in charge of all the infantry for the whole army was there, and he saw what was going on and without saying anything to me, he decided that this is going to be the ration for emergency for *all* the infantry. And I was appalled because . . . it was designed as the sort of thing you could put in your pocket for a couple of days at most, not as a sustenance diet."

The result was the development of the K ration, the universally detested, if effective, field chow for the American GI. The "K" stands for Keys. The Wrigley Company in Chicago won the contract to produce it and turned it out by the millions.

In another experiment for the war department in which he analyzed the sweat of subjects who exercised in warm rooms, he determined that vitamins are not lost in sweat, and therefore there was no need to feed soldiers in the tropics vitamin supplements.

Ancel was fascinated by another aspect of diet and nutrition: starvation. What happens when the human body gets little or no food? To find out, he did a series of now famous tests known as the Minnesota Experiment. Besides studying the effects of starvation, he felt it imperative to find the best way to rehabilitate the undernourished and starving.

The full knowledge of what was going on in German concentration camps was not yet public, so the Holocaust had no influence on the study. But starvation, limited or full, was hardly unknown in wartime; the first scientific studies of hunger and starvation had begun around the time of World War I. "I had various reports that people were starving in some parts of Europe," he remembered. Of particular concern were Norway, Denmark, and the Netherlands.

Much of his work appeared in the chillingly titled two-volume publication *The Biology of Human Starvation*. In 1944 Ancel and his colleagues took thirty-six conscientious objectors — all of whom volunteered for the study — and put them on carefully measured near-starvation diets. The volunteers had prepped for the study by eating well: during a three-month control period the normal calorie intake for each subject was determined, an average of 3,492 calories. When they were ready, plump and satisfied, the researchers cut their intake to half their normal diets. The meals weren't bad; there just wasn't much of them.

The psychological effects of the diet were profound, affecting every aspect of the men's lives, from their dreams to their behavior. They thought about little else but food ("I have no more sexual feeling than a sick oyster," one remarked), and they fell into the depths of apathy.

The study is famous among psychologists and was of great interest to Terman, but the psychological aspects were not of special interest to Ancel. Like many physical scientists, he found the social sciences mushy; he liked real numbers meaning real things. The psychological aspects of the study were left to others on the team.

Ancel and his colleagues found that recovery from starvation was not rapid or complete in all respects, even for these men who had had at least some nutrients. The dizziness and apathy disappeared quickly, but the weariness, loss of sex drive, and weakness lingered, even after twelve weeks. It took three months for their table manners to become reasonably civilized. Some became more depressed when their diets were improved. Simply giving food to the starving does not end the effects of starvation.

Unfortunately, the results were not finished in time to help the victims of the Holocaust when the war ended. "We were a little too late to help them as much as we might," he said. "We should have had the answers two years earlier."

By 1948 Ancel was named director of the Laboratory of Physiological Hygiene, making $13,000 a year and running an operation with more than forty employees. He and Margaret had one son and two daughters and a home on Lake Owasso near St. Paul.

Some time after the war ended, Ancel had noticed a newspaper obituary of an American businessman who died of a massive coronary. It struck him that he was seeing more such items in the newspapers and wondered if there was some kind of coronary epidemic affecting Americans.

He started a study with Henry Taylor and other staff members in 1948 looking at the health of 286 Minnesota executives to see what characteristics of the men, all in apparent good health, could warn of eventual heart attacks. Twenty-seven of the subjects suffered heart attacks during the study and the only common denominator was a cholesterol count in their blood over 240. The cholesterol count turned out to be a better predictor than electrocardiograms and was an enticing clue to one of the causes of coronary heart disease.

Ancel was not the first to notice the relationship between diet and heart disease. He was the first, however, to put it into context and to get the message across to the public. His work has probably had greater influence on our welfare than the work of any other person in Terman's study.

Evidence of a link between what we eat and how long we live goes back to the beginning of the century. A Dutch scientist reported in 1916 that the people of Java, then part of the Dutch East Indies, were far less prone to arteriosclerosis than were their Dutch masters. The Javanese ate less fat and had less cholesterol in their blood. But the serum cholesterol of Javanese stewards on Dutch steamers who ate a Dutch diet equaled that of their Dutch shipmates.

World War II provided further evidence, if indirectly. In Scandinavia and Holland it was discovered that deaths caused by coronary heart disease decreased during the German occupation when wartime restrictions changed the diet to include less fat. It went up again as soon as the Germans left and the Danes, Norwegians, and Dutch returned to their traditional diet.

"Well, we now know that in a severe shortage of food, especially a shortage of meats and things like that, the cholesterol level in the blood goes way down," Ancel said. "Putting these things together I said, 'Okay, let's see if I could do an experiment.' " He did. It ran for eight years at Hastings State Hospital, a Minnesota mental institution, and produced what is now called the Keys equation, which predicts the serum cholesterol level from the quantity of fatty acids in the diet.

In 1951 Ancel went to Oxford University as a visiting professor for a year. At a United Nations nutrition meeting in Rome he was told by an Italian physiologist, Gino Bergami, that coronary heart disease was of little concern in Naples. Intrigued, he took a leave from Oxford and he and Margaret went to Naples to see for themselves. Bergami was right; only rich men had heart attacks there. The average Neapolitans ate red meat, lean, only about once a week, "butter was almost unknown, milk was never a beverage except in coffee or for infants, *colazione* on the job often meant a half loaf of French bread crammed with boiled lettuce or spinach," Ancel wrote. They ate pasta every day, and about one-fourth of the calories in their diet came from olive oil and wine, both containing little or no saturated fats. Pasta, olive oil, and wine, apparently, are good for you. Tests taken by Margaret revealed that these Neapolitans had serum cholesterol counts around 160 or 170, well below what Ancel was used to seeing in Minneapolis.

Visits to a Neapolitan hospital revealed that among cardiac patients valve problems far outnumbered angina or other typical symptoms of coronary heart disease; heart attacks were uncommon. A trip to Spain, which also had a relatively low fat diet, showed similar results; heart attacks were rarely seen except in the private hospitals catering to the upper class.

Back in Minnesota, the Hastings tests showed that decreasing fat and increasing carbohydrates in the diet or the reverse had a definite effect on cholesterol in the blood. The pattern was clear.

Ancel, along with Paul Dudley White (famed as President Eisenhower's cardiologist) and several other colleagues, returned to Naples to do further tests. They confirmed the earlier findings, which were released late in 1952.

Studies around the world followed. The Bantus of South Africa almost never suffered from coronary heart disease. In Bologna, Italy, where the diet differs radically from that of Naples, obesity and heart disease were common. In Sardinia, cholesterol levels were low despite the abundance of eggs in the diet; the Sardinians ate little meat and only small amounts of dairy products.

When Paul Dudley White asked the pathology department at

Kyushu Medical School hospital for a sample of a diseased Japanese heart, the best it could do was the heart of a physician who had spent thirty years in Hawaii eating, presumably, an American diet.

Ancel and Martti Karvonen, later to become surgeon general of Finland, studied the phenomenal rate of coronary heart disease in Finland. The Finns had a diet with staggering amounts of fat. "A favorite after-sauna snack," Ancel wrote, "was a slab of full-fat cheese the size of a slice of bread on which was smeared a thick layer of 'that good Finnish butter.' " The Finns died of heart attacks at a rate even higher than did Americans, and 15 percent of the sample had a cholesterol count over 300.

Ancel's crowning achievement was a project known as the Seven Countries Study, which ranged around the world collecting data.

The prototype of the Seven Countries Study was a trial in southern Italy. (They found that fly specks on the test paper altered the cholesterol values; they discovered that fly specks contain cholesterol.) In the course of the international study, researchers measured the blood cholesterol and many other characteristics and dieticians analyzed the diets of hundreds of representatives of the populations, sixteen groups of men in seven countries, a total of 12,786 men aged forty to fifty-nine, with follow-up examinations scheduled every five years. Funding came from the Commonwealth Fund, the same people who backed Terman's gifted study.

The Seven Countries Study is still going on, thirty-four years after Ancel began it. In the United States the researchers studied 2,571 men employed by the railroads in the Pacific Northwest. After twenty-five years almost 1,500 had died, and the study continues, comparing the characteristics of the living and the dead.

By 1960 Ancel's scientific work became available to the public when he and Margaret published *Eat Well and Stay Well*. The book, which became a best-seller, 108,000 copies in the first edition alone, was the first to emphasize to the public the dangers of high-fat, cholesterol-rich, high-calorie diets. This led to a *Time* cover.

Keys was the first to suggest that eggs, dairy products, and marbled beef could be harmful in excess. He claimed that Americans eat too much. He found the American diet was almost 40 percent fat calories, was loaded with saturated fatty acids, and averaged 3,000 calories a day when 2,300 would do. The extra weight these calories bring, he wrote, lead to increased risk of cancer, heart disease, and diabetes.

"Sunday dinner is no longer special," he said. "We have Sunday dinner every day."

Other research by other scientists, particularly a widely publicized study of residents of Framingham, Massachusetts, have proven Keys's theory, and his work is now considered part of medical wisdom.

Ancel, at age eighty-seven, in 1991, still maintained an office in Minneapolis and his house on Lake Owasso, but lived the rest of the year in southern Italy. He had a computer in each of his homes and worked seven or eight hours a day on his epidemiological studies.

"With friends we bought land stretching from the road down to the sea seventy meters below," he wrote, "the slope of Monte della Stella rising 1,131 meters [almost 4,000 feet] behind us. Across the sea 220 kms due west is the Costa Smeralda [Emerald Coast] of Sardinia; the same distance south is the eastern tip of Sicily and the Strait of Messina, the passage between the Tyrrhenian and Ionian Seas where the whirlpools and racing currents . . . terrified sailors in the days before steamships. A beautiful five-hour drive takes us to the Adriatic and the car ferries to Greece and Yugoslavia, convenient for the continuation of work on the subjects of the Seven Countries Study. This is far from the rigors of winter in Minnesota; year 'round we enjoy the outdoors almost every day.

"My next door neighbors are a former student of mine, now a professor in the University of Perugia, Italy, a retired professor of cardiology at Northwestern University Medical School, and the former surgeon general of Finland. Perugia is famed as the headquarters of the Mafia in southern Italy, but Italian friends say that does not mean I am a 'mafioso.' "

"I have poor vision in one eye due to macular degeneration," he wrote from his Minnesota home. "I have had two bouts of TIA [temporary ischemic attack] which much disturbs my sense of balance so I can do no physical work. I am largely confined to my computers and word processors. My wife Margaret is a great help; she checks the errors she sees on the monitor."

The American Heart Association has established an annual Ancel Keys Lecture. He is an honorary citizen of two towns in Italy. The oldest known surviving Termite, Keys is still producing scientific papers, Margaret acting as his copy editor. His mind is full of names and numbers and things to say.

Jess

ALTHOUGH DESI ARNAZ is frequently cited as the originator of the idea, Jess and Harry Ackerman were the ones who decided to film "I Love Lucy" in front of three film cameras and a live audience.

"The truth is that no one particular person came up with the idea," Jess wrote in 1973. "It developed in conferences and was dictated by necessity. . . . The fact surfaced that Ralph Edwards was doing his television show ["Truth or Consequences"] with moving film cameras. We called in his production manager, Al Simon, who saw no reason why a comedy show couldn't be done that way. After all, in motion pictures before they knew how to cut sound, they used as many as six cameras. Furthermore, he told us that a George somebody [Fox] had developed a system for keeping the cameras in sync. We hired Al and George whatever his name was."

Ackerman knew Ball was "dead without an audience." Jess knew that by filming in this way he could guarantee that each of CBS's affiliates would get a first-class print of the show, as required by the contract. CBS's New York office resisted the innovation and Ackerman and Jess had to put their careers on the line trying to convince them.

Jess, meanwhile, had joined his two cowriters from "My Favorite Husband," Bob Carroll, Jr., and Madelyn Pugh, grinding out scripts for the show. "He and Bob and Madelyn wrote thirty-eight scripts in as many weeks," one colleague said. "Amazing!" His director's chair on the set said "JESS OPPENHEIMER — Boy Producer." Ball called him "The Brains."

A motion picture studio was renovated to accommodate the unusual stage Jess wanted. On September 8, 1951, three hundred people took their seats in the newly constructed bleacher in the General Services Studio for the first filming of "I Love Lucy."

Jess, who had been described by Melita Oden as having no discernible sense of humor, had created the seminal comedy program in the history of television and became one of the country's best-paid comedy writers and producers. The show revolutionized television in another way: the manner in which the episodes were filmed made it possible for the program to be rebroadcast by independent stations, virtually creating the syndication market. "Lucy" has never been off the air. Much of the economic basis of all American commercial television derives from Jess's creation.

"I, too, have been thrilled by the success of 'I Love Lucy,'" he wrote Terman. "It's one of the crazy things where the right combination suddenly happens and, although you're doing all the very same things for years, it suddenly goes crazy and becomes a tremendous hit."

He described television as "an unbelievably demanding monster with a tremendous appetite for material. For anyone to commit himself to writing and producing a half-hour motion picture every week for as far into the future as the eye can see or the ulcers will stand is completely insane, but we are so much a slave to the technical progress that is being made that we go right on signing contracts for our own destruction. I could even forgive science for discovering the atom bomb if they could only un-invent television and let me return to radio."

Jess stayed head writer, producer, and part owner of the first 153 programs of the show, which ran for six years and was rated first for four of them. When the show was sold to CBS for $5 million, Terman wrote Jess: "You have certainly reached the top of the heap." Carl Reiner told Jess's son that Jess and the "Lucy" team were the models for the another great comedy hit on television, "The Dick Van Dyke Show."

The relationship with Ball did not end well. Several years after Jess left the show, he was disturbed to see that her new shows for CBS ("The Lucy Show" and later "Here's Lucy") were using the same "Lucy" character and plots he had created for "I Love Lucy." (The Lucy in the new shows even had the same maiden name —

McGillicudy.) CBS claimed that the Lucy character in the new shows was totally different and that the story ideas were all new and original. Jess saw this as a matter of principle. He had left the show, he said, precisely because he felt that they had run out of fresh ideas and that they had done everything that could be done with those characters and that format. He asked CBS to stop using his work or at least to acknowledge that it was his work and to pay him as provided in his contract. He finally (reluctantly, said Estelle Oppenheimer) sued and won a monetary settlement from CBS. Unfortunately, one of the necessary defendants in the suit was Ball's new production company, "which Lucy took very personally," Jess's son remembered.

"She never spoke to him again," Estelle said. "Never. Never spoke to Jess again, even though he was still crazy about her." He wrote a foreword to a biography of Ball calling her the greatest person he ever worked with.

"He felt very hurt about it, he really did," Estelle continued. "He was almost forced into suing because there was no way to get them to stop. He really didn't want to. He said, 'I hate airing dirty linen in public.' All of his friends — I guess we pushed him to do it."

Busy as he was, Jess continued tinkering, garnering more than twenty patents, including, ironically, a new kind of laugh track machine that stops the actors long enough to pause for the synthetic laughter. He also invented the in-the-lens prompter, which is still in use. Originally called the Jayo Viewer, it is the way everyone from television anchors to the president of the United States knows what to say when the camera is on. He developed several devices to help children with handicaps such as his. His inventions often came, he told Terman, after he explained them to Estelle and she said "That's impossible."

Jess even came up with one for Terman, an IQ test in the form of a game for home use. Terman said it was a neat idea, but if he agreed to help, he would get thrown out of the American Psychological Association because untrained (and unpaid) people would be administering the test and would likely misuse or misinterpret the results.

Jess was responsible for finding one of the missing Termites. While he and his family were remodeling their new Brentwood home in 1961, they lived in a West Los Angeles hotel. They frequently ate at a small sandwich shop, called the Squirrel Cage, and occasionally spoke with the small, sad man named Irving who was the owner, cook, and head waiter. One day Irving and Jess began chatting about their childhoods. They discovered they had gone to the same high school, Lowell, in San Francisco and probably knew each other forty years earlier. Then Irving revealed he had been a member of the Terman study.

Jess immediately contacted the Terman office. In a memo for the file, Melita Oden wrote:

"It was really a sad case. . . . Irving was a 'whipped man.' He has long been operating a little restaurant which amounts to little more than a lunch stand. His business had recently failed and he is selling the place and was planning, at least temporarily to get a job as a short-order cook. . . . The Oppenheimers talked with Irving quite a bit and he confided in them about his troubles and lack of success, and Jess says he is sure that is why Irving hasn't filled out our last questionnaire. He lives with his mother and apparently leads a rather lonely and defeated life. Jess also says that Irving would be at the lower end of the success ladder in any appraisal of achievement."

It turned out that Irving had been married briefly when he was a young man. The marriage ended disastrously, without children, and Irving moved back in with his mother, going from job to job, small business to small business. The meeting with Jess was the last contact the Terman office had with Irving. He disappeared again.

Jess and Estelle lived in their Brentwood house for twenty-eight years. He was one block from his office and one block from the Brentwood Country Club where he played golf every day. "That was his small world, he said," Estelle recalled. He had a workshop at home. "I think he was as proud of his carpentry as he was of his writing," Estelle said. He was in his shop so often his son thought at first his father was a carpenter. Carpentry looks more like work than does writing.

"He was not 'on' like many joke writers we know," Estelle said. She did not recall his being particularly funny at home, although his son, Gregg, when he was grown up and a lawyer in Los Angeles, remembered him as a joke teller. He collected a bunch of corny "high school" jokes he repeated constantly and came home every day with a dirty joke from the golf course.

"His mind was always working. He was always preoccupied with some invention or some thought. It took a little while to get his attention. He was wonderful," Estelle said.

If Melita Oden found him pushy and forward as a child, those who knew him as an adult found the opposite. "He was anything but pushy and forward," Estelle said. "He was so laid-back and almost shy, to a degree that when asked to give lectures, he wouldn't. 'I'll answer questions,' he said, 'that's fine.' "

Terman, besides taking pride in Jess's accomplishments, found that he liked Jess and his family enormously. After one family visit to Stanford, he wrote: "I have never met a family who impressed me more favorably. They are all extremely attractive in appearance (Gregg is very handsome) and charming in personality. They were all characterized by a complete lack of pretentiousness and by genuine friendliness. I asked Mrs. Oppenheimer if their household was anything like 'I Love Lucy,' and she said, 'No indeed, not at all.' Then Jess said that their home life is completely separate from his professional life, and that they rarely go out in Hollywood, that they live in an area of professional people, chiefly lawyers and doctors, and had little to do with show business socially."

In 1956 Jess left CBS and joined NBC as an executive. He produced several segments of three popular and well-respected anthology programs, "Kaleidoscope," "The U.S. Steel Hour," and "Chrysler Theater." He worked on "Get Smart," "The Debbie Reynolds Show," "Angel," and such retrospective programs as "CBS Salutes Lucy: Her First 25 Years" for CBS, two versions of "NBC: The First 50 Years," and the "General Motors 50th Anniversary Show." He was nominated for an Emmy half a dozen times and won two.

Jess retired in 1978, three years after suffering a heart attack. He continued writing and playing golf daily until his death in December 1988 due to complications from major colon surgery.

"I have lost a dear friend and a true genius of our business," said Ball on Jess's death. "I owe so much to his love of the business, his creativity, and his friendship."

Said William Asher, director of most of the Lucy episodes, "Jess has left a legacy for the world, for which he should be thanked and revered. As for me, he quite simply taught me everything I know about comedy."

Melita Oden was wrong.

Shelley

IN 1950 Terman, who had a weakness for beautiful, smart women, filled out a field report on Shelley Mydans, but admitted in pencil on the bottom, "Ratings possibly biased, as she is one of my most favorite subjects."

Shelley and Carl eventually settled for good in Larchmont, New York.

In 1955 she reported from vacation in Portugal that all was well. Carl was assigned to Time-Life's London bureau and the family was comfortable in a house in Hampstead. "I've been fortunate enough to attain a little spiritual growth in the past year and have been attending a wonderful 12th century church down near Smithfield market. I've also been working on another book but this one takes a great deal of research and more thought and planning, and I'll feel lucky if I can do so much as to get a good start on it this year."

The novel, *Thomas*, about St. Thomas à Becket, made the *New York Times* best-seller list and earned more than $100,000, helped no doubt by the publicity generated by the coincidentally popular play and movie on the same subject. Later, after two years in Tokyo and three in Singapore, Shelley published another successful novel, set in eighth-century Japan.

Shelley filled out her forms regularly, a chore, it seemed, but one she accepted. She, like many others, bristled a bit at the questions Terman constructed to try to measure the success of his now aging kids.

"I've published two books since 1959," she wrote in 1972, "but I wonder if this kind of external accomplishment means much. I wonder if this questionnaire is really getting at the important aspects of one's life? Are earnings and honors the mark of the gifted?"

Perhaps not, but Terman seemed incapable of finding any less material way to measure success and was particularly stumped trying to measure the success of the women in his program.

"Please forgive me for not returning your 1977 questionnaire," she wrote to Terman's successors. "I didn't seem to fit into any of your categories and it was difficult for me to frame my answers."

She wasn't going to fill out the 1978 form either, but instead wrote a letter describing her life, which by then included three books and several magazine articles.

"A great deal of my energy since my 'retirement' has been absorbed in moving from place to place, adjusting to new customs and languages, schooling for the children, etc. Since 1949, we have lived in Tokyo, Palo Alto, London, New York, Moscow, Larchmont, Tokyo again, Greenwich, Connecticut, Singapore, and again Larchmont for periods ranging from two to five years. My husband retired in 1972 at the age of sixty-five, but continues to do exactly the same work as he did for thirty-five years before that. Our gross income for the past five years has stayed approximately the same. . . ." She did not remember ever telling Terman that marriages work best when the husband is "the whole show," and she retracted that statement looking back in retrospect. "That's a quote from that era, isn't it. I take it back. I've matured a little, and had my consciousness raised."

In 1991 Shelley was working on another book, this one about the patriarch Abraham and his life in Mesopotamia before he heard the word of God.

"He is the Father of the three great religions of the Western world," she said. "And most scholars think now that there was such an individual, and they pinpoint him at about 1800 B.C. This is a fascinating period. Archeologists are digging up a lot of what life was like. So bit by bit, I am writing a novel about the youth of this man and what affected him.

"This is, of course, fiction. I am not trying to be scholarly. But I'm picking things up from the scholars in the field like a magpie. That is what I really am. I pick up things from anybody who knows something. But I am lazy. If you are going to write anything about me, you ought to say first attribute: lazy."

In 1991 her son, Seth, was a reporter and a former foreign correspondent for the *New York Times*. Her daughter, Shelley, was a lawyer in Sacramento in the California Attorney General's office.

Her sister, Rosemary, a singer on the New York stage, had died of leukemia in 1971. Her brother, Sandy, was in a rehabilitation center, suffering the effects of a stroke. Shelley thought the Terman study may have stunted his achievement in life.

"I think it changed Sandy's life — that along with my mother's belief that he was a perfect little boy. It took him five years to get through high school. I think perhaps his attitude was: 'I'm a near-genius (as we believed we were graded in the Terman study) and I don't have to work.' So he never lived up to his potential.

"Sandy is charming and made friends easily and all that and supported his family in very good style. But I sometimes think he is something like an iceberg; you only saw a little tip of Sandy and everything else was going on underneath."

The study, she said, affected her, producing lazy study habits.

"But I thought I was okay, partly it was the family, but partly it was knowing you were something special."

The Tadashi Family: Emily

EMILY TADASHI remarried in 1936 to Edward Goodwyn, a photographer. He was barely able to make a living, so the family's economic condition scarcely improved. One of her sons told Terman that no one in the family was optimistic about the marriage, that Goodwyn was not nearly as bright as his mother. Goodwyn, however, provided something like a normal family life for the children, and a non-Oriental cover. Patience, one of the daughters, changed her name in high school from Tadashi to Goodwyn.

Emily and most of her family had adopted the Baha'i faith, a gentle religion that originated in Persia. Even in her poverty, Emily retained a nobility that impressed all who met her. One field-worker wrote in her file:

"My first impression of Mrs. Tadashi is quite confirmed. She is very extraordinary and magnetically vital. Her mind works rapidly and relevantly and her comments are full of wisdom and humor. She finds time to do a great deal of reading and has worked out a philosophy to live by. Her favorite virtues are courage, a sense of justice, and sincerity; if one has those, then it is time to think of the many traits that added to others give charm of personality."

A few years later another Terman field-worker wrote: "Mrs. T is a wonder — brave, cheerful, witty, and spiritually unbeaten."

Some found her emotional. She never seemed to care how she dressed. One of her children said she read while she was dressing and sometimes went into town with mismatched stockings.

In 1933 she asked Terman to write a letter of recommendation so she could take a civil service test. She had been living as housemother at a school for the deaf in Berkeley and needed civil service accreditation. By this time, for reasons unknown, she had changed her first name and was now Florence Goodwyn.

Emily Talbot Tadashi, sometimes known as Florence Goodwyn, the beautiful daughter of an Episcopal bishop who left a life of comfort and predictability to follow the man she loved into poverty and loneliness, died at the age of fifty-eight in 1947. If her soul was embodied in any of the children, it was in her daughter Sophie.

The Tadashi Family: Sophie

OF ALL THE CHILDREN, Sophie isolated herself the least and found the purest peace. It just took her a while.

Sophie was born in 1909, a middle child and one of great beauty. The Terman field-worker described her as a "flower-like girl with dainty Japanese prettiness, perfect manners, a charming naturalness about her gracious courtesy."

She appeared to visitors a happy child, but she wrote later that she was not always happy at all.

"My own memory is of a childhood over which there hung a dark cloud. True, there were happy hours, but the overall impression is of vague fears, incomprehensible difficulties and general unhappiness between grandmother, mother, and father. I was not a very happy girl until I went to college, and even then I did not feel socially accepted. I felt that I was waging a fight with society to prove something, and I threw an enormous amount of effort into school work."

As a child she wrote poetry, some of it based on texts from the Baha'i faith.

"I hate to be resolved into a statistical table. You know, when I was in high school, an idiotic friend of my mother's told some news reporters that we were a family of geniuses and the resultant publicity made me feel an awful fool. I took some kidding about it too. But on the whole, I think your testing made me conceited."

In 1927 she asked Terman for a letter of recommendation for a Stanford scholarship. "I have been especially interested in psychological work," she wrote him, "although I intend to earn a teacher's certificate in order to have a regular occupation in reserve. My brother

[Alfred], who is also prepared for university, is willing to stay out for a year or two in order to help me get started."

Stanford rejected her, giving no reason; she was one of the few Terman could not help. But he wrote a letter for her to Berkeley, and she was accepted there.

She did not have much of a social life at Berkeley, despite having grown into a remarkably beautiful young woman. She learned to make up her eyes in such a way that it increased her racial ambiguity and added to her exotic grace.

She lived in a rooming house near the campus. Her landlady, a Mrs. Blochman, told Barbara Burks, a field-worker, she never had a boarder from the school she liked as much. Sophie always volunteered to do more work around the house than was required and learned to cook to relieve her landlady of that burden.

"She said Sophie seems very happy at the university, that she is doing splendidly in her studies, and has made a good social adjustment. She takes her lunch every day and eats it in one of the women's lounging rooms where a number of the other girls eat. Mrs. Blochman doesn't think Sophie's Japanese blood prejudices people in any way against her — says 'I don't believe people think anything about it.' I think it is probably true that the people she meets are gracious to her, and like and respect her, but I doubt whether she has the intimate friendships with girls that a white girl under similar circumstances would have. Mrs. Blochman mentioned no special college friendships that Sophie had made when I specially inquired about this."

She spent time with some cousins from her mother's side and a mixed American-Persian couple whom she probably met at a Baha'i service. Barbara Burks became something of a surrogate mother to her, visiting Berkeley and reporting back to Emily that all was well. Terman kept up a steady barrage of letters to the Berkeley student aid office trying to get scholarships for her. He did not succeed her freshman year, but apparently she did get one subsequently. He may have contributed anonymously himself.

She hoped to become a teacher even if that meant a fifth year in college. Money was always a concern in the Tadashi family. Once Sophie tried to earn $50 by donating blood (she apparently had a rare type), but her veins were too small and it took much too long to "bleed." She feared she would not be able to do that again. Then she got into the greeting card business. She marched into local greeting card stores and convinced the owners that they needed a campus representative. She even sold a box to Burks. She sang for pay in the Unitarian choir.

She found a boyfriend at Stanford, apparently through the American-Persian couple, but they dated for less than a year.

In 1932 she became engaged to a Russian-Jewish chemist, Michael Golub, then teaching at Fordham University in New York. It is not clear how she met him, but she told Burks she was so happy she was "almost unconscious." She had hoped to finish her senior year at Berkeley, but Michael wanted her to come to New York and finish college there if she wished. Burks told Terman that Sophie was working on a novel. She left college and moved to New York. Michael's family was upset about the marriage, and this produced some painful moments for her. The family had fled Russia during the revolution and had lived in China for several years before immigrating to the United States. Having an Oriental (and non-Jewish) daughter-in-law was not a blessing, they felt. Her in-laws "hate Japanese," she wrote Terman, "but I can't take it seriously any more." New York was freer of anti-Japanese sentiments than California was, but it had its own prejudices: Fordham, a Catholic school, did not know Michael was Jewish and he feared that if it found out, he would be fired.

By 1938 Sophie had three children (all one-quarter Japanese, one-quarter white Anglo-Saxon Protestant, one-half Jewish), whom she described as "willful and ingeniously naughty" when she wrote to Terman for advice on their education.

Michael was commissioned in the army at the start of World War II and was sent overseas. Sophie and her children moved to her brother Alfred's ranch in the Sierra foothills.

Michael had actively discouraged Sophie from cooperating with the Terman people. Alfred told Terman that Michael was very distrustful, thinking people were always trying to get money from him. Sophie told Alfred she was no longer interested in the study and was not cooperating, but her files are filled with long, handwritten letters to Terman, asking for his advice and support — and receiving it always.

After the war, Michael got a job with an industrial laboratory in Cleveland and the family reassembled there.

Michael was sometimes a difficult man to live with, Sophie told Terman, and the problem of her mixed blood — and that of her children — was part of the difficulty. Caught as a child between two worlds, she now found herself caught by a third.

"Dr. Golub is a clever man, much cleverer in many ways than I," she wrote Terman in 1946, "and when we disagree I never can oppose him with any conviction, any strong conviction, that is, because too often, I want to agree with him. My sentiments are in accord with his; my reason is not. Now, for a long time, I have felt that the children should be acquainted with their mixed heredity, not only because I wish them to be aware of, and if possible, proud of my racial background, but more practically, as a sort of defense against receiving information about me from outsiders who may be antagonistic.

"It is not likely to happen as all of the people I know seem to be well disposed towards me, but every year that passes brings me a new surprise at the number of people who know that Dr. Golub has a 'Japanese wife.'. . . Because of the recent war, this information might startle the children, especially if they think we kept it a secret, as if we were ashamed — which I have never been. . . .

"It is complicated by the fact that, although the children know we are Jewish, we do not live as Jews. Our home life is comfortable and the only religious instruction I have given them is the knowledge that there is good in all religions. . . . We try to follow the Golden Rule and to love one another. . . . So you see, it troubles me severely all the time to think that by living without labels, in this rather unhappy world, all kinds of prejudice will one day rise up and overwhelm our children."

Michael did not want her to tell them, believing, he said, the matter was simply unimportant.

"Now, when people say 'What church do you belong to?' I want the children to say 'We are Jews.' My husband says that is not strictly true since we don't go to a synagogue and anyway, it's no one's business but our own." Since she was not Jewish, it was not technically true either. But Michael wasn't making a theological point; he feared that since his family lived in a Christian neighborhood, being open about the family's Jewishness would just make the children's lives harder. There is always the possibility he is right, she told Terman. "Now you see why I can't argue with him. It is making me very unhappy because either way I may be making a serious mistake."

Terman advised her to tell the children about her heritage. Golub frowned when she showed him Terman's letter.

"If you didn't have a problem to worry about, you would probably invent one," he said, dismissing her concern. She took matters into her own hands.

One day, after Michael had left for work, Sophie took out her family picture album to show her daughter, eight-year-old Rachel. When she got to a picture of her father, Rachel pointed and said, "He looks just like a Jap."

"That's not strange," Sophie said, trying not to show her emotions. "He was a Japanese gentleman."

Rachel smiled and said offhandedly, "That so?" and kept turning the pages of the album, commenting on the pictures. Sophie kept as calm as she could. Later, her two younger sons joined them.

Jon said, "Aunt Patience looks Chinese."

"No wonder," said Rachel. "Her father was a Jap — Japanese," she added, correcting herself.

"Oh," said Jon, slightly surprised. Then he turned to Sophie. "Why then our grandfather was Japanese."

"That's right," she said.

"Let's see his picture."

She turned back to Akio's picture and the boy stared at it. "He looks kind — he's nice," he said approvingly.

"Very nice. Handsome, too," she said. "Also rather naughty. He used to gamble and lose all his money."

"You don't look a bit Japanese, mother."

"Oh, well, I'm only half. You children don't look it either. For that matter, you're only one-quarter, you know."

And that, she told Terman, was all it took.

In 1948 she wrote Terman about her life and her six children: "Once in a while I marvel that I should be blessed with a whole half dozen angels, but that feeling is usually obscured by a feeling of harassment. Most of the time I am overwhelmed by too much housework, too little money, anxiety about the future of the civilization into which we have borne our children, and most of all, about their education and their future."

The family moved to Philadelphia when Michael got a job as a biochemist at the Fox Chase Cancer Center. The work was interesting, the pay low.

"Both of us are ridiculously uninterested in becoming rich and idealistic enough to hope that in spite of the thin family purse, this country will be willing to educate our monsters," she wrote Terman.

Sophie was beginning to bristle a bit about the questionnaires she was getting from the Terman office: "You assessed youngsters on the basis of learning ability and personality, but you assess adults by a more worldly measure of financial standing and recognition by a public which has never shown any great ability in distinguishing between knaves and fools and good public servants.

"I consider myself a successful person. I was a lovely, ambitious, discontented girl with, I think, an unusual capacity for happiness. Right now I wouldn't change places with anyone. Day in, day out, I lead a richer, more fulfilled life than I ever dreamed of. I have the love of my husband, a most discriminating man, and the love of my children, but more than that, I believe that I have their respect — that I cherish and struggle to maintain. . . .

"Why don't you ask your 'children' to judge themselves as people? I venture to say that the majority of them would feel as I do. Because intelligence must include the ability to find one's place even in a muddled world." There is no record that Terman responded.

She was writing and had finished three unpublished novels, four short television scripts that were produced in Philadelphia for educational television, and a few poems that were published in small magazines. She helped set up her suburban town's first library.

"We live in a small community and I am rather conspicuous in an eccentric sort of way," she wrote Terman in 1943. "I have a great deal of energy and I am amused at human beings and I enjoy my own idiosyncrasies. . . . I am lucky to have six children because I am very intense about them, and if I had one or two to mother, I am afraid I should have smothered them."

By 1953 Terman was writing letters of recommendation to colleges for Sophie's children, starting with her son Aaron. Rachel was working as a waitress in Boston and was reported to be happy. Jon, after a difficult time in high school, straightened out and went to Rutgers.

In 1959 Sophie Tadashi Golub went back to school to get a teaching certificate. She did so over the objection of her husband who was old-fashioned enough to protest her working. She confessed to Terman's successor Robert Sears that she and Michael were "already out of sympathy" with each other by then.

"Among my friends I have noticed that the better educated a woman is, the more difficult is her adjustment to marriage and motherhood. It may be that Dr. Golub's upbringing in a society in which women are at worst a chattel and at best a toy has made it difficult for him to accept a partnership."

She began going to a Quaker meeting and continued her education, getting a master's degree in education. She taught reading to the retarded and was "extremely happy" with her job. She was, by now, a grandmother, and her children were happy as adults. Two were housewives, one a secretary, one a teacher, one a tree surgeon, and one a musician.

She wanted to become a Quaker, she wrote, but her husband wouldn't approve. He was very protective, she said, and she felt as though she often let him down. After a while, she stopped caring what he thought, but she sometimes wondered if she had let herself down as well.

The knowledge of being gifted made her self-conscious, she wrote. "I was too self-conscious anyway. But in bad times I kept trying to 'live up to' a questionable potential.

"I 'trained' to be a wife and mother, but I became unhappy and prepared to support myself in case I left my husband."

She did leave Michael in 1966, to his amazement and confusion, and lived alone and independently for eighteen months. They reconciled and lived together for a few months before he died of a heart attack.

"It was a shock," she wrote Sears. "We had a few happy months. I tried to be less egotistic. Intellect doesn't seem very important."

She went to Japan twice to visit her Japanese cousins, trips she described as "inexpressibly enlightening," and on her return moved into a racially mixed neighborhood.

By 1977 she moved back to California, settling in the Central Valley. She designed a small house for herself "that fits me like a shell."

At the age of sixty Sophie was teaching full time, tending her garden, and raising vegetables for "family, friends, and freezing." In 1977 she had a heart attack but recovered.

She made her peace with the Terman study. In her last letter to Sears, she wrote: "The consciousness of your benevolent eye upon me has mitigated various periods of my life when I might have felt neglected."

Sophie died of another heart attack in 1982.

Chapter Twelve

THE GOLDEN DATA BASE

TERMAN LEFT BEHIND an amazing collection of data and a trained and willing corps of subjects. Many of the Termites eagerly read all the reports generated by Terman's office and continued a long, personal correspondence with Robert Sears, who became Terman's successor in 1956. The study was, for many, an important part of their lives.

Sears, himself a Termite, was joined by his wife, Pauline, a psychologist, and later Lee Cronbach, another Termite-psychologist. They acted as Terman's scientific executors and the keepers of the golden data base. They and scores of social scientists from around the world mined the mountains of information and the mailing lists to find out as much as they could about these unique people. The mining continues to this day.

Melita Oden was the direct link to Terman, putting together a survey in 1960 that expanded on Terman's efforts to find out why some men succeeded and others failed.[1] She and Terman had raised intriguing questions in their earlier work. In 1960, with the Termites about age fifty, at the cusp of their careers and lives, she hoped that now she could find some answers.

Oden got filled-in questionnaires from 664 men and 524 women. One hundred thirty Termites had died, 83 men and 47 women, a mortality rate of 8.6 percent, as opposed to the 12 percent to be expected in the white American population overall. Sixty-one percent of the deaths were from natural causes, mainly heart disease in the men, cancer in the women. Fourteen men and eight women had committed suicide.

More than 90 percent of the men and almost the same percent of the women reported themselves in good or very good health. Less than 2 percent of men and women said they were in bad shape. Seventy percent of the men and 64 percent of the women said that they were in satisfactory mental health; about 10 percent had serious mental difficulties. Thirty-four Termites had been hospitalized for mental problems. Oden found no difference statistically between the men and women in that regard. Ten of the people institutionalized had drinking problems. Two of the men and four of the women suicides had been hospitalized for mental disease; the other suicides had shown no overt signs of problems.

Oden reported no change in the negligible criminal rate. Except for the one man imprisoned in the 1930s for forgery, no subject had been in trouble with the law and that single adult felon did not repeat his transgressions. The rate of homosexuality remained the same (about 2 percent) as in the 1955 study (see page 211). The educational level of the subjects remained remarkable: eighty-seven men and twenty women had earned their doctorates.

Ninety-four percent of the men and 91 percent of the women were married, a slight increase (four men and six women had married since 1955). Twelve men and fifteen women waited until they were over forty to marry. The divorce rate was 23 percent, equal for men and women. Divorced or widowed men were more likely to remarry than divorced or widowed women in the study. Men and women who did not graduate from college were more likely to be divorced than college grads. Women who graduated from college were less likely to marry than nongraduates, especially those with graduate degrees.

The Termites had produced 2,600 offspring, a median of 2.7 per gifted parent, a fertility rate just below what would be required to maintain the gifted population. They had four hundred grand-children; one woman already had fifteen. The gifted men tended to have more children in their families than did gifted women. Oden arranged for Stanford-Binet tests for 1,571 of the Termites' children, either administered by field-workers or, in the case of children who lived out of state, by officials in their schools. The average score for boys and girls came out the same at 133, just below the gifted cutoff, an improvement over the earlier tests. The girls once again were somewhat more variable than the boys, which either says something about girls or about the Stanford-Binet. An astonishing 16 percent of the gifted's children were gifted themselves, a percentage vastly above the 1 percent that would be expected in the general population. Less than 20 percent had IQs below 120.

Almost half the men were in the first occupational group, the professionals in the Minnesota scale, with lawyers (10.4 percent) the largest single profession and engineers and college faculty next. Almost 40 percent were semiprofessionals or managers, mostly at middle management levels. Only 1.1 percent were in the semiskilled category. Less than 3 percent (18) were retired or unemployed. Eight of the unemployed had mental problems; seven were disabled by poor health, including one man with multiple sclerosis.

The male Termites were doing well so far as income was concerned. The income reached an average of $13,464, with a range of $5,000 to $300,000. Median family income was $16,140. Income rose with age, as would be expected with successful people. The lowest income group included four carpenters, three small business owners, two clergymen, two office clerks, the dean of a small denominational college, a lawyer, an electrician, and a decorator. Four percent earned more than $50,000. Oden pointed out that income was deceptive because many of the most successful subjects were in academe, which generally pays poorly.

Three men were members of the National Academy of Science, including Fred Terman and Norris Bradbury, former director of Los Alamos National Laboratory. Six Termites were in *International Who's Who,* forty were in *Who's Who in America,* and eighty-one, including twelve women, were in *American Men of Science.* Terman's kids had earned 350 patents. They had produced more than 2,500 articles and papers, 200 books and monographs in the sciences and humanities, more than 400 short stories, not counting the work of the professional journalists such as Shelley Mydans. Anthony Boucher (William A. P. White) acted as editor for L. Sprague de Camp at *The Magazine of Fantasy and Science Fiction,* a Termite team. Artists greatly outnumbered musicians.

The gifted also had been enormously active in civic affairs; citizen of the year awards abounded. None was elected to high office, but several had achieved considerable power in appointed offices, including two ambassadors and five executives in the State Department.

Others served on the Federal Reserve Board, the Atomic Energy Commission, NASA, the Department of Justice, United Nations agencies, and the U.S. Senate staff.

Politically, the Termites had moved, with the rest of the United States, to the right. More of them said they were Republicans than ever before (60 percent of the men, 56 percent of the women). This was just as the United States was moving from the Eisenhower years to the Kennedy administration. The younger men tended to be Democrats; age seemed to make no difference among the women.

The Termites had known they were included in the gifted group for at least twenty-five years, maybe longer. Did they think they had lived up to their intellectual capabilities? No one would expect many of these extraordinary people to feel they had fully lived up to their potential — " 'reasonably well' is a more realistic response," Oden said — and indeed 68.3 percent of the men and 63.4 percent of the women said they had lived up to their capabilities fully or reasonably well.

Self-Ratings on Fulfillment of
Intellectual Capabilities

	Men (Percent)	Women (Percent)
Fully	2.5	2.0
Reasonably well	64.8	61.4
Considerably short	24.8	27.7
Far short	6.1	6.6
Largely a failure	1.1	1.0
Ambiguous reply	0.7	1.2

The ratings for men and women were quite similar. Oden said the seven men who listed themselves as failures would not be so regarded by others; they had serious social and emotional problems, but would otherwise be considered successful by all outward appearances. The women who thought they had failed did not seem to be any less successful than the other women. Apparently, these men and women had set their own goals in life and found themselves wanting; probably, their standards were much higher than the standards others set for themselves.

Education was a key factor in self-ratings of fulfillment; the better educated the respondents, the more likely they were to think they had fulfilled their capabilities. People with some college felt better about themselves than people with none, a finding that runs contrary to some results in earlier reports where those who started but did not finish college seemed to show considerable frustration in life. Men with graduate degrees were more satisfied than men with only under-graduate degrees; no difference was found with the women.

The higher up the occupational rung, the more fulfilled they were. College faculty were the most satisfied, followed by physicians and lawyers. Teachers and school administrators below the college level ranked ninth. People high in business and industry were not as happy about their achievements as were the professionals, who generally worked for themselves.

The largest percentage of people, when asked what motivated them in their work life, reported a "drive for excellence." The smallest percentage said it was money. This was true for both men and women; everything else was somewhere in the middle. The Termites reported they got more ambitious as they got older, and, oddly, it was then that money became important. Apparently, Terman's kids were driven by things other than money until they noticed retirement loom-ing ahead of them.

What gave them the most satisfaction in life in general? Men said work first, then their marriages, and then their children; women who did not work full time put their children first and then their marriages. Women who worked full time put their work first to an even greater extent than did men.

Said Oden, "An earlier volume in the series of publications on the Terman study was *The Promise of Youth*. Now after forty years of careful investigation there can be no doubt that for the overwhelming majority of subjects the promise of youth has been more than ful-filled."

But some still did better than others, so Oden decided to replicate the experiment she and Terman carried out a generation earlier sep-arating the most successful from the least successful. What was differ-ent, however, was that here she measured only occupational success, "vocational achievement"; unlike Terman before her, she did not attempt to make cosmic judgments about the lives of the men.

Merely setting up the experiment provided interesting results because things had changed for many of the subjects. When she and Helen Marshall started going through the files they had no trouble finding over two hundred men who were unambiguous successes, but they couldn't find more than sixty men who were clear failures. Partly, this was the result of a quite inexplicable difference in mortality: eight of the men in the A group in the 1940 study had died in the twenty years since Terman selected them as models of success, but twice that many in the C group had died. Since the health statistics on the two groups in 1940 were not that far apart, it was not clear why that should be. Six of the deaths in the A group were from natural causes, one committed suicide, and one died from other causes, but five C's died from other causes, two committed suicide, and nine died from natural causes.

More interestingly, there had been significant changes in the classifications. Some A's had not kept their record of success, and some C's proved to have simply taken their time deciding how they wanted to go through life and had become more successful. The attrition rate in both classifications was a whopping 45 percent; 46 percent of the A's dropped down, and 45 percent of the C's moved up. Four of the A's dropped all the way to the C group; in all four cases alcoholism was a factor. Two C's moved up so far that while they did not quite make the A group, they were so close and promising that Oden put them at B+.

Oden then decided the best thing to do was to shrink the groups. She and Marshall limited the study to the hundred most successful and the hundred least successful. Picking the C's was more difficult, she wrote, as they were a more diverse group.

The average age of both groups of men was just shy of fifty.

The A's included twenty-four college faculty members, eleven lawyers, eight scientists, two architects, five physicians, four authors or journalists, three engineers, an economist, two architects, and a landscape architect. Thirty were top-level business executives, six were high-ranking officials in the State Department, two were heads of philanthropic organizations, one served as a high city official, and two were in show business (Jess Oppenheimer and the unnamed film director). One man was in agribusiness, scarcely to be called a farmer.

Five C's were in the top occupational classification, the professions, but apparently weren't very good at what they were doing. The C group included two lawyers, a man described as a dilettante with a Ph.D. in biology, a chemist and a mathematician working as lab technicians, a tax consultant, an accountant, and six civil servants in state or municipal employ. Four men were either policemen or firemen, which Oden (and Terman before her) did not consider to be living up to their potential. Nothing was said of the police chief mentioned in an earlier survey. One man inherited considerable wealth and promptly retired, apparently having more brains than ambition. Others were either chronically unemployed or simply stopped working years ago. Oden did report that one man who had been quite successful earlier and then had a precipitous decline seemed poised to make a comeback, but he was still classified as a C. One man was characterized as a hypochondriac who felt he was too ill to work, but not ill enough to stay away from the race track. Alcoholism was a factor in many of the sad tales in the C group.

That the two groups differed in earned income was built into the selection process. The 1959 median individual annual income for the A's was $23,900, the C's $7,178. The median income for white males in the United States that year was $5,000, so the C's were still doing better than most. The difference between the A and C groups in family income was just as wide, $33,125 versus $8,500.

Another striking difference between the two groups was education. While 92 percent of the A's (ninety-two A's, since each group had 100 members) were college graduates, only 40 percent of the C's were. While 72 percent of the A's had graduate degrees, only 8 percent of the C's had advanced degrees (six had law degrees). The undergraduate major most favored by the A's was science or engineering. Most C's majored in social science. More C's than A's majored in humanities. More C's than A's supported themselves in college. A's were far more active than C's in extracurricular activities. The A's grades were much better: almost 92 percent had a B or better average, while only slightly more than 50 percent of the C's could match that. More than 60 percent of the A's graduated with honors compared to slightly less than 11 percent of the C's. More than 90 percent of the A's said they had had enough education, while only 50 percent of the C's thought so.

Going back into their early years, Oden found again that the two groups were equally matched in elementary school but the A's were accelerated more than the C's, perhaps an important difference. The C's were about half a year behind the A's. In high school the divergence continued. Twenty percent more of the A's earned precollege credits despite having twice the extracurricular activities. Something was already at work in these boys that would head them on very different roads. Oden wondered if it could have been a difference in intelligence. She went back to the old records and found that the average Stanford-Binet scores for the A's was 157.3 and for the C's 149.7. Her statistical tests labeled that difference significant, but could a difference of seven points really mean that much? She didn't think so. Terman found little significant difference in his 1940 test and although these were not exactly the same men, she didn't believe this was anything other than a statistical artifact of the study. The results of the Concept Mastery test showed a similar difference, but that probably reflected the better education of the A's. The C's still did better than the average Ph.D. candidate.

The A's reported themselves healthier than the C's. They were more apt to report their good health as a contributing factor in their success, while C's were more likely to blame ill-health for their problems. The A's were also taller to an extent that she said was statistically significant.

In the 1940 study Terman found that the C's had a much more difficult time adjusting socially and emotionally to life. Oden found that this dissimilarity grew as they got older. Twenty-six in the C group reported having serious problems adjusting to life; six of them had been institutionalized at one time or another.

Fifteen percent of the C's reported they were heavy drinkers; only 3 percent of the A's had that problem. Oden also found, like Terman before her, that the C's had almost double the percentage of teetotalers.

She went through the data to see if any character traits could be said to be related to placement in the groups. The information came from the men, their wives, and their parents. As in the previous study, three traits stood out: an ability to set goals and achieve them, perseverance, and self-confidence. These traits ought to be self-evident for successful people, but Oden showed the traits were remarkable enough when these men were children to be noted. Other traits, such as lack of moodiness, happy temperament, cautiousness, and coolness seemed not to matter.

Field-workers, none of whom knew who was classified as what, reported that the A's were more physically attractive than the C's, more poised, more articulate, more alert, more attentive, more curious, more original, and friendlier. It is impossible to know which is cause and which is effect: do people become like that because they are successful, or do they become successful because they are that way?

Another problem of cause and effect has to do with marriage. The A's were by every count more happily married than the C's, enough so that Oden found a strong statistical relationship between marital happiness and success. But which was the cause and which the effect? she asked. She felt marriage tended to foster success, pointing out that every one of the A's was married, while only 82 percent of the C's were. The A's had far fewer divorces. The A wives were better educated, but only five of them, one-twentieth, worked full time; more than a fourth of the wives of C men worked, usually in low-paying jobs and apparently because the families needed the money.

The C's who were married produced fewer children, and almost a third of the C marriages were barren. Oden had many of the children tested and found the average IQ for the A children was 140 and the C 132, a difference that passed her statistical test for significance.

Politically, the two groups were not far apart, although the C's tended to be a bit more conservative.

Oden then looked at the all-important family factor. Did these two groups come from different types of families as Terman found in 1940? The answer again was yes: the two groups differed in such things as education of parents, occupation and marital status of the parents, interests of the father, and size of the home library. Success seemed to run in families.* The successful men reported that their parents, particularly fathers, encouraged independence and initiative. A larger percentage of A's admired their parents, both mothers and fathers, and wished to emulate them. A larger proportion of A's reported that their parents, both mothers and fathers, were affectionate.

Oden could find no socioeconomic differences between the fami-

* The proportion of Jews in the A group was double the proportion of Jews who were C's despite the fact that only 10 percent of the Terman kids were Jewish.

lies of the two groups. She also could find no difference in the religious beliefs of the subjects or their families. The home library of an A was more likely to have at least 500 books. More A's came from stable homes.

What Oden did find was a marked difference in what the men remembered about their parents' attitude toward education. The parents of the A's stressed it far more than did the parents of the C's. This turned out to be one of the strongest conclusions in her study; the difference was unmistakable. The pressure to succeed in school was much greater on the A's. Most of the parents of A's encouraged their children to forge ahead, not just go at a comfortable pace; they demanded or encouraged high grades and insisted that their children go to college.

> In the total picture, the variables most closely associated with vocational success are a home background in which the parents place a high value on education, encourage independence and initiative, and expect a high level of accomplishment; good mental health and all-round social and emotional adjustment; and the possession of certain traits and characteristics of personality. . . .
>
> The correlates of success are not possessed exclusively by the A's for there are no factors favorable to achievement that are not also found among some, albeit a minority of the C men, but the magic combination is lacking.[2]

A few of the C's, she noted, deliberately chose to go through life as they were, and she was measuring only occupational success. "In any case one must conclude . . . that intellect and achievement are far from perfectly correlated."

The Termites were a resource social scientists in and out of Stanford could not resist. Pauline and Robert Sears and Lee Cronbach, besides doing their own research, opened the files to scores of scientists and occasionally even let them contact the subjects. The Searses and Cronbach also began the monumental task of trying to put the data on computer tape, so researchers could make use of it without having to camp at Stanford.

"There were 1,528 cases to start with," Robert Sears told Daniel Goleman in an interview in *Psychology Today* in 1980. "We are still in touch with more than 900. More than 300 are dead, so we have 75 to 80 percent of the living still being followed. The total number of variables we will eventually code for each person will be in the neighborhood of 4,000. Let's say we have 4,000 codes for each and about 1,000 cases. That's 4 million pieces of information!"

The task is still not done, and some of the coding was not done as carefully as it might have been, some scientists have complained. Nonetheless, as a social science resource, the Termites are unique and many have taken advantage of their kindness and their time.

The Sears team was, of course, one of the most active. In 1977 Robert Sears used the 1972 survey and earlier data to try to understand what he called the "life satisfaction" of the gifted men. Their average age was sixty-two and they ranged from fifty-two to seventy-two, from still in their prime to well into their mellower years. Sears wanted to see if he could detect anything in their early lives that predicted satisfaction later on; he was looking for the antecedents to happiness. He measured four things: satisfaction through the years with work, satisfaction with family life, duration of work life, and stability of marriage. Sears wrote:

> Age sixty-two seemed a good time to ask these men to focus on both the past and the future. With a long life of accomplishment already behind them, they would be in a position to evaluate its joys and sorrows, its successes and failures, and its *might-have-been* as well as its *was*. And they were nearing the time, if they had not already reached it, when a hard look at the future was necessary.[3]

Sears used six categories of goals: occupation, family, friends, richness of cultural life, service to society, and joie de vivre. He asked such things as "How important was each of these goals in life, in the plans you made for yourself in early adulthood?" and "How satisfied are you with your experience in each of these respects?" Family life was the most important to these men when they were younger, and they seem to have found the satisfaction with their families they sought. Surprisingly, they put joy of life in second place, just ahead of occupation. What gave the most satisfaction when they were approaching their autumn years? Family, jobs, and friends. Most middle-class men are supposed to be fixed on their work and money, but Sears found that for this group family was first.

The most satisfied men were healthy and well educated. They felt that as young men they had chosen their professions, not just fallen into them, and so they had control over what they did for a living. They had a feeling of self-worth, enjoyed the competition and complexities of their jobs, and were ambitious.

Sears wanted to see to what age these men worked and what happened when bright, successful men retire. He couldn't really measure this at that time because the sample was still too young and many of the men were well below normal retirement age. He did observe a slight tendency for men who were well satisfied with their work to keep working.

The men who continued to work were those who were better educated, most successful from the ages of thirty to fifty, ambitious, well integrated with their work, and somewhat healthier. In short, the same attitudes that brought them success also kept them at their jobs.

Most of the married couples had taken Terman's Marital Aptitude test at about the age of thirty, and Sears found that the couples who were the most happily married in 1972 had generally done well on that test; the test was a good predictor. Good mental health, of course, was an antecedent to a happy marriage; the most happily married were also the best adjusted when they were children and the most sociable when they were in high school. They had a favorable attitude toward their parents, especially their fathers. The only problem area was the work pattern of the wife; men who had working wives tended to be less happy with their marriages.

Seventy-one percent of the men were married to their first and only wife, a rate that matches the general population. Only 3 percent were never married. The rest of the men were either divorced at least once or widowed. The men with stable marriages were closer to their parents, especially their mothers. Sears believed the men with stable marriages had apparently resolved whatever conflicts they might have had as children by the time they were forty and the divorced men apparently hadn't.* Sears also found that the more money a man made, the less the chance of divorce in the first marriage, while the more money a woman made, the greater the chance of divorce and the less the chance of remarriage.

---

* Going back to Terman's masculinity-femininity test, Sears reported that the men with the most stable marriages were the boys who had the highest masculine scores by the age of ten. Other research, by Terman and others, indicated these scores dropped as they got older. Neither Sears nor anyone else was able to explain what that meant, if anything.

Another researcher, Robert T. Michael, went into the women's files to see if he could find any precursors of divorce or marital stability. He found that the women with the most stable marriages tended to have been older when they wed, less educated than their husband, of the same religion as their husband, and Catholic or married to a Catholic.[4]

Carole Holahan, of the University of Texas, studied attitudes toward marriage of a group of Termites at the age of thirty (1940), a group of thirty-year-olds in 1979 drawn from the list of Stanford alumni, and the same Terman subjects forty years later. Over the course of years, apparently, the Termites became more egalitarian in their attitudes toward marriage, with the women showing the greatest change. The Terman women grew to think it less important to marry a man older than they and came to believe more strongly in a single standard for sexual behavior. Both men and women showed a decline in the belief that men should dominate a marriage, although the women felt more strongly about it than the men. Both men and women came to feel that the woman ought to work or be financially independent, but showed less agreement on whether the woman should be given a definite household budget. Both men and women came to feel they should say "I love you" more often.

Although the Terman women were ahead of their time, young women in 1979 were still ahead of them, a generation gap perhaps not as wide as with other women in their seventies, but a gap nonetheless. The modern women were even more egalitarian. They believed even less that the man should be older than the woman or that the man "should wear the pants in the family." Holahan found that the differences between generations was sexual: the modern men did not differ from the male Termites when they were thirty, but the contemporary women certainly did. The modern men still tended to believe in the double standard. The modern men believed more than the Terman men at seventy that fathers should take an active role in child rearing, and they tended to be more emotionally expressive in their marriage. The differences between the Terman men at age thirty and the Terman men at age seventy were not as great as the differences between the Terman men at age seventy and the modern men at thirty, Holahan found.

The contemporary couples seemed to be less happy with their

marriages and more likely to contemplate divorce than their older counterparts.

Other researchers were able to round out the picture of the gifted a bit more. Arleen Leibowitz found that the amount of preschool education the gifted children received from their parents at home was not related to family income and seemed to have no relationship to how much schooling the children eventually received.[5] Mothers with the highest IQs were the most likely to invest time in preschool education. The time and quality of the in-school education were more important factors. When she looked at acceleration in school, she found that the Terman men were accelerated at a more rapid rate than the general population, that these men earned more money throughout their lives than men of similar ages, and that the greatest difference was in the early years. She attributed this to their getting into the work force earlier and were thus always a year or two ahead of other men their age. "We cannot conclude," Pauline Sears wrote about the Leibowitz study, "that either home instruction or acceleration will improve IQ or increase adult earnings in gifted children."

Edwin S. Shneidman, a psychologist at the University of California at Los Angeles, went back through the files to see if he could find a precursor to suicide among the gifted.[6] He was given the files of thirty white men from the Terman study. Five of the men had killed themselves (all by gunshot) in their fifties, ten died from natural causes, and fifteen were still alive. He didn't know which was which and tried to predict from the files the five most likely to have committed suicide. He got four out of the five and narrowly missed the fifth. The seeds of self-destruction had been sown at least as early as the age of thirty. He found that the men who were most likely to kill themselves in middle age had some of the following traits: felt rejected by their fathers, were disturbed when they were adolescents, had married more than once, were alcoholic, were unsuccessful or at least disappointed with themselves, were lonely, had a wife who was not helpful. None of them were overtly crazy, he found.

And, finally, the researchers could explore old age. In 1986 Holahan wanted to find out how the Termites were doing physically and emotionally and mailed out more questionnaires. The average age of the Termites was now seventy-six. She found that about 40 percent of them had not suffered any physical deterioration in the previous five years that concerned them. They tended to compare themselves with others of their age rather than look back at the kind of physical health they once had.[7]

By and large, the Termites were doing fine physically although they tended to report less energy and vitality, which should be expected. The most worrisome health problem was loss of hearing for the men and loss of energy for the women.

Holahan found that the psychological well-being of the subjects was largely the result of what they expected their last years to be like when they were fifteen or so years younger. Health and psychological well-being seemed unrelated to occupations in men, but career women were better off psychologically than other women, in part because they reported fewer bouts of depression. Both men and women reported themselves to be "pretty happy."

She did not find a strong relationship between physical health and psychological well-being. She did find a strong relationship between psychological well-being and how happy the Termites were with their work lives. Social activities and recreation had the strongest relationship to both physical and mental health. Marriage did not seem to affect either, but having children positively, if modestly, affected the men, curiously not the women.

How did Terman's "kids" age mentally? Shneidman and Gordon Strauss, his colleague at UCLA, tracked down forty-five of the Termites then in their seventies and put them in front of tape recorders.[8] They were able to interview thirty-five of them, all men, as the men passed through their seventh decade to see if they could determine how the men were aging mentally. Shneidman and Strauss transcribed every word of every interview into a computer and programmed the computer to count the total number of words spoken and then to sort the words to count the number of unique words used (if the word *and* was used a thousand times, it would be counted a thousand times in determining the total number of words spoken, but only once in determining the number of unique words used). They wanted to see what happened to the vocabularies of the gifted men. Most cognitive psychologists believe that one thing that does not deteriorate with time is vocabulary; Shneidman and Strauss were the first to test this in gifted people.

In 171 interviews between 1981 and 1989, the Terman men spoke a total of 1,029,749 words and used 26,290 unique words. The range of unique words was from 3,297 to 4,858.* Over the decade Shneidman and Strauss saw a gradual decrease in the total number of words and, in most cases, a more modest decrease in the number of unique words. The ratio of unique words to total words actually went up for 77 percent of the men — they were using fewer words but with more variety.

The researchers also found that the decreases in vocabulary were noticeable when the men were talking about several specific subjects: occupation, family, and education, although family and occupation were still at the top of the list overall. Words about health moved from fourth to third, probably reflecting a growing concern about that topic. Use of the word *wife* declined by 40 percent, but was still the second most common of the key words (nouns and verbs, mainly). By the end of the decade, the word *doctor* was used more frequently than *family*, *job*, or *retire*. The words *die*, *death*, and *cancer* were infrequently spoken throughout.

Shneidman and Strauss also found some interesting patterns in the interviews. "For any particular person in our study there turn out to be certain important life events or incidents which the man recites each time he is interviewed," they wrote. No matter how recently the story was recited or how many times, it would come out again. It could be a triumph or a defeat or any pivotal incident in that person's life. Interestingly, it was never told the same way twice and frequently more detail came out with the telling. One man retold the gruesome accidental death of his wife five times and each time more details flowed from him. He was seventy-nine at the fifth interview.

The Termites in the UCLA study also seemed to be still growing. "In several instances," the researchers reported, "we observed what we can only call a process of maturation occurring in the late seventies which seems to represent dramatic change from patterns well established over the previous fifty plus years of adult functioning." The researchers had thought that by the time someone got to be seventy-five that person would be pretty well set in his or her ways and thinking, but the interviews with the Terman men showed the opposite.

* Strauss points out that the 1987 edition of the *Random House Dictionary* has about 300,000 unique words and that Herman Melville used 17,560 different words in *Moby Dick*. People use more words when writing than when speaking. The man with the largest vocabulary of English words was probably Shakespeare; his plays contain more than 20,000.

They found that the decreases in total vocabulary and "inferable cognitive function" (how well the men appear to be thinking) are more evident in men who have withdrawn from life than in those still intellectually active. "For individuals of high intelligence, not only does the brain work better, but it lasts longer, especially if it is occupied," Shneidman and Strauss reported.

Sometime in the first decade of the next century, the last of Terman's kids will pass away. She — and it likely will be a she — will be the last of one of science's greatest treasures. She will probably have done her mentor proud.

Chapter Thirteen

EVERYONE'S KIDS

THE MANY FLAWS in Terman's study are well documented, and, certainly, what we can learn from comparing his bright, kind, and open Termites with the rest of humanity is limited. But the seventy years of research have many things to teach us. What was learned from the group itself filled volumes. The results of the study may be helpful for parents who think or know they have gifted children and perhaps even for the gifted themselves. More important, the research may have lessons for everyone with children, gifted or otherwise.

It should be said that in retrospect many of Terman's findings seem to be commonsensical. And while what he found applied to people who were unusually bright, there is no reason to doubt that much of it also applies to others.

It must be repeated that no one knows what Terman actually was measuring with his Stanford-Binet and Concept Mastery tests. This has been the subject of endless controversy for most of this century. The definition of intelligence itself is equally controversial, a matter of whom you ask and when. All kinds of things are dragged into the debate: politics, ideology, sensitivities, egotism. The debate about definition easily drifts into a debate about social philosophy between people who see themselves as "democrats" and people the "democrats" call elitist. Terman saw his kids as special and thought such gifted children should have special treatment. From that standpoint he was an elitist, and he would have considered that label a compliment. If you think that smart people are special and if you support special educational programs for the gifted, you, too, can be called an elitist.

As he grew older, Terman's concept of the origin and manifestation of intelligence changed. He backed away from ideas of racial inequality and eugenics, somewhat embarrassed that he once espoused them. Politically, he moved to the left, becoming a New Deal Democrat and a passionate admirer of Adlai E. Stevenson. He was endlessly troubled by the sexual imbalance in his sample and his inability even to phrase the questions he needed for his women subjects. He had set out to prove that intelligence was largely a matter of genetics (until his last volume, the series was called Genetic Studies of Genius) and he ended up with a study that proved beyond question that intelligence, or whatever he was measuring, was far more complicated than that.

The definition of intelligence and the efficacy of intelligence testing are best left for other volumes. Let us accept that, whatever those tests measured, the people in Terman's studies were unusually bright, intellectually gifted in many ways, and notable for their success by conventional standards.

The Terman study is believable despite its faults. While Terman was lax in finding control groups or other studies that might support or provide a context for his own, we know from work done elsewhere that the Termites were in no drastic way different from other mentally gifted people. None of Terman's findings is directly contradicted by other similar, long-term studies. One of the best known, the so-called Grant study of 268 men at a "highly competitive liberal arts college" (read Harvard) was begun in 1937.* The Grant study found some differences, but nothing contradictory. Given the standards of admission to Harvard, men in the Grant study were intelligent and had a record of accomplishment as children. They were selected, in fact, because of their mental health; they were as "normal" a collection of young men as Harvard could produce. They were boys who, in the words of one Harvard administrator secure enough not to cringe from a cliché, were "able to paddle their own canoe."[1]

The Harvard men generally came from the same socioeconomic group as the Termites. They probably were less intellectually gifted, because admission to college took into consideration factors other than Stanford-Binet scores. They were better educated; everyone in the Grant study was by definition a college student.

* The study is named for its benefactor, William T. Grant. The study is still continuing, under the guidance of George E. Vaillant.

The study came up with some differences in the lives of its subjects and the Termites over time:

- While the same percentage of subjects were married, the Terman subjects had a higher divorce rate.
- The Terman subjects had fewer children (possibly because many were in the height of their reproductive years during the depression).
- More Grant men went to graduate school, but their overall record of graduate work was less distinguished than that of the Terman men.

In almost every other regard, from the rate of homosexuality to the percentage of subjects listed in *Who's Who*, the records of the two groups were almost identical. The conclusions of the Grant study, despite linguistic differences, were much the same as Terman's. The intelligence of these men made it easier for them to adapt to life, to find health and satisfaction, and to continue to grow.

Another comparable study, the survey of Rhodes scholars (see page 167), also verifies the context in which we can look at Terman's work. So, whatever the flaws, Terman's study must be taken seriously as a view of what happens when gifted children grow up.

In some ways the most egregious error Terman made was getting too close to his subjects. The sexual and racial imbalances in the sample can probably be explained, but *not* excused, as the products of his time; his meddling in the lives of his subjects cannot. Perhaps they would have ended up the same way, but the mere fact these people knew Terman was studying them changed their lives, and his active interference certainly changed the paths they took. We've seen several examples of Terman's tampering with his own results. Would Beatrice have burned out in her twenties if Terman hadn't pushed her into Stanford? Pressure from her mother was certainly one of her burdens, but a girl in her mid-teens was suddenly, without any preparation, thrown into a most demanding college. Terman could have refused to help until she was old enough and had more schooling or could have gone out of his way to discourage her mother, but he did not. In fact, what he should have done was nothing. Not every Termite with the chance of early college took it. Robert Minge Brown, who became a Rhodes scholar, a successful San Francisco attorney, and president of the Stanford Board of Trustees, was encouraged by Terman to enter Stanford at the age of thirteen. "I refused because I had a certain amount of common sense." He waited until a more normal age and, also because he was an athlete, had little trouble fitting in.

Not all people go through life knowing that when they are troubled, when they need advice, when they need help getting into a school or getting a job, when they need money, no matter how long they live, there is an office and a psychologist they can call and be welcomed. Free. Even if they needed only the therapy of opening their heart to someone by correspondence, the Terman subjects knew where to go. Mail flew, even in the later years when Robert Sears was in charge of the office. Sears and many of his adopted kids had long, sensitive conversations by mail about the most intimate details of the subjects' lives. In one correspondence it is not clear who was doing the learning, Sears or an unusually reflective, perceptive grown kid.

However, being in the study was not always an advantage. In several cases the Termites felt being in the study was a burden. Several subjects said that knowing they were gifted and knowing they were being watched changed their lives for the worse. Shelley Mydans thinks that happened to her brother. In Oden's last survey she asked the Termites if being in the study changed their lives. A quarter of the men and almost a third of the women said it had. Another almost 5 percent of the men and 8 percent of the women said it was possible but they weren't sure. That didn't necessarily count those who did not attribute events in their lives to Terman's actions, but who had in fact been affected by his meddling. Rumors persist that not a few of the suicides stemmed from the individuals' feelings that they had not lived up to what was expected of them as people who had been selected as special. The author found no evidence that is so, but some of the unhappiness of a few of the Termites can be traced back to disappointment and frustration, and being in the Terman study undoubtedly was a factor.

The files are full of letters from Terman to his kids recommending another Termite for a job. Jess Oppenheimer got several about subjects wanting to get into show business, and he met with every one of them. Many of the subjects got into prestigious colleges or graduate schools because they were in the Terman study and because the most famous psychologist in the nation wrote letters for them. When one of his girls was rejected by Stanford, Terman leaned on the admissions office and got it to change its mind. He told the girl the office had made an administrative mistake.

Terman's intervention was usually for the good. None of the Tadashis could have gone to college without his help.

Terman acted with good and kind intentions. But Terman was studying what would happen to these children when they grew up, what kind of people they would turn out to be, and in many cases did everything he could to determine those results. The relationship between subject and scientist in the Terman study was entirely understandable, human, unprecedented, and wrong. This does not invalidate all or even most of the results. One could only wish Terman had behaved himself.

Terman was still the best friend gifted Americans had for most of the century. His mission in life was to liberate them from prejudice and fear, and he succeeded. He destroyed the misconception that mentally endowed people were somehow physically deprived. His subjects were if anything healthier, larger, and longer-lived than the average person.

He most certainly proved that extremely intelligent people don't have to be eccentric, maladjusted, or egocentric. They accepted convention and respectability and succeeded grandly. Rebels were scarce among the Termites, and Henry David Thoreau's different drummer would have found few followers. They did not change life; they accepted it as it came and conquered it.

Terman proved that success, if not intelligence, ran in families. Whether it was genetic or environmental or, more likely, both is impossible to divine from his study. Unquestionably, however, certain families primed their children for success in life and others sent them off with a handicap, even with their exceptional intelligence. But what worked for the Termites is probably a good prescription for everyone else. (The only caveat necessary is that what Terman found for his subjects as a whole did not necessarily apply to every individual in the study, and what is good for most people is not necessarily good for all individuals.)

The single greatest determinant of success was education. The better educated parents instilled the importance of education in their children. It may account for the large number of Jews in the study, a people whose holiest object, after all, is a book. It probably accounts for the rise of Asian-Americans in the 1980s, cultures that have always valued literacy and science. The homes of the most successful subjects typically had at least a five-hundred-book library. Getting good grades and extracurricular activities were thought of as a norm and were actively encouraged. In these families whether a son or, in most cases, a daughter should go to college probably was never an issue, even when paying for it was. There are few if any examples of Termites' fighting their families to get an education.

The happier people were the ones with the most education. The most frustrated, at least among the men, were those who started college but never finished. They seemed to have more trouble coping. People with graduate degrees were more satisfied than people with only undergraduate degrees. The evidence is compelling and uniform throughout the study.

The evidence also seems compelling that gifted children should be treated differently by schools. At the very least they should be allowed to accelerate at a moderate rate through grades. Terman's suggestion that they should be accelerated fast enough to get them into college by the age of seventeen seems sound and supported by his data. In most cases this means accelerating them a year at the most. If nothing else, it gets them out into the world faster. The advantages of acceleration appear to greatly outweigh the disadvantages; most of Terman's A men had been accelerated, while the C men had not.

Families were important in other ways. The Terman researchers found that the families of most of the highly successful subjects were close and affectionate, and the role of the father was surprisingly strong. The fathers were not passive, and they did not leave child rearing exclusively to the mother. The children admired and respected both parents.

Success was expected. The parents, particularly the fathers, were successful people and the tone of family life, it might be inferred, was that this simply was how one went through life: one succeeded. They were lucky. Few of the Termites' families went through serious financial hardship, even in the depression.

There were, however, no guarantees. Intelligence was never an insurance policy against failure. Desirable family characteristics did not necessarily produce success. The study included two half-sisters raised by the same mother. Both went to Stanford. One became a successful, wonderfully happy, and well-known free-lance writer in New York; the other died miserably of alcoholism. One never knows.

The subjects with the happiest marriages came from happily married parents. Whether happy family life as children was the cause or result of success is immaterial: the two are intrinsically intertwined.

Some attributes that lead to success stand out. The most successful of the Termites were people who had the ability to set goals for themselves and the perseverance to achieve them. They were taught by their parents to be independent and to take the initiative. They were instilled with self-confidence. One important fact that stands out is that whatever the attributes that lead to success were, they were in place by the time the Termites got to high school. The A's and the C's in the various studies were similar in most ways until high school. In high school these children diverged. The lesson for us all is that postponing helping any child to acquire these attributes is not doing him or her a favor.

One thing their high level of intelligence gave the Termites was armor, both economic and emotional. While, as Elder found, the older Termites were affected by the depression more than Terman guessed, their experiences — with exceptions — were in no way comparable to what many other Americans went through. Divorced or widowed women seemed to be able to cope better. Intelligence gave them some independence and more choice.

Stable marriages also seemed to be a factor in success, but cause and effect are unclear. Does success help build more stable relationships? Probably. Do more stable relationships help one find success? Probably.

Another factor in success that seems to pop out of the Terman study is the importance of work. The happiest, most satisfied people were the people who were pleased with their work and were good at it, even exceeding family life in its importance in many cases. It was true across the group. Men in particular found satisfaction in life generally when they had decided for themselves what they wanted to do by the time they were thirty and then did it — well. Merely being that focused certainly helped, but these were men who chose their occupations; they did not settle for a job because they couldn't think of something better to do. None of Thoreau's "lives of quiet desperation" here. In a few cases, they also had the courage to change their lives in mid-career. The actress Eleanor Sully comes to mind; she became a public health educator.

And is it accidental that the happiest Termites were professionals, people who generally worked for themselves? They were men and women in control of their lives. The happiest of the lot were college professors. Tenured college professors are generally the most independent of characters, running their own classrooms, research, and their own students — and frequently the worst paid. The Terman subjects did not seem to like occupations requiring teamwork or bureaucracies. The very successful people in business and industry were satisfied people, but their level of satisfaction seemed to be below that of those in the professional categories.

Women's lives are complicated by factors that don't affect men's lives. Half the women said they did not live up to their full intellectual potential; a third said they failed to use their capabilities. Career women seemed satisfied with their lot, particularly if they devoted all their time and energies to their careers and did without children. The unhappiest women were those who were forced to work for subsistence or felt the need to work for additional income, usually the divorced or widowed. Women who were happy being homemakers were happy indeed. But many homemakers, when asked if they would take that path if they had to live their lives over again, said no. They would have worked harder to find a career. By and large these were also people who had relinquished control of their lives. Something that probably is no surprise to modern feminists is that highly educated women who find themselves as housewives have a quick recipe for frustration.

So we have some solid ideas from Terman's landmark study about the meaning of the gift of intelligence as he measured it and some clues about success in life. But look at what the Termites did not turn out to be. While many of the Termites were capable of originality and some had considerable talents, none were great original thinkers or artists.*

No scientist even came close to winning a Nobel Prize. (Two men who would become Nobel laureates were rejected for the study.) No writer won a Pulitzer. While Jess Oppenheimer was able to make a huge contribution to popular culture and Ancel Keys affected the national diet and thereby undoubtedly saved many lives, none of the

---

* Terman admitted he was not an original thinker himself; he believed he was a synthesizer, one of the most important roles in science.

Termites proved to be the stuff of legend or history. There were no Einsteins or Newtons or Mother Teresas. No one founded a major industrial giant* or discovered a cure for an intractable disease. True, the sample was small enough to make such eminence highly unlikely, but the evidence is that these were not the kind of people who would be Einsteins or Mother Teresas. They certainly were successful, admirable, productive, and happy people, but there was among them no one of historic genius.

There were no Paul Gauguins either. Whatever Terman was measuring, artistic creativity seemed almost incidental to it. He assumed at the beginning that child prodigies in the arts had to be very intelligent, tested many, and found that was just not so. Many Termites became flourishing writers, but none of them produced anything resembling great literature. Except for Henry Cowell, who was a special case in many regards, none made a name in music or in art. One man became a successful film director, but he was no Alfred Hitchcock. Terman devised a method of quantifying and measuring verbal, mathematical, and logical skills, but his tests could not measure those elusive gifts of talent and imagination. Intellectual skills and artistic creativity are surely not mutually exclusive, but one does not necessarily go with the other. An Albert Schweitzer could be a great scientist and a fine musician, but he was twice-blessed. Paul Gauguin, existing in abject poverty in the South Pacific, selling his paintings to survive, living with native women while his wife and daughter scraped by in Europe, would have been at the bottom of the C list. Terman had no illusions about that; he admitted this shortcoming.

Terman thought it might be too early to see who would later be considered an immortal, and that's true. It's just no longer very likely.

Terman's contributions to the social sciences and to society are historic whatever his flaws. It takes a man of great complexity to do something as complicated and meaningful as the gifted study. Nonetheless, everything should be taken with a grain of salt. The Terman kid who may have had the greatest impact on our society was a comedy writer.

---

* Terman's son, Fred, came the closest with his encouragement of Hewlett and Packard and his influence on the creation of Silicon Valley.

NOTES

Publication information for books and articles cited in the Notes may be found in the Bibliography.

CHAPTER ONE. INTELLIGENCE TESTING

1. Gould, *The Mismeasure of Man,* p. 68.
2. *Ibid.,* p. 157.
3. Minton, *Lewis M. Terman,* p. 6.
4. *Ibid.*
5. Minton, *ibid.,* quoting essay by Terman in Murchison.
6. Terman, papers, 1935.
7. The dissertation was published in 1906 as *Genius and Stupidity: A Study of Some of the Intellectual Processes of Seven "Bright" and Seven "Stupid" Boys.*
8. Ernest R. Hilgard, interview with author, Feb. 14, 1991.
9. *Ibid.*
10. Olga McNemar, interview with author, Jan. 7, 1991.
11. Terman, *The Measurement of Intelligence,* pp. 6–7.
12. *Ibid.,* pp. 91–92.
13. Gould, *Mismeasure of Man.*

CHAPTER TWO. THE STUDY

1. Seagoe, *Terman and the Gifted,* p. 82.
2. Terman, *Genetic Studies of Genius,* p. 4.
3. *Ibid.*
4. *Ibid.*
5. *Ibid.* and Seagoe, p. 88.
6. Terman, *Genetic Studies of Genius,* p. 20.
7. *Ibid.,* p. 27

8. Seagoe, p. 89.

9. Terman, *Genetic Studies of Genius*, p. 29.

10. *Ibid.*, p. 33.

11. From interviews with Shockley and Alvarez, n.d.

12. Seagoe, p. 96, and Rodney Beard, interview with author, Dec. 8, 1990.

13. Terman, *Genetic Studies of Genius*, p. 47.

14. Minton, *Lewis M. Terman*, p. 142.

15. Terman, *Genetic Studies of Genius*, p. 51.

16. *Ibid.*, p. 52.

17. *Ibid.*, p. 54.

18. *Ibid.*, p. 57.

19. *Ibid.*, p. 66.

20. *Ibid.*, p. 83.

21. Beard interview.

22. Terman, *Genetic Studies of Genius*, p. 139.

23. *Ibid.*, p. 251.

24. *Ibid.*, p. 517.

CHAPTER THREE. GENIUSES OF THE PAST

1. From Terman's speech to Sigma Xi at Stanford in 1941.

2. Gould, *The Mismeasure of Man*, p. 184.

3. Seagoe, *Terman and the Gifted*, p. 217

4. Gould, p. 184.

5. Quoted in *ibid.*, p. 186.

6. Terman, Volume 2, *Genetic Studies of Genius*, p. 146.

CHAPTER FOUR. THE BATTLE OVER TESTING

1. Quoted in Gould, *The Mismeasure of Man*, p. 180.

2. Quoted in Minton, *Lewis M. Terman*, p. 106.

3. *Ibid.*, p. 196.

4. *Ibid.*, p. 193.

CHAPTER FIVE. THE PROBLEM WITH SEX

1. Seagoe, *Terman and the Gifted*, p. 142.

2. Minton, *Lewis M. Terman*, p. 141.

3. Quoted in *ibid,* p. 170

4. *Ibid.*, p. 172.

5. *Ibid.*, p. 174.

6. Seagoe, p. 142.

7. Minton, p. 182.

8. Terman, *Psychological Factors in Marital Happiness.*

9. Olga McNemar, interview with author, Jan. 7, 1991.

10. *Ibid.*

11. Minton, p. 165.

12. Ernest R. Hilgard, interview with author, Feb. 14, 1991.

CHAPTER SIX. THE PROMISE OF YOUTH

1. Terman, *The Promise of Youth,* Volume 3, *Genetic Studies of Genius,* p. 8.

2. *Ibid.,* p. 24.

3. *Ibid.,* p. 277.

4. *Ibid.,* p. 61.

5. *Ibid.,* p. 60.

6. From the personal files of the Terman study.

7. From Seagoe quoting unpublished papers.

8. Terman, *The Promise of Youth,* p. 161.

9. *Ibid.,* p. 329.

10. *Ibid.,* p. 266.

11. *Ibid.,* p. 475.

12. *Ibid.,* p. 468.

CHAPTER SEVEN. LITERARY JUVENILIA

1. The poems used in this chapter and the study of them come from *Genetic Studies of Genius,* Volume 3, beginning p. 361.
   Identity of the poets: "Night" was written by the child Terman called "Edith." The poem here called "How Wonderful Is Death" is an excerpt from "Queen Mab" by Percy Shelley. "The Happiest Day, the Happiest Hour" is by Edgar Allan Poe. "Death" is another poem by Edith. "A Glove" was written by the child called "Beatrice."

CHAPTER EIGHT. THE GIFTED GROW UP

1. Terman, *The Gifted Child Grows Up,* Volume 4, *Genetic Studies of Genius,* p. 370.

2. From the personal files.

3. Terman, *The Gifted Child Grows Up,* p. 73.

4. *Ibid.,* p. 119.

5. *Ibid.,* p. 122.

6. *Ibid.,* p. 129.

7. *Ibid.,* p. 137.

8. *Ibid.,* p. 281.

9. *Ibid.,* p. 310.

CHAPTER NINE. HOW TO MEASURE SUCCESS

1. Glen H. Elder, interview with author, June 3, 1991.
2. Terman, *The Gifted Child Grows Up*, p. 311.
3. *Ibid.*, p. 313.
4. *Ibid.*, p. 324.
5. Elder interview.
6. Elder, "Talent, History, and the Fulfillment of Promise."
7. Elder interview.

CHAPTER TEN. TERMAN'S LAST REPORT

1. Terman, *The Gifted Group in Midlife*, Volume 5, *Genetic Studies of Genius*, p. 47.
2. *Ibid.*, p. 78.
3. *Ibid.*, pp. 136–139.
4. *Ibid.*, p. 152.
5. Terman, "Scientists and Nonscientists in a Group of 800 Gifted Men."
6. Seagoe, *Terman and the Gifted*, p. 248.
7. Minton, *Lewis M. Terman*, p. 252.
8. *Ibid.*, p. 253.
9. Seagoe, p. 182.

CHAPTER ELEVEN. TERMAN'S WOMEN

1. Terman, *The Gifted Group in Midlife*, p. 106.
2. Sears and Barbee, "Career and Life Satisfactions Among Terman's Gifted Women."
3. *Ibid.*, p. 54.
4. *Ibid.*, p. 60.
5. *Ibid.*, p. 60.
6. Sears, "Terman Studies: New Findings from 1977."
7. Holahan, "Lifetime Achievement Patterns, Retirement and Life Satisfaction of Gifted Aged Women," p. 746.

CHAPTER TWELVE. THE GOLDEN DATA BASE

1. Oden, "The Fulfillment of Promise: 40-year Follow-up of the Terman Gifted Group."
2. *Ibid.*, p. 92.
3. Sears, "Sources of Life Satisfactions of the Terman Gifted Men," p. 120.
4. Robert T. Michael, from Sears, "Terman Genetic Study of Genius," p. 90.
5. Arleen Leibowitz, *ibid.*, p. 93.
6. Edwin S. Shneidman, from "Perturbation and Lethality as Precursors to Suicide in a Gifted Group."

7. Carole Holahan, from "Antecedents of Health and Well-Being in Aging for Terman's Gifted Men and Women."

8. Edwin S. Shneidman and Gordon D. Strauss, "Some Patterns of Cognitive Aging Among Superior Septuagenarians."

CHAPTER THIRTEEN. EVERYONE'S KIDS

1. Vaillant, *Adaptation to Life,* pp. 37–38.

BIBLIOGRAPHY

Note: The bibliography is incomplete. In order to preserve the privacy of certain subjects, I have omitted all references to material that could help identify them.

"Lucy and the Gifted Child." *Time,* June 28, 1954, 59–60.

Ackerman, Steve. "Three-Camera Method." *Los Angeles Times,* Feb. 23, 1991.

Burks, Barbara Stoddard, Dortha Williams Jensen, and Lewis M. Terman. *The Promise of Youth: Follow-up Studies of a Thousand Gifted Children.* Genetic Studies of Genius, vol. 3. Stanford, Calif.: Stanford University Press, 1930.

Elder, Glen H., Jr., Eliza K. Pavalko, and Thomas J. Hastings. "Talent, History, and the Fulfillment of Promise." *Psychiatry.* In press.

Goleman, Daniel. "1,528 Little Geniuses and How They Grew." *Psychology Today,* Feb. 1980, 28–53.

Gould, Stephen Jay. *The Mismeasure of Man.* New York: Norton, 1981.

Holahan, Carole Kovalic. "Antecedents of Health and Well-Being in Aging for Terman's Gifted Men and Women." In *American Psychological Association* in San Francisco, 1991.

Holahan, Carole Kovalic. "Lifetime Achievement Patterns, Retirement and Life Satisfaction of Gifted Aged Women." *Journal of Gerontology* 36 (June 1981): 741–749.

Holahan, Carole Kovalic. "Marital Attitudes over 40 Years: A Longitudinal and Cohort Analysis." *Journal of Gerontology* 39 (Jan. 1984): 49–57.

Jensen, Dortha Williams. "A Study of Literary Juvenilia." Ph.D. dissertation, Stanford University, 1930.

Keys, Ancel. "From Naples to Seven Countries—A Sentimental Journey." *Progress in Biochemical Pharmacology* 19 (1983): 1–30.

Keys, Ancel. *Journal of Abnormal and Social Psychology* 47 (1952): 736.

Keys, Ancel. Telephone interview with author, Aug. 10, 1991.

Keys, Ancel. Telephone interview with author, June 15, 1991.

Keys, Ancel. Telephone interview with author, July 4, 1991.

Klinger, Karen. "Growing Up Gifted." *Mercury-News,* June 1, 1980, 1A–3A.

MacPherson, Virginia. "Dennis O'Keefe Is No Terman Booster Now." *San Francisco Chronicle,* Aug. 23, 1947.

McGraw, Carol. "Creator of 'Lucy' TV Show Dies." *Los Angeles Times,* Dec. 29, 1988, 3.

Minton, Henry L. *Lewis M. Terman: Pioneer in Psychological Testing.* New York: New York University Press, 1988.

Murchison, C. A., ed. *Trails to Psychology: A History of Psychology in Autobiography.* Worcester, Mass.: Clark University Press, 1932.

Mydans, Shelley Smith. Personal communication, Aug. 7, 1991.

Mydans, Shelley Smith. Telephone interviews, June 30 and July 4, 1991.

Oden, Melita H. "The Fulfillment of Promise: 40-Year Follow-up of the Terman Gifted Group." *Genetic Psychology Monographs* 77 (1968): 3–93.

Oppenheimer, Estelle. Personal communication, July 20, 1991.

Oppenheimer, Estelle. Telephone interview with author, June 25, 1991.

Oppenheimer, Estelle. Telephone interview with author, June 19, 1991.

Oppenheimer, Gregg. Personal communication, Aug. 19, 1991.

Oppenheimer, Jess. "All About Me." *Journal of Learning Disabilities* 1 (1968): 68–81.

Seagoe, May V. *Terman and the Gifted.* Los Altos, Calif.: Kaufmann, 1976.

Sears, Pauline S. "A Long-Term Perspective on the Gifted: The Terman Genetic Studies of Genius, 1922–1972." In *NSSE Yearbook on the Gifted Child.* Chicago: National Society for the Study of Education, 1977.

Sears, Pauline S. "The Terman Genetic Studies of Genius: 1922–1972." In *NSSE Yearbook.* Chicago: National Society for the Study of Education, 1979.

Sears, Pauline S. "Terman Studies: New Findings from 1977." In California Association for the Gifted in Los Angeles. 1977.

Sears, Pauline S., and Ann H. Barbee. "Career and Life Satisfactions Among Terman's Gifted Women." In *The Gifted and the Creative: A Fifty-Year Perspective,* ed. Julian C. Stanley, William C. George, and Cecilia H. Solano. Baltimore: Johns Hopkins University Press, 1977.

Sears, Pauline S., and Robert R. Sears. "From Childhood to Middle Age to Later Maturity." In American Psychological Association in Toronto, Ontario, Canada.

Sears, Robert R. "Sources of Life Satisfactions of the Terman Gifted Men." *American Psychologist* (1977).

Shneidman, Edwin S. "Personality and 'Success' Among a Selected Group of Lawyers." *Journal of Personality Assessment* 48 (1984): 609–616.

Shneidman, Edwin S. "Perturbation and Lethality as Precursors to Suicide in a Gifted Group." *Life-Threatening Behavior* 1 (Spring 1971): 23–45.

Shneidman, Edwin S., and Gordon D. Strauss. "Some Patterns of Cognitive Aging Among Superior Septuagenarians." In American Association for the Advancement of Science in Washington. 1991.

Terman, Lewis M. *Genetic Studies of Genius, Mental and Physical Traits of a Thousand Gifted Children.* Stanford, Calif.: Stanford University Press, 1925.

Terman, Lewis M. *The Measurement of Intelligence.* Boston: Houghton Mifflin, 1916.

Terman, Lewis M. *Psychological Factors in Marital Happiness.* New York: McGraw-Hill, 1938.

Terman, Lewis M. "Scientists and Nonscientists in a Group of 800 Gifted Men." *Psychological Monographs* 68, 378 (1954).

Terman, Lewis M., and Catharine Cox Miles. *Sex and Personality: Studies in Masculinity and Femininity.* New York: McGraw-Hill, 1936.

Terman, Lewis M., and Melita H. Oden. *The Gifted Child Grows Up: Twenty-five Years' Follow-up of a Superior Group.* Genetic Studies of Genius, vol. 4. Stanford, Calif.: Stanford University Press, 1947.

Terman, Lewis M., and Melita Oden. *The Gifted Group in Midlife: Thirty Years Follow-up of the Superior Child.* Genetic Studies of Genius, vol. 4. Stanford, Calif.: Stanford University Press, 1959.

Vaillant, George E. *Adaptation to Life.* Boston: Little, Brown, 1977.

Walsh, Eileen. "Gifted Kids of Yesteryear Return to Campus." Stanford University *Campus Report,* Nov. 12, 1986, 12.

Young, Kimball. "The History of Mental Testing." *Pedagogical Seminary* 31 (1923).

INDEX